S-
a

12|19.

Margaret Kenna
February 1972

Three Styles in the
Study of Kinship

Three Styles in the Study of Kinship

J. A. Barnes

TAVISTOCK PUBLICATIONS

First published in 1971
by Tavistock Publications Limited
11 New Fetter Lane, London E.C.4
Printed in Great Britain
in 11 point Baskerville
by Butler & Tanner Ltd
Frome and London

SBN 422 73820 4

To Frances

Contents

CONTENTS

Figures

. . . the true road of anthropological science, which is to out-line and explain differences and not to keep them hidden behind confused notions.

Lévi-Strauss (1957: 903)

Le preuve de l'analyse est dans la synthèse.

Lévi-Strauss (1960e: 140)

Acknowledgements

Part of Chapter 2 was written during 1965–1966 while I was in Churchill College, Cambridge, as an Overseas Fellow. I am much indebted to the Master, the late Sir John Cockcroft, and to the Fellows of the College for their hospitality. The greater portion of the book was written at the Institute of Advanced Studies, Australian National University. I am grateful for this opportunity to record my deep appreciation of the stimulus derived from participation in the vigorous intellectual life of the Institute. I am also very conscious of the ample provision of time and facilities for scholarship which made work in the Institute so pleasurable. I was greatly helped and encouraged by Anne-Marie Johnson and owe much to the comments made on early drafts of portions of the book by my colleagues Paula Brown Glick and L. R. Hiatt. I wish to thank the Faculty of Economics and Politics, University of Cambridge, for assistance in preparing the final typescript.

Preface

Most books on kinship contain descriptions of selected social institutions – families, marriage patterns, clans and lineages, kinship terminology, and so on. There are no descriptions of this kind here. This book is on the study of kinship, not on kinship itself. The reader primarily interested in kinship, or in some similar substantive division of social and cultural behaviour, may well ask what need is there for a book whose subject-matter stands at one or more removes from the empirical world. I therefore begin with an attempt to explain and justify what I am trying to do.

This extended analysis of the writings of three anthropologists, Murdock, Lévi-Strauss, and Fortes, in the field of kinship was begun in an effort to assist the transformation of social anthropology from an intuitive art to a cumulative science. For several decades sociologists and social anthropologists have maintained as an article of faith that their dual discipline aims at the discovery of social laws, at the formulation and validation of significant generalizations about culture and society. I have no quarrel with this article of faith but find it chronically embarrassing to have to present such an apparently meagre set of works as our only claim to scientific salvation. In social science there are plenty of high-level tautologies masquerading as laws, and innumerable low-level generalizations which stand up well to test but which cannot readily be linked together in an embracing logical scheme. There are taxonomies galore, many of which sharpen our vision and enable us to see contrasts and connexions previously overlooked. But taxonomies in social science, unlike those in evolutionary biology, have no temporal implication and cannot be proved or disproved, only used or discarded.

There are many people who maintain that this state of affairs is inevitable. Man, they say, is born free, unlike the atom. There is no inexorable regularity in human affairs, and the only generalizations possible about social life are merely statistical summaries of past events, with no predictive power. Other people argue that the fault lies in the phenomena we chose to generalize about. We are too much concerned with accidental features that are the result of specific historic sequences, whereas if only we were to shift to using broad enough categories, everything really significant would be explained by ethology, general systems theory, or something similar. There is merit in both these views. On the one hand the laws of social science must necessarily be of a different order from the laws of physics, if only for the reason that men modify their behaviour in the light of knowledge of the laws to which it is supposed to conform, whereas the planets continue in their courses in blissful ignorance of whether Ptolemy, Newton, or Einstein wears the mantle of orthodoxy. On the other hand brains, men, and societies are nothing but gigantic configurations of law-abiding atoms. It is scarcely surprising that at a sufficiently empty level of generality there are similarities in all thoughts, all systems of interaction and symbolic interchange, all mammalian behaviour, all primate societies, and so on. Indeed, these two contrasted criticisms pose problems for social science that will become more acute in the future. We need to know to what extent the generalizations of social science are self-negating or self-fulfilling prophecies. Once we know how the system works, we think we also know how to make it work differently, and on the other hand, once the mode and mean are published, they become available as approved norms, as for example with Kinsey, so that *what is* changes into *what must be*. The tools of sociological analysis are continually being blunted with the patina of culture. From the opposite point of view, it is just as important to know what limitations are placed on us because we are merely human, what features of social life must be present if we are to survive as a species, what forms of social experiment must fail with our present set of genes, and what potentialities there are in the human psyche that are not yet fully used.

Between these limits lies a vast area of human behaviour where we can take man's membership of genus *Homo*, species *sapiens*, for granted and can also neglect the effect of feedback from the investigator to the societies he studies. This is the central area of social science, and it is in this area that the article of professional faith essentially applies. Here, if anywhere, can we hope to find that interconnected set of empirically validated and distinctively sociological propositions which was the goal of nineteenth-century positivism and which, in varying guises, has remained the target for social science ever since. So far there has been only modest progress. Two explanations immediately come to mind. Either we are not going about the job properly; or else the goal is illusory. Perhaps both explanations are true. The second explanation contradicts the basic article of faith, and most social scientists plump for the first. In a sense, this book also is based on the assumption that the absence of an ordered structure of propositions about one selected portion of social activity, kinship, is due to the inadequacies of the investigations that have been carried out, rather than because those forms of social action and thought that fall under the rubric of kinship are intrinsically unordered, random, chaotic, arbitrary, and unpredictable. But this is not because I reject the second explanation as heretical. I dislike articles of faith, and like to convert them if possible into tested propositions. I would very much like to know to what extent and in what ways, at what level of specificity and within what limits or probability, human affairs are orderly, predictable, and determinate. Articles of faith, like norms generally, as I argue in the first chapter, tend to be drawn in terms of black and white, all or none. We declaim either that we can one day have an all-embracing social science (despite the poor showing so far), or else that human ingenuity and freedom of choice will defeat all attempts at hard and fast generalization about human behaviour (despite the fact that everyday life depends on continual success in predicting the actions of our fellows). From this forced choice science offers us the hope of escape to some calibrated multidimensional continuum with which we can discover and describe how free man is and how much he is bound. My strategy is thus made plain. Assume that the reason for the non-emergence of an accepted, verified, logically organized social science lies with social scientists rather than with their subject-matter; put this to rights so that then, and only then, may we discover how much of a social science is possible.

Strategy is one thing and tactics another. I have no magic formula for building a brand-new edifice of concepts, methods, and techniques which would embody all previously discovered high-level and low-level generalizations in one logical deductive structure, whose design has eluded so many of my illustrious predecessors. Instead of starting afresh, I have tried to work with existing materials; even so, I have not got very far. I have selected three of my colleagues and tried to look at their work, not from a distance in terms of the substantive propositions they establish or suggest, but from close up, in terms of the kinds of problems they set themselves, the analytical categories and verification procedures they use, and the range of application of their results. Instead of looking at their work as a synthesis, I have, as it were, taken it to pieces, in order to study the parts and to see how they fit together.

This process of argumentative dismemberment must, I fear, be rather uncomfortable for the three authors I have chosen and I must crave their indulgence. Evans-Pritchard has remarked that in anthropology every writer tends to be closely identified with the views he advocates, and that it is difficult to criticize views without appearing to criticize their author as well. Therefore I must state explicitly that I am here concerned only with modes of analysis and not with personalities; I hope that the critical attention I have given to the works of these three anthropologists will be recognized as adequate evidence both of the importance I attach to them and of my admiration for their authors, even when I think they are wrong. At the same time I hope I can escape the ill-will of those many colleagues whose work I might have selected for review, but did not. This neglect should not be taken as indicating that I think their work unimportant. The three anthropologists whose work I examine were chosen so as to establish as sharp a set of contrasts as possible, to delineate, I hope, a triangle of extreme polar types that may serve to calibrate the views and styles of most other writers on kinship. Almost all contemporary students of kinship seem to me to belong somewhere within this triangle in respect of aims, concepts, procedures, and styles of argument. I do not attempt to develop a calculus for locating any given writer in relation to the vertices of the triangle, but I think this could be done if necessary.

The trio was chosen because it seemed that I could treat all three anthropologists as independent cases, a consideration that receives particular (and misplaced) emphasis in one of the analytical schemes we shall examine. During the first half of this century, while anthropology was becoming a professional discipline, studies of kinship were dominated by Boas, Rivers, Kroeber, Radcliffe-Brown, and Malinowski. Then in 1949 three books on kinship appeared simultaneously, though each had been in gestation before or during the years of the war. Because they appeared together, it was apparent that there had been no collusion between the authors. The books, *Social structure*, *Les Structures élémentaires de la parenté*, and *The web of kinship among the Tallensi*, differ radically from one another, yet during the couple of decades that have followed their publication each has had a major effect on anthropological thinking, an effect that has by no means been limited to the study of kinship. In the last few years other approaches to kinship, for example componential analysis and human ethology, have received increasing attention, and throughout the period other more centrally placed writers have written on kinship without identifying themselves at all closely with any one of the three I have chosen. But these three writers, and in particular the three books mentioned, provide as good a starting-point as any for a comparative analysis of post-Malinowskian studies of kinship.

It seemed essential to choose for scrutiny writers whose main impact has come after 1945. When I began to think about this book some twelve years ago the traditions of analysis dominated by Malinowski and Radcliffe-Brown were still alive and powerful, particularly in Britain. Although later writers had begun to make their influence felt, a great deal of undergraduate teaching and professional debate still centred on discussions of what Malinowski and Radcliffe-Brown really meant, and their books were an essential part of the literary culture of the subject. I thought that a decisive break with the past was called for, and that anthropology should change its style of publication and the organization of its findings so that it was no longer necessary to keep on going back to the classics for fresh enlightenment. I believed that in this respect, though not in others, we should strive to copy the natural sciences where, so Fortes (1963a: 424) tells us, 'Everything that has not been superseded, whether in theory or in method, or in the matter of experimental data, is embodied in the current body of accepted knowledge, the orthodoxy of the day.' I still think that this is a desirable goal. Nisbet (1966: 19–20) is quite right to argue that whereas a physicist can learn very little that is new about his discipline by reading its classic works, the sociologist can always go back to the classics for information and stimulus. But this is a reflection of the pre-scientific state of contemporary sociology, and I do not believe that it must always remain like this, even though the goal of emancipation from the classics seems to lie further away than I had thought. Indeed, even though I may have succeeded in making some sort of break with the past by excluding Radcliffe-Brown and his contemporaries and predecessors from detailed consideration, I have completely failed to replace or supersede the books and articles on kinship written by the three authors whose work I examine in detail. I hope that the long-term effect of my analysis may be the development of a truly cumulative theory of kinship, but in the short term I hope that its effect will be to encourage others to tackle the works of Murdock, Lévi-Strauss, and Fortes more effectively. Certainly this analysis is not a substitute for what they have written, nor is it in any sense a book of readings or snippets. It is intended as an extended commentary on works that still need to be tackled whole.

The field of kinship was chosen mainly because I thought that I would find here more glory and more knock-down argument, as Humpty Dumpty might have said. The study of kinship has been the central and distinctive feature of social anthropology ever since Morgan, and has reached a level of sophistication that makes it, more than any other branch of the discipline, impenetrable to the specialist in some other branch of social science as much as to the layman. In the study of kinship there are more specialized terms, more definitions, and more would-be theorems, than in, say, the anthropological study of politics or of religion. Here then, there seemed to be a greater proba-bility of finding mature and developed logical structures that could be dissected and compared.

Of necessity I have been forced to treat each writer very much in his own terms, in his own vocabulary, and using his own range of interests and data. The goal of a unified theory of kinship implies the establishment of a single paradigm of concepts, theorems, and accepted procedures of investigation. Unfortunately, with three, and more, rival approaches currently in play, the study of kinship, like social anthropology as a whole, is still at what Kuhn calls the pre-paradigmatic stage of intellectual development (Kuhn 1962: 20). I have tried to put each of the three writers into intellectual and historical context (Scholte 1966), but I am well aware that I have not developed a meta-language into which all three bodies of writing might be translated and related to one another. To do this would be a major undertaking, but it may be a necessary step before the great leap forward to a paradigmatic stage in social science can be achieved.

All three writers are based in the northern hemisphere and their latest work has therefore not always been available to me while I have been writing. In particular this book has been finished before the publication of Fortes's Morgan lectures, *Kinship and the social order*. Had I been able to include this book in my analysis, many paragraphs of Chapter 3 would have been expanded, but almost all the arguments would, I think, have remained unchanged. Likewise Simonis's critique, *Claude Lévi-Strauss ou la 'passion de l'inceste'*, arrived too late to be used. I have tried to base my study not only on the better-known books and articles by the three writers but also on a wide range of their publications; nevertheless I have had to omit from my review several works which have not been available at all in Australia. A fairly complete list of Murdock's works is available in his festschrift volume (Goodenough 1964: 599–603) and an inaccurate list of Lévi-Strauss's works has appeared three times (*Arc* 1965a; *Current anthropology* 1966; Simonis 1968: 357–363). I have therefore included in my bibliography only those works by these two authors that I have referred to in the text. No bibliography of Fortes's writings seems to have been published previously and I have tried to list them all, including those I do not refer to. In the text, when indicating references or the source of quotations, I have often omitted the name of the author when no confusion is likely.

Although I have attempted to make an analysis of all the published work of these three anthropologists, I have probably often taken them much too literally and have divorced statements from the context in which they were made. For purposes of this analysis I have made the heuristic assumption that all three writers are consistently aiming at scientific, and not artistic, explanation (cf. Hammel 1968: 161), even though I think this assumption does not tally with the facts. Indeed, I argue elsewhere (Barnes 1971) that Lévi-Strauss can sometimes be better understood if we make the opposite assumption. In this enterprise my main exemplars have been Abelard's *Sic et non* (1122) and Parsons's *Structure of social action* (1937). Since the penalties of scholastic heresy are now not so great, I have been able to be more outspoken than Abelard; on the other hand I have tried to let my three senior colleagues hold the stage to a greater extent than, I think, is the case with Parsons's book. The product of a union of the expository modes of two such ill-assorted giants has proved to be decidedly rabbinical, but at least I have enjoyed watching it take shape.

When this study was planned several years ago, I intended to cover a much wider field. My polar triangle was to have been a tetrahedron, with the Manchester empiricists led by Gluckman forming the fourth pole. This chapter would have been the hardest of all to write, for I have been fairly closely associated with this group of writers, even if in somewhat anti-podean and iconoclastic fashion. These four chapters were to make up only the first half of the book; the second was to consist of a series of case studies, showing how anthropologists from all four corners of the tetrahedron, along with centrally based colleagues, converged on delimited bodies of ethno-graphic data in tackling ostensibly common problems that had become controversial. I had planned chapters on the stability of marriage, the contrast between cognatic and unilineal, the relation between kinship and politics, and so on. Only one of the case studies was completed, and this has been published separately as *Inquest on the Murngin* (1967c). This appeared at about the same time as the second French edition of Lévi-Strauss's *Les Structures*, containing a revised chapter on the Murngin (1969: 181, f.n.1, 184, f.n.2; 185, 192–195). I have said nothing here about these revisions, and I doubt if and useful purpose would be served by doing so at this stage. I consider that my analysis of the issues raised over the Murngin by Lévi-Strauss, Murdock, and others still stands. In any case, despite Lévi-Strauss's plea for the study of hypothetical societies simulated by computer, it is scarcely possible to continue to discuss the Murngin in an artificially maintained ethnographic vacuum that would be quite alien to the fundamental anthro-pological tradition of empirical inquiry. For the recent field investigations in northeastern Arnhem Land made by Shapiro (1969 and references therein) convince me that the Murngin, as they are defined in the literature of the Murngin controversy, do not exist and never have existed.

As originally designed the book would have been a monstrous blunderbuss, and the fragments that remain are quite massive enough; nevertheless the volume would have been improved had it been possible to include an analysis of the Manchester group, whose object of study seems to be 'what actually happens'. But this chapter, and the other case studies, will have to be written by someone else, for I have now to direct my attention elsewhere.

1 Safety in numbers

*In scientific anthropology, it would seem,
there is safety in numbers.*

Murdock (1940a: 369)

1 Safety in numbers

1 Introduction

George Peter Murdock has had a major influence on theoretical studies in kinship and social organization. The publication of his book *Social structure* marked the establishment of a distinctive trend in comparative anthropological inquiry. His interest in comparative studies based on information about a large number of societies from all parts of the world led him to initiate the Cross-Cultural Survey, later to grow into the Human Relations Area Files. He founded the journal *Ethnology* to provide an outlet for publications in this field for articles which 'specifically incorporate or relate to some body of substantive data' (Murdock *et al.* 1962a: 2). His 'World ethnographic sample' (1957a) has been used by many other scholars for a great variety of investigations. Its replacement, the *Ethnographic atlas*, which appeared in instalments in *Ethnology* over many years before being published separately, continues as a sampling frame for general use. We can have no hesitation in identifying a distinct school or sub-branch within social anthropology, characterized by its own method of cross-cultural analysis. Two collections of papers, *Readings in cross-cultural methodology* (Moore 1961) and *Cross-cultural approaches: readings in comparative research* (Ford 1967), provide an ostensive definition of the school and indicate its range of interests.

Yet although quantitative world-wide cross-cultural studies 'have been appearing of late at a geometrically increasing rate' (Murdock 1967: 3), the fundamental assumptions common to

3

these studies do not command unqualified professional support. Now that professional activities as a whole, and not merely cross-cultural studies, are expanding rapidly and new band-wagons threaten to create an indigestible intellectual traffic jam, it is no surprise that a line of inquiry marked out some thirty years ago should have many competitors. More surprisingly, those who have followed other lines have for the most part been content to ignore the cross-cultural method and to develop their own techniques without reference to it. A few writers have stated briefly their unequivocal mistrust of the method, but usually without examining Murdock's arguments and assumptions in detail. For some reason or other, most of the sustained discussion of cross-cultural method has been about blemishes and limitations in the practical application of the method rather than about fundamental principles. Criticism has been directed more at the way ethnographic data should be selected and coded for analysis than at the type of analysis performed. Yet there are many social anthropologists, in the United States as well as in France and Britain, who have no enthusiasm for the cross-cultural endeavours of Murdock and those who have followed him; the quantitative aspect of these studies has met with particular disapproval. A striking example of this lack of enthusiasm was the absence from Britain for many years of any copy of the Human Relations Area Files; this cannot have been due solely to shortage of funds. Silence among the critics cannot be explained by uncertainty about the stated aims and premises of cross-cultural research, for Murdock has set out the assumptions underlying his inquiries, as he sees them, with great gusto and forcefulness. The technique of inquiry he has developed has its roots in the work of one of the founders of anthropology, E. B. Tylor. It is one instance of what Köbben (1952: 131, 137–138) calls the holo-geistic method, whose practitioners seek to 'identify associated variables that transcend the vagaries of historical contact and local conditions' It aims at nomothetic, rather than idio-graphic or genetic, explanations and its statistical procedures are similar to those used very widely in cognate disciplines

4

such as psychology and sociology, and in the natural sciences. The intellectual credentials of the school thus seem to be impeccably traditional and scientific. The results of applying the techniques of cross-cultural inquiry now form a substantial part of the contemporary literature in social anthropology. We cannot merely ignore them because, for example, we happen to find the structuralist dialectic more exciting, or the ethological approach more firmly based on verifiable fact. If we think that quantitative cross-cultural studies as now carried out are along the wrong lines, we should give our reasons. This is what I try to do in this chapter. I concentrate my attention on Murdock's principal theoretical work, *Social structure* (1949a), and on the strenuous efforts he has made since that book was published to improve his sample of societies and to meet other criticisms.

One distinctive feature of the cross-cultural movement, if we may call it that, is that it has acquired not only a common set of intellectual aims and research techniques but also specialized bibliographic institutions and several key published documents. The Cross-Cultural Survey was established at Yale University in 1937 under Murdock's leadership as part of the Institute of Human Relations. Extracts of published and unpublished ethnographic material on selected societies were classified according to a scheme set out in the *Outline of cultural materials* (Murdock *et al.* 1938, subsequently revised). Material in foreign languages was translated into English. During World War II several handbooks were produced with the help of the Survey. In 1949 the Human Relations Area Files were developed from the Survey. Whereas the Survey is confined to Yale, the Files were established to allow the extracted ethnographic material to be distributed to other universities (Murdock *et al.* 1950: xii–xiv). Both the Survey and the Files were designed to facilitate the formulation and testing of cross-cultural generalizations using quantitative methods. The societies included in the Files were chosen so as to form a fair sample of all known cultures (Murdock 1940a: 369). Later, as the number of societies increased, the objective shifted slightly; the

5

societies in the Files are now seen as forming a collection from which a satisfactory sample can be drawn with minimum effort. Naroll (1968: 254) comments that recently societies thought to be of strategic interest to the United States government tend to have been selected disproportionately. The goal of the Survey is, or was, to cover 'a representative ten per cent sample of all the cultures known to history, sociology, and ethnography' (Murdock 1949a: viii). When writing *Social structure*, Murdock used a sample of 250 societies, 85 of them taken from those covered by the Survey at that time.

While the Survey and the Files may be seen essentially as bibliographic aids, a commitment to quantitative cross-cultural inquiry has also led Murdock to construct a series of standard samples of cultures and/or societies. His *Outline of world cultures* (1954a) establishes a list of all known cultures and suggests a suitable sample. His 'World ethnographic sample' (1957a) contains 565 cultures whose main characteristics are indicated in succinct coded statements. The sample has been used by many other ethnologists as a basis for their own inquiries. A revised version appeared in 1961 (Murdock 1961; cf. Köbben 1967: 9). Publication of the 'Ethnographic atlas' began in 1962. With the twenty-first instalment the Atlas reached a total of well over 1,100 societies. Finally, Murdock has constructed a standard world sample of 200 cultures. A new organization, the Cross-Cultural Cumulative Center (CCCC) will use this sample to re-test correlations found earlier and 'to intercorrelate the findings of different studies and thus raise the rate of scientific accumulation from an arithmetic to a geometric level' (Murdock 1968b: 306). Other institutions have followed Murdock's lead, and a Permanent Ethnographic Probability Sample is being established at Northwestern University (Naroll 1968: 254).

Although the principal stimulus to develop the Survey, the Files, the Atlas, and so on has been the requirements of the cross-cultural method, Murdock has claimed from the start that these research tools can have other uses. The Survey, he writes, 'should prove useful in nearly every type of research

6

which anthropologists and other social scientists have hitherto pursued' (Murdock 1940a: 363). Some anthropologists who criticize the cross-cultural method are nevertheless ready to support the Atlas and similar documents as providing them with handy cues, directing attention to new portions of the ethnographic corpus that may merit closer scrutiny. The Files may be seen as a convenient set of indexed extracts from a huge body of scattered literature, and the Atlas provides an even more succinct key to the contents of ethnographic monographs. It is obvious that, as the amount of ethnographic writing continues to increase, we need more effective ways of finding our way around the literature; and it may well be that the Atlas adequately earns its keep as an index alone. However, the use of the Atlas as a pointer back to the literature is quite distinct from its use as a lead forward to statistical cross-cultural inquiries, and it is with the latter that we are here mainly concerned.

In the Files we have a relatively expensive and elaborate tool for library research. Murdock has been the driving force behind their development and he has been the obvious person to announce the achievements and possibilities of this undertaking. Typically, he has tried to assess quantitatively the efficacy of the Files as an aid to research. He states that with their help one of his articles (1950b) was written in a total elapsed time of twenty-five hours (1950c: 720; 1953: 485), whereas without their aid he would have needed at least twenty-five days. Similarly Udy (1964: 169) reports that he was able to extract all the information he needed ten times faster by using the Files than by reading through the source monographs themselves.

It is therefore not surprising that to many observers Murdock has become identified with a set of ethnographic data organized in distinctive fashion in the Files, as well as with a theory of functional relations between cultural items and a statistical technique for establishing these relations. Thus Nadel is led to note, rather peevishly, his suspicion that 'for Murdock, nothing anthropological is scientific unless it is (a) based on the

Human Relations Area Files and/or (b) contains some acknow-ledgement of Clark L. Hull's learning theory' (Nadel 1955: 346). A more accurate assessment is made by Leach when he says that, although Murdock may be generally associated with a particular style of cross-cultural comparison, the volume of his collected papers 'is a valuable reminder that Six-Gun Pete has had other aces up his sleeve' (Leach 1966: 1518). Similarly, the vigorous diversity of methods, range, and ethnographic content of the articles appearing in *Ethnology*, and the even wider range of interests shown by his pupils in the *festschrift* presented to their teacher (Goodenough 1964; cf. Fox 1966), give convincing evidence that Nadel was wrong.

In part, the scope of articles appearing in *Ethnology* under Murdock's editorship is explained by the division he draws between ethnographic accounts and comparative studies; we shall have more to say on this later. However, this is only part of the explanation, for he has always held that the cross-cultural method is not the only way to arrive at propositions that are valid transculturally. He has often expressed his approval of the inquiries conducted by Mead in Samoa into the biological and cultural causes of adolescent stress, and by Holmberg among the Siriono into sex anxiety in a society with chronically uncertain food supply, for these investigations were made in field situations where the appropriate variables occurred naturally in the combinations desired. If experimenta-tion with human beings was possible, these are situations one might well construct artificially (Mead 1928; Holmberg 1950; Murdock 1950a: 573; 1951b: 1; 1954b: 27; 1957b: 252; 1966: 97). But since, like astronomers, we cannot experiment, we have to rely mainly on the other method distinctive of anthropology, that of subjecting hypotheses to quantitative comparative tests. Although most of his book *Social structure* is aimed at 'scientific results of universal application' (1957b: 249), Chapter 8 and Appendix A, where he discusses the evolution of social organiza-tion, deal with historical (or prehistorical) reconstruction, though some of the ethnographic evidence educed is expressed quantitatively. Elsewhere, as in his book *Africa*, he has pursued

8

of those animals with a pronounced social life, such as termites, is inherited and, unlike human culture, does not have to be inculcated (1940a: 364-365). Although learning principles are essentially the same for man and most mammals, man's ability to use language makes his form of life distinctive. All human cultures, because they are carried by men, have a great deal in common. These common aspects make possible generalizations that are true for all humanity or all cultures.

This reference to all human cultures explains why Murdock is perennially preoccupied with constructing an adequate ethnographic sample. Only in this way can he be sure that his propositions are genuinely expressive of a character of human activity as a whole, and not true merely of human beings in Africa, or during the Middle Ages, or at a subsistence level of economy. We might argue that, despite their limited reference, propositions that are true for only one segment of human experience, whether this is delimited temporally, spatially, or by cultural and social criteria, are nevertheless of scientific value and worth the effort needed to establish them. But for Murdock these propositions are definitely of lesser value; hence his appeal to sociologists, political scientists, and others to find in the pages of *Ethnology* data from a sample of societies 'extensive enough to be truly representative of the total range of variation in human behaviour, a more extensive field than is provided by the materials on European and American culture to which their attention has traditionally been limited' (Murdock *et al.* 1962a: 1-2).

In this chapter we are not concerned with the whole range of Murdock's writings as an anthropologist, nor with the qualities that his work has in common with that of his colleagues. Our scrutiny is directed to the distinctive features of the cross-cultural method, as exemplified in the work of Murdock and those associated with him. Hence I cannot follow his example, and construct a sample of cross-cultural ethnologists or of articles and books using the cross-cultural method, which could be analysed quantitatively. Instead of picking at random, I try to exercise judgement and discretion to bring to light the

primary historical interests with minimal reliance on qu
ethnographic data (1959a: 40), and one of his many com
against British social anthropologists is their alleged co
lack of interest in history (1951a: 468).

Murdock's training during World War I and imme
thereafter was decidedly unorthodox for a recruit to the a
pological profession in the United States at that time (
356–358). His eclectic background in social science and l
and his early association with sociology at Yale, show
selves in the battery of disciplines on which he draws
explanation of social phenomena. Whereas many of his
orthodox contemporaries have tried to establish a disti
cultural level of discourse, freed from the taint of reducti
Murdock tries to manufacture from carefully selected po
of cognate disciplines a comprehensive theory of l
behaviour and of culture (cf. Lévi-Strauss 1963a: 306
theory impinges on the activities of individuals as w
groups, and relates to instrumental behaviour as well as
construction and transmission of symbols. In keeping wit
broad frame of reference Murdock looks to the common
acteristics of social behaviour at all times and all places, r
than in some delimited temporal, geographical, or ecol
context. The quartette of disciplines – sociology, hist
anthropology, behaviouristic psychology, and psychoanal
specifically invoked by Murdock in *Social structure* (1
xi–xvii; cf. 1949b) could well be applied to an analysis c
social behaviour of a single community or tribe. Althoug
has published the findings of his own fieldwork in B
Columbia, Oregon, and Truk (1934a, 1936, 1938, 1
1958b, 1965b; Murdock and Goodenough 1947), it is
that analysis at this level is not Murdock's main inte
Indeed, another of his criticisms directed against his Br
colleagues is their concentration on the intensive study
few societies (1951a: 467). His preferred universe of disco
is the whole of human social life, whether contemporary
extinct, tropical or arctic, tribal or industrial. He is not c
cerned with social life among other animals, for the cult

B

structure of thinking underlying the cross-cultural method and to test it for logical consistency. First, I describe briefly the theories used by Murdock, what data provide grist for the cross-cultural mill, and how these are put into standard form. Then I discuss a crucial analytical step, the use of synchronic data to infer the existence of diachronic processes. The next section deals with the need for statistical techniques and is followed by a discussion of the encoding procedure characteristic of the cross-cultural method. Lastly I discuss the concept which, for me, constitutes the Achilles' heel of the method, the sampling unit. The chapter ends with a brief assessment of the value of Murdock's work in the recent development of social and cultural anthropology.

2 Data and disciplines

Murdock begins his book *Social structure* with the sentence: 'This volume represents a synthesis of five distinct products of social science – one research technique and four systems of theory' (Murdock 1949a: vii). In this chapter I am concerned more with Murdock's 'research technique' than with the systems of theory that he employs, for it is essentially the research technique that marks off the writings of his school of cross-cultural inquiry from other contemporary publications in anthropology as well as from the products of other modes of comparative investigation. The research technique is distinctive, whereas the four systems of theory are widely employed in social science, even if Murdock's selective amalgam of the four is idiosyncratic. Despite Murdock's tendency to identify comparative studies in anthropology with that particular variety of comparative inquiry which he has developed, there have in fact been many studies using other techniques to assess evidence from a large number of diverse societies and cultures (cf. Lewis 1956). Similarly, many anthropologists have used statistical methods for purposes quite distinct from those envisaged by Murdock (cf. Kluckhohn 1939; Mitchell, J. C., 1967).

In this chapter we shall confine our attention to one particular application of statistical methods, and for brevity I use the label 'cross-cultural' in this restricted sense. As already mentioned, the cross-cultural method was not developed from scratch by Murdock, but had its origins in the work of Tylor (1889), Steinmetz (1896; cited in Naroll, 1962: 5–6) and others (cf. Köbben 1952). Murdock has, however, written extensively about the assumptions and aims of the method, and our attention will be concentrated on what he has to say.

Yet before we can come to grips with the research technique specific to the cross-cultural method, we must look briefly at the four theories, at how they are used and at the ethnographic data they are called upon to explain. Only after we have discussed theories, data, the verbal arguments linking them, and the model of society which emerges from this linkage, can we begin to consider to what extent the quantitative research technique provides adequate tests of the theories and of the various testable propositions derived from the theories. In this section we shall therefore introduce a few definitions, sketch the range of information about the real world which Murdock handles, and classify the kinds of explanation he seeks to establish.

It will help our discussion of Murdock's cross-cultural method to follow a terminology based on that used by Textor (1967: 20–21). By cultural 'characteristic' I mean some aspect of culture such as 'mode of marriage', 'settlement pattern', 'mean size of local communities', or 'linguistic affiliation'. Characteristics typically appear as the names of columns in Murdock's 'World ethnographic sample' and in the Atlas. By 'attribute' I mean the value taken by a cultural characteristic in a given society. Thus 'marriage with bride-service', 'migratory or nomadic bands', 'communities with fewer than fifty persons', and 'Khoisan language stock' are typical attributes, and are the values that happen to be taken by the four characteristics mentioned in the culture of the Kung Bushmen of the Kalahari, the first society listed in the Atlas. Murdock himself uses a variety of terms – trait, element, item, etc. – for our 'characteristic' and 'attribute' (cf. Murdock 1932: 204–205). The essence of the cross-cultural method is the establishment of statistical associations between pairs of attributes.

The number of attributes associated with a given characteristic must be at least two ('present' and 'absent'). In the Atlas, most characteristics have more, with a maximum of 128 attributes for 'linguistic affiliation'. The 'World ethnographic sample' provides information on thirty characteristics. Some of this information was presumably employed in *Social structure*, but the information on inheritance, extra-marital intercourse, the sororate, the levirate, and niece terminology used in that book is not given in the 'Sample', though this does list information on some characteristics, such as the utilization of plants and animals, which are not made use of in the book. The Atlas, as published in 1967, contains information on about 85 cultural characteristics, and additional characteristics dealing with behaviour between kin have appeared in an instalment (Murdock *et al.* 1965: 242–243). The scheme of characteristics and attributes is flexible, for these can be chosen to suit the interests of the investigator. We shall comment later on the neglect of physical factors, and the comparatively cursory treatment of political institutions, in the Atlas, as well as on the way in which population size is handled (pp. 19, 30f., 92f.).

The distinction between 'characteristic' and 'attribute' is sometimes arbitrary, as is seen in Textor's manipulation of 'raw' and 'finished', i.e. dichotomous, characteristics and attributes (Textor 1967: 20–21). The attributes associated with any one characteristic must form a mutually exclusive set of categories which together exhaust all possibilities, whereas the various characteristics can be chosen merely for convenience and scientific interest. Thus, for example, the information on marriage between cousins which is spread among three characteristics in the 'World ethnographic sample' (second letter of columns 10, 11, and 12) appears under one characteristic (column 25) in the Atlas. The existence of polygynous families living in one dwelling is treated in the Sample (second letter of column 7) as an attribute which contrasts with seven other

13

forms of household, whereas in the Atlas (first letter of column 14) it is contrasted with nine other types of domestic family. Thus it seems that Murdock does not see the characteristics as necessarily constituting the dimensions of culture, with the attributes indicating the values taken on the various dimensions by particular cultures. Nevertheless many of the characteristics are used in this way.

The characteristics are selected as far as possible to apply significantly to all kinds of societies and cultures in all parts of the world. The attributes have a narrower range of application, for only one attribute for each characteristic fits any given society. Nevertheless they too are chosen so that they apply widely. Both characteristics and attributes are essentially etic, not emic, categories (Conklin 1964: 50 f.n.: Sturtevant 1964: 101–103). Thus, for example, every society has some form or other of family organization, and of settlement pattern. Attributes indicating 'absence' are supplied for characteristics such as 'type of high god believed in' and 'type of genital mutilation practised'. The use of a limited number of attributes does less injustice to the facts when the various states of the characteristic encountered in reality fall naturally into one or other of several discrete categories. For instance, this is the case, many anthropologists would maintain, with characteristics such as kinship terminology for cousins, mode of marriage, and type of patrilineal kin group, at least in so far as these relate to cultural norms rather than actual behaviour. Other characteristics can be assigned a limited number of attributes only by arbitrary chopping, as for example 'mean size of local communities', which has eight attributes in the Atlas. The replacement of these arbitrary attributes by continuous variables would be an obvious improvement in the scheme. Some critics have objected in principle to the use of a limited number of discrete attributes for classifying ethnographic information, as we shall see when we come to discuss encoding (see below, pp. 61f.).

In the Sample and in the Atlas, both of which are arranged in tabular form, each row is identified with a chosen society, and each column with a characteristic. Symbols appearing in a given column indicate the various attributes. The same or slightly variant forms of presentation of ethnographic information are used in many other cross-cultural studies (e.g. Stephens 1961, Textor 1967: Appendix 7). The choice of attributes and/ or characteristics varies from one study to another.

The distinction between characteristics and attributes is procedurally important. Many of statements in *Social structure* and other cross-cultural studies describe how many sample societies, or what proportion of the societies, possess each of the several attributes associated with a single selected characteristic. For example, one of the characteristics used in many cross-cultural studies is the rule of post-marital residence. In *Social structure* there are six attributes associated with this characteristic, i.e. all rules of residence reported in the ethnographic literature are grouped into six classes. Murdock (1949a: 17, 32) reports the number of sample societies in each class. Likewise he states the number of societies which have independent nuclear families with monogamy, or with infrequent polygyny, or which have dependent polygamous families with polyandry, or with polygyny, and so on. No inference drawn from these statements depends on the precise number of societies listed in each category, and hence problems of sample construction are not critical. The reader gains the knowledge that polyandry is rare, polygyny fairly common, and monogamy relatively infrequent, and that independent and dependent families are about equally frequent. At this level of specificity, the sample provides confirmation for impressions that many readers will have already gained from unsystematic ethnographic reading.

Simple distributional statements of this type may be of real interest, particularly when certain attributes are found to occur in no societies at all. Thus for example, Murdock (1949a: 12) supports his argument about the structure of the nuclear family with the statement that the nuclear family exists as a distinct and strongly functional group in all the 250 sample societies, and that in none of them is a man allowed to marry or copulate with his mother, sister, or daughter (1949a: 2, 12). His sample includes the Nayar of Kerala, but with Fawcett and Pannikar as his sources, this society seems not to need special mention. He asserts that the nuclear family is a universal human social grouping. On the other hand, the apparent partial exceptions to his generalization about incest presented by the evidence from Azande, Bali, Dobu, Egypt, Hawaii, and the Incas are noted with the comment: 'By their special circumstances or exceptional character these cases serve rather to emphasize then to disprove the universality of intra-family incest taboos' (1949a: 2, 12–13, 266).

In general, however, simple distributional statements do not bear upon the presence or absence of functional relations between attributes. To obtain statistical evidence for a functional relation, at least two cultural characteristics must be considered together.

The data for cross-cultural analysis are items of ethnographic information, as Murdock calls them, arranged according to society and characteristic and equated with one or other of the available attributes. Statistical methods are used to establish correlations between selected attributes or sets of attributes. These correlations in themselves have no explanatory value; they merely demand explanation in terms of some theory about the characteristics of culture. Murdock distinguishes three kinds of explanation for the empirically established fact that certain attributes, i.e. cultural traits, appear together in the same society more often than would be expected if they were randomly distributed (1960b: 183–184). First, the explanation may be what Murdock calls genetic. If the members of one society are descended from the members of a second society, or if they both are descended from a third, then it is likely that, despite possible changes in habitat and despite the passage of time, there will be many similarities in the cultures of the two societies. Thus for example there are many similarities between the cultures of twentieth-century Australia and twentieth-century Britain. This may be explained, at least in part, by reference to the 'genetic' connexion of the populations of both societies to the population of nineteenth-century Britain. A second kind of explanation appeals to the phenomenon of diffusion. Members of one society may copy the behaviour of members of a neighbouring society in one or other cultural aspect, and after a while the cultures of the two societies will display similarities. Murdock often labels this kind of explanation 'historical', and much of *Social structure* is devoted to a demonstration that historical explanations cannot be found for most of the empirically discovered correlations between cultural attributes. On the other hand Murdock is ready to admit that some similarities between cultures are due to copying. Most of the refinements that have been successively introduced into his sampling procedure have been aimed at eliminating from the sample similarities of this kind.

Similarities due to genetic connexion result, in effect, from the process whereby within a society each generation more or less accurately copies the culture of its predecessor, whereas similarities due to diffusion result from the possibility of observing the behaviour of contemporary members of a neighbouring society and of copying it. The third kind of similarity, the kind with which Murdock is mainly concerned, is caused by the adaptation of the various attributes present in a single culture to one another. Murdock writes that 'The shared habits that constitute a culture . . . also become progressively adapted to one another so that they tend to form an integrated whole. They exhibit what Sumner has called "a strain towards consistency" ' (Murdock 1956a: 259; Sumner 1906: 5-6; cf. Murdock 1937b: xvii; 1941: 145; 1949a: 137–138, 197–198). Any given attribute or characteristic may influence any other to a varying extent and at a varying speed. The temporal dimension in the relation between attributes is methodologically important, for Murdock makes use of the concept of 'cultural lag' enunciated by Ogburn (1922: 200). Thus we have a model of culture in which the various parts are continually adjusting to one another, but at various speeds and intensities. The adjustments, if they were allowed to proceed undisturbed, would eventually bring the culture to a position of stable equilibrium or perfect

17

integration. Owing to the effects of external factors, historical accidents, and non-cultural influences, this position of complete integration is seldom attained by any culture. Nevertheless, a statistical examination of an adequate sample of societies will reveal which aspects of culture have the strongest effects on one another. Between these attributes we have what Murdock and his followers describe as a functional relationship.

Murdock is strictly concerned with all human culture, and not with propositions or generalizations that are true only of one part of the world. Every major region of the world must be included, for otherwise theorems might be regarded as proved when in fact they were not true of cultures in some part of the world (cf. Driver and Schuessler 1967: 336–347). A good example of this danger is to be found in a paper by Driver, who provides statistical evidence interpreted by Chrétien to imply that the only type of kin avoidance which occurs alone is that between mother and son. Driver comments that his statistical evidence is drawn only from cultures in North America and that Chrétien's conclusion does not apply to Asia (Driver 1966).

Conversely, the sample must be stratified so that one source of variation, that of location, is eliminated.

Murdock writes:

> . . . if some areas are discovered to yield negative coefficients of correlation while other areas with a larger total number of cultures yield positive coefficients, it must be concluded that the apparent statistical confirmation of the hypothesis is fictitious and accidental and the hypothesis must either be rejected entirely or modified and tested again (1940a: 369).

In other words, geographical location cannot be accepted as an explanatory factor for variations in culture. Many people would agree that in the past there has been a tendency among anthropologists specializing in one particular area to describe cultural features as, say, typically Australian or typically West African, as though that was as far as explanation need or could go. Nevertheless to deny any explanatory value to geographical position is equally unsound. It may be that living in a world of snow and ice, or in a rain forest, or on an isolated island, has no critical influence on social structure, or at least on those aspects of structure with which Murdock deals. But this has to be demonstrated and not assumed *a priori*. None of the characteristics listed in the Atlas tell us anything at all about the physical environment in which the sample societies operate. It is curious that although one of Murdock's formal assumptions is that 'forms of social structure are . . . created by forces external to social organization, especially by economic factors' (Murdock 1949a: 137), and although he mentions 'the available sources of food' as a factor affecting the sex division of labour, and hence indirectly the rule of residence, he nowhere examines systematically and statistically how available sources of food and other economic factors impinge on social institutions. Nor does he provide the necessary coded information to encourage others to do so, though Textor (1967: 69–70) has done this, drawing on unpublished codings made by Moore (1962). Similarly, although overpopulation is mentioned in *Social structure* as a cause of social change (1949a: 203), the Atlas contains no data on population density. The assumption of the causal priority of economic factors, combined with an apparent lack of interest in how the factors work, may perhaps be explained by Murdock's preference for dealing with culture as an heuristically closed system. He does not assert that cultures exist in isolation from their external and physical environment, but his area of interest is restricted to the interconnexions between the different parts of culture, and excludes the links between these parts and the environment. In his cross-cultural inquiries, he assumes the existence of continual varying influences from outside which prevent cultures from attaining perfect integration, but these influences are regarded as impediments in the study of culture and not as cultural-physical relations worthy of study on a world-wide cross-cultural basis in their own right. Yet in his book on Africa, where he deals with phenomena that are avowedly historical, i.e. specific in time and place, he makes admirable efforts,

19

sometimes successful, sometimes not, to take account of changes in physical environment and changes in available food resources.

The geographical tests foreshadowed in Murdock's 1940 article, in which one geographically restricted part of the sample would be checked against another, might also be used to determine the existence of correlations between environmental factors and cultural attributes. In *Social structure* they are applied neither for this purpose nor to check the validity of correlations found in a world-wide sample, as Murdock proposed. The only results of area testing included in the book are given in *Tables 57* and *58*, showing how many sample societies possessing each of the attributes of selected characteristics are found in each continent and in each culture area of America, while *Table 59* lists societies speaking Malayo-Polynesian languages and possessing one or other combination of attributes for kinship terminology and rule of descent. This evidence is adduced only to disprove diffusionist theories of cultural development and not to test Murdock's own propositions. His conclusion from the tables that 'the almost random distribution of the traits of social organization . . . render practically useless all historical interpretation based on expectations of diffusion' (Murdoch 1949a: 196) has been challenged, on his own evidence, by Wilson (1952) and Driver (1967). Recently Sawyer and LeVine (1966), Driver and Schuessler (1967: 336–347), Barry (1968), and Murdock (1957a: 686; 1968a) himself have shown how correlations between attributes can vary radically according to the geographical limits of the societies in the sample used (cf. Naroll and D'Andrade 1963: 1053–1054).

Thus far the argument provides us with a model of society or culture in which certain attributes have a functional relation to certain others, and with a sample of societies chosen so as to provide statistical evidence for these relations. The next step is to provide explanations for the various relations that are established. For explanation at this level Murdock turns to the four disciplines, identified as behaviouristic psychology, sociology, historical anthropology, and psychoanalysis, dealing with

20

human learning, society, culture, and personality, and collectively labelled 'lesocupethy' (LEarning, SOciety, CUlture, and PErsonality THoerY)(Murdock 1949b; 377; 1949a: xi–xvii). The four disciplines, originally independent, are thought of as dovetailing together, so as eventually to constitute, by judicious selection and mutual interaction, a single theory about acquired behaviour. For instance, Murdock (1949a: 292–300) uses 'unassimilated Freudian theory' to explain the 'universal appearance of incest avoidance tendencies'; sociological theory explains why these tendencies are established within the nuclear family in all known societies; the principle of stimulus generalization, taken from behaviouristic psychology, explains the tendency for incest taboos to be extended beyond the nuclear family; anthropological theory explains why the directions in which extensions are made correlate with the rule of descent – patrilineal extensions in societies with patrilineal kin groups, matrilineal extensions in matrilineal societies.

Yet despite this proclaimed disciplinary eclecticism, for many of his conclusions Murdock falls back on less sophisticated arguments. He sometimes supports his case with a mode of argument unkindly called 'the fantastic anecdote' or the 'if-I-were-a-horse technique'. For example, in advancing his views on the sequence of stages whereby a matrilineal matrilocal society changes into a patrilineal patrilocal one, he begins by asking the reader to 'conceive of such a community as a small settlement containing two matri-clans, each localized on one side of the main village thoroughfare' (1949a: 216). The sequence of changes that follow may be plausible, but it is not derived from any historically verifiable instances of change, nor is it clearly connected with any of the four disciplines. Likewise, although he supports his discussion of the nuclear family with statistical evidence indicating that it is found in all societies, his description of the functions, activities, and structure of this primary group is oversimplified and dogmatic, and unrelated to the ethnographic evidence freely available (Murdock 1949a: Chapter 1; cf. Steiner 1951; Levy and Fallers 1959).

In similar fashion he discusses how a change to a state of affairs in which the principal means of subsistence is secured by the activities of men, rather than of women, 'seems to promote' patrilocal (i.e. what I call patrivirilocal; cf. Murdock *et al.* 1962b: 117–118) residence after marriage. Murdock argues that the division of labour by sex is such that men's skills have to be exercised in a terrain they know, whereas women can practise their skills anywhere; hence, under these conditions men rarely shift from one community to another when they marry. He refers to statistical evidence, drawn from more than 75 per cent of the sample societies, about the tasks assigned to men, and he refers briefly to circumstantial evidence from the Crow, but most of his argument is presented deductively and is based on his assumptions about the nature of culture. Thus, for instance, he refers explicitly to patrilocal residence in aboriginal Australia, and explains it by reference to the occasions when 'a tribe moves into an area where game is plentiful and dependable, so that subsistence comes to depend primarily upon the chase rather than upon the collecting activities of the women' (1949a: 206, 213–214). He cites no evidence on the extent to which Australian Aborigines relied on the products of men's hunting and women's collecting. For sedentary communities, Murdock's assertion has been criticized by Kloos (1963) who uses statistical evidence to support his own proposition that, in sedentary communities with a matrilocal rule of residence, the statistical association with local endogamy is a function of ascribed leadership and not due to environmental handicaps facing the man who marries out.

Much of *Social structure* is taken up with examining in turn various cultural characteristics, whose attributes are shown to be correlated with various attributes of other characteristics. We have in effect a series of statistically supported functional relations, each with its separate explanation. In his discussion of kinship terminology Murdock diverges from this style of argument. Here he attempts to provide indirectly a proposition for which direct statistical support cannot be obtained. This he does by using 'the postulational method' (Murdock 1940a:

22

369-370; 1949a: 127). The basic postulate is itself derived from thirteen assumptions about human behaviour in general and about kinship behaviour in particular. Some of the assumptions are so general that it is difficult to see how they could be refuted; for instance, we have the assumption 'that all human behavior, including that which is called cultural, conforms to the fundamental principles of behaviour as these are being laid bare by psychologists', and that 'terminological classification of kinsmen is but a special case of linguistic classification'. These assumptions are better seen as statements about the strategy Murdock proposes to adopt in seeking explanations than as axioms which form part of these explanations. Two assumptions assert the operation of certain psychological processes identified by Clark L. Hull in the classification of relatives. One other assumption is mainly a matter of definition, the distinction between 'inherent distinctions' and 'subsidiary criteria'. Other assumptions are more substantial, as for example the assertion that the forms of social structure are created by forces external to social organization, especially by economic factors.

With these assumptions Murdock is able to lay down a basic postulate stating the conditions under which two kin types tend to be called by the same term. Each of the six inherent distinctions – generation, sex, affinity, collaterality, bifurcation, and polarity – tends to produce differences in terms. Certain aspects of social structure and of associated cultural behaviour increase similarities between certain types of kin and increase dissimilarities between certain others, and the terminology is affected accordingly. Murdock examines the effect on kinship terminology of the presence or absence of polygyny, the various rules of marriage residence, the several forms of the family, consanguineal kin groups, and special marriage rules. The various configurations of conditions are arranged to yield twenty-six theorems, most of which are divided into several sub-theorems. Each sub-theorem is a statement about various conditions under which specified pairs and trios of kin types are called by the same term.

In this method, the validity of the postulate is established

23

only if all the theorems derived from it are proved to be true. If any one theorem that has been deduced from the postulate is shown to be empirically false, then the postulate is disproved. We should note that most of Murdock's assertions about culture cannot be refuted simply by discovering a single society in which the assertion seems to be false. As we shall see later, Murdock argues that the laws of social science have to be expressed in tendencies, i.e. in stochastic terms (see below, p. 51). Single negative instances, or 'misses' as Naroll would call them, may be of interest but do not provide decisive evidence. However, when he adopts the 'postulational method', with its more rigorous form of argument, Murdock does have to deal with the possible decisive single negative instance, but in the guise of a single disproved derived theorem rather than of a single aberrant society. In fact his basic postulate states more than is strictly necessary for deducing his theorems, and hence is more vulnerable to refutation than it need be. According to the basic postulate, identity of kinship terms occurs 'in inverse proportion to the number and relative efficacy' of the relevant 'social equalizers'. All the derived theorems are of the simple form 'ABC tends to be associated with XYZ' and do not depend in any way on the quantitative relations entailed by the reference to 'inverse proportion' in the basic postulate. We shall discuss what sort of quantitative meaning Murdock has in mind when we come to consider his statistical procedures in a later section.

He adduces the usual kind of statistical evidence in support of each of the 120 derived theorems and sub-theorems. Societies are grouped into those in which the required conditions are present, and those where they are absent, and also into those where the required pairs or trios of kin types are called by the same term, and those where they are not. From this a two-by-two table is constructed, and the likelihood of the existence of a correlation assessed statistically. Some of the theorems receive stronger statistical support than others, but none is disproved, and Murdock interprets this result as decisive validation for his basic postulate.

24

3   Culture or society?

We have seen how Murdock organizes his ethnographic data and, in outline, how he uses this data to provide statistical evidence to support statements about culture. These statements are derived in part from several social sciences and refer particularly to the existence of functional relations between different aspects of culture and to the way in which cultures change. We now turn to a closer examination of the way in which he uses the idea of culture, first, by looking at the contrast between culture and society, and then at another contrast, between culture and behaviour. This examination will, I hope, enable us to see more clearly what connexion there is between events in the real world and the coded input to the statistical procedure used in the cross-cultural method.

So far I have tried to make a clear distinction between 'culture' and 'society', using 'culture' for a collection of customary habits of thought and action, together with appropriate material equipment, and 'society' for an organized and relatively self-contained group of people sharing a culture. This is how Murdock sometimes uses these words, but there have been several shifts in his usage that throw light on the development of his ideas and that bear on the problem of how the sampling unit is defined in cross-cultural inquiries.

Some sort of distinction between society and culture has long been recognized. Just what distinction this is, or should be, is a question that has been discussed by many writers. For our purposes, it is sufficient to observe that certain individuals are linked to one another by a network of rights and duties, and interact with one another with some measure of regularity; they thus form a society. In so far as they share a pattern of expectations, evaluations, and symbolic meanings, they have a common culture (cf. Nadel 1951: 79–80). It is obvious that many people can think alike without having anything to do with one another, and that many people who came into contact with each other every day hold radically different views about good and evil, the nature of the universe, and the right way to behave. For example, Holmberg has shown that there is scarcely any contact at all between one Siriono band and another, even though they appear to follow the same way of life (Holmberg 1950: 50–52); on the other hand there are many well-known examples of plural or stratified societies where, despite daily contact between members of different strata, their mode of existence, scale of values, symbolic systems, and social organization differ radically. Hence units of common culture, if these exist, cannot necessarily be equated with the units of mutual interaction which we call societies. Yet although Murdock refers in one of his earliest papers to 'the fundamental distinction between the social and the cultural' (1932: 209), in much of his subsequent work he seems to assume that a sample of cultures and a sample of societies can be isomorphic and that it is mere pedantry to insist always on the distinction between them.

Tylor (1889) refers to his sampling units as 'peoples', while Hobhouse, Wheeler, and Ginsberg (1914) use terms like 'tribes' and 'social groups'. In the early paper just mentioned Murdock writes enthusiastically about the study of culture and argues that 'the proper study of sociology is culture' (1932: 210). It is therefore not surprising that the organization established at Yale in 1937 was called the Cross-Cultural, rather than Cross-Societal, Survey. In his explanatory article on the Survey, Murdock stresses its concern with culture. Yet it seems that at this stage what he had in mind as his unit of study is not so much a distinctive culture as the culture of a distinctive group. He says 'The habits which the members of a social group share with one another constitute the culture of that group' (1940a: 365). Since this formulation is followed immediately by an attack on Lowie for asserting that 'a culture is invariably an artificial unit segregated for purposes of expediency' (Lowie 1937: 235), I assume that Murdock puts forward his statement as a definition. Thus two separate social groups whose cultures are identical would, by this definition, generate two cultures. The sample containing 250 units which Murdock used is described in 1937 and 1940 as a sample of cultures, but in 1949, in *Social structure*, the same sample becomes
26

a sample of societies (1937c: 460; 1940a: 369; 1949a: viii). The *Outline of world cultures* is said to be a classification of 'The societies and cultures of the world' (1954a: ii). The 'World ethnographic sample' is a sample of 565 cultures, while the Atlas that has superseded it is a sample of 862 societies (1957a: 667; 1967: 7). Yet we cannot simply treat the two terms as synonyms. In another paper where he refers to the units of the Human Relations Area Files both as cultures and as societies, Murdock (1953) also deals at length with the distinction between the two terms. He attempts here to relate a series of cultural units of decreasing uniformity – local cultural variant, sub-culture, culture, culture cluster, and culture area – with a parallel series of culture-bearing social units of increasing size – community, sub-tribe, tribe, nation, and region. He draws an analogy with biological taxonomic differentiation into sub-variety, variety, etc., and makes 'culture' and 'tribe' correspond to 'species'. In the discussion accompanying the proposed classification, Murdock draws attention to some of the difficulties of applying these categories to the ethnographic evidence. He gives a formal definition of a culture as 'including all local cultural variants exhibited by communities within a particular geographical area which speak mutually intelligible languages and have essentially similar forms of economic adjustment', a community being defined as a local group – 'a band, village or neighbourhood – which seems to be the smallest social group to carry essentially a total culture'.

Culture clusters and nations appear in this scheme, as I understand it, as optional taxonomic levels that are present only when peoples with different cultures have been united under a single government. Under these conditions, 'Social unity exceeds cultural unity and gives rise to institutions, usually economic and often religious as well as political, which, though cultural, are not truly a part of the component cultures' (1953: 479). Murdock mentions that wherever they exist, culture clusters have been used as the units of classification in the Files rather than the constituent tribes, i.e. cultures.

From these comments it becomes apparent that the analogy

27

between a biological genus and a culture, cluster or nation is very weak; a genus contains several similar species whereas a nation contains, on this definition, several tribes characterized by the fact that their cultures are different rather than similar. We should also note that culture clusters, as defined in 1953, are quite distinct concepts from the clusters of genetically related culture-bearing units (earlier called 'cultural types') which appear in the Atlas (Murdock 1966: 99; 1967: 3–4; Murdock *et al.* 1963: 249). We shall consider this latter class of clusters when we discuss sampling procedures (pp. 92–95).

The difference between culture and society might seem not to matter for cross-cultural inquiries if we are content to regard the input to the inquiry, whether this be the content of selected lines of the Atlas or information from some similarly arranged source, as statements about the state of culture at a particular point on the earth's surface, at a particular moment of time. We would then have to concern ourselves neither with the delimitation of the area within which people share a common culture nor with the range of social interaction around the reference point. In a later section (pp. 75ff.) we shall discuss some of the complications in statistical handling that this interpretation of ethnographic data entails. But even before we come to consider statistical and sampling problems, the ambiguous status of the units in cross-cultural analysis in some instances causes difficulties from which the notion of 'culture at a point', as we might call it, provides no escape. In a nation, as Murdock defines it, we have at least three cultures or partial cultures. Some cultural institutions link the two (or more) segments of the nation, while apart from these each segment has its own culture which, by definition, differs from that of the other segment (cf. Murdock 1964a: 301). How can this degree of local diversity be represented in a single line of the Atlas, when for each characteristic one and only one attribute can be selected?

For example, let us look at the Hima herders and Iru tillers who are politically and socially united in certain east African societies and who are specifically mentioned in Murdock's
28

discussion of nations. Internal cultural diversity among one of these peoples, the Nyankole (Regional identification and code number: Ad45 787), is indicated in an instalment of the Atlas by supplementary comments on the coded attributes stating that the cultures of the two segments of the 'nation' differ in respect of kin terms for cousins, prohibitions on marriage with cousins, and settlement pattern (Murdock *et al.* 1966: 116, 118, 129). But it is not clear to me how this internal cultural diversity can make itself felt in the usual form of statistical analysis. The significance of diversity, when subjecting ethnographic data to the cross-cultural method of analysis, is further obscured by the fact that in the separately published version of the Atlas, these comments on the Nyankole are omitted. On the other hand, comments about an ethnic form of class stratification do appear for two other 'nations' in the same area, Rundi (Ae8 309) and Ruanda (Ae10 640), although these comments did not appear in the instalments (Murdock *et al.* 1962b: 539; 1965: 118; 1966: 129–130; Murdock 1967: 11). The other non-industrial 'nation' mentioned by Murdock, the League of the Iroquois, is said to contain 'five tribes with distinct languages and cultures'. It is represented in the *Social structure* sample by one of its constituent tribes, and in the 'World ethnographic sample' it appears under its own name, without any indication of internal diversification. In an instalment of the Atlas there is a comment that the selected tribe had moieties, while two other constituent tribes did not. This is the only indication of the existence of 'distinct languages and cultures', and even this comment disappears from the separately published version of the Atlas (Murdock 1949a: 361; 1953: 479–480; 1957a: 684; 1967: 38; Murdock *et al.* 1965: 121). These changes may perhaps all be due to the continual correction and improvement of the coded information contained in the Atlas but equally they suggest that the system is unsuited to cope with this kind of observed intra-unit diversity. This conclusion is confirmed by the treatment of China. Although China, excluding Tibet and Mongolia, 'is, and has long been, essentially a single society', it nevertheless contains several

29

distinct cultural types, each of which is represented in the Atlas by a separate culture (Murdock *et al.* 1963: 249–250; Murdock 1967: 22). The definition of 'nation' contains almost the only formal recognition in Murdock's analytical scheme of internal diversity as a significant cultural characteristic. One of Leach's criticisms of the cross-cultural method is that its range of attributes is inadequate for classifying even the culture of a society as undiversified as the Kachin (Leach 1964a). We shall see later that although Murdock makes poor provision for internal diversity, he is concerned with diversity of two other kinds; diversity of behaviour rather than of culture, and the diversity of a sample of cultures.

Murdock's analysis is tuned to examine cultures which are ostensibly homogeneous, despite his entirely commendable desire to include as part of his evidence information about complex industrial societies. This concentration on technologically simpler rather than on complex societies also shows itself in the emphasis given throughout his work to face-to-face relationships rather than large-scale political and economic institutions. The chapter in *Social structure* entitled 'The community' is the shortest in the book, chieftainship is mentioned only briefly, and almost nothing is said about legal institutions. In the 'World ethnographic sample', two characteristics (double column 14) deal with social stratification, one with five attributes and the other four. The Atlas contains rather more information about these aspects of culture, with nine characteristics (columns 31, 32, 67, 69, and 71) which, broadly speaking, are significant in the classification of complex rather than simpler societies. Nevertheless the complex societies of Murdock's 'Circum-Mediterranean region', i.e. Europe, Turkey, the Caucasus, the Semitic Near East, and the overseas settlements in America, South Africa, and Oceania, fit uneasily into the cross-cultural scheme, as Murdock (1966: 108) seems to admit. The handling of one of the complex societies outside this region, China, in cross-cultural inquiries has been the subject of considerable controversy, as we shall see later. Writing in a sociological journal about the significance of face-to-face relations, Murdock (1950c: 714) says that 'Sociological analysis can advance only if we segregate towns and cities as a fundamentally distinct category from the universal phenomenon of a small local community with its maximum population of not more than a thousand'. In his effort to break down the ethnographic parochialism within which so much of the sociological analysis of complex societies is conducted, Murdock may have failed to make adequate provision in his own analytical scheme for these 'fundamentally distinct' phenomena and the specialized social institutions that go with them.

4   Culture or behaviour?

What people would like to do, or think it would be right to do, or expect they will do, usually differs from what they do in fact. The distinctions are sometimes hard to draw and it is often hard to get reliable evidence on these different aspects of human behaviour, but the distinctions are clear enough in principle. In practice the picture of social life built up from one point of view may differ radically from that built up from another. Murdock discusses these distinctions in several of his works and despite his early statement, noted above, that 'the proper study of sociology is culture', tends to equate sociology with the study of what people actually do. Anthropology for him is more concerned with 'ideals to which behaviour should conform' (1940a: 366; 1954b: 22). Whether or not this characterization of the two disciplines is correct does not concern us here; our task is to determine what kind of evidence Murdock himself deals with.

In his 1940 statement of objectives he says that he is trying to study the common aspects of all human cultures, and goes on to discuss some of the characteristics of culture formation. He then distinguishes culture from behaviour. An element of culture is a traditionally accepted idea that a particular kind of behaviour should conform to an established precedent. Behaviour may differ from the culturally prescribed precedent because of the individual actor's impulses or 'the nature of the circumstances'. Hence an ethnographic monograph, which reports ideal norms, is poles apart from a typical community study, which reports the statistical norms of actual behaviour (1940: 366). He goes even further when he writes that anthropologists 'are primarily concerned with the culture patterns which define proper conduct and scarcely at all with the actual social interaction by which such patterns come alive in the behaviour of individuals' (1950c: 717). When he writes that 'the norms of man's social interaction are as definitely a part of culture as are the norms of his reactions to the external material world' (1955: 362), the ambiguous term 'norms' presumably refers to expectations and ideals rather than to actual frequencies of behaviour.

If then Murdock's sample is assembled for the purpose of studying culture, it would seem that we have to deal with ideal or correct patterns of behaviour rather than with the actions people actually perform. It is this premiss that enables Murdock to use, in many instances, dichotomous attributes whereby a tribe is classified as either having, or not having, some specified cultural trait. Much ethnographic reporting describes valued norms rather than observed behaviour. For example, it is often easier to determine whether or not a tribe has a rule of exogamy than it is to discover how often the rule, if it exists, is broken. Cultural rules, Murdock implies, can be determined by asking about them, for '. . . as every ethnographer knows most people show in marked degree an awareness of their own cultural norms, an ability to differentiate them from purely individual habits, and a facility in conceptualizing and reporting them . . .'. An exception is made for grammatical rules, which are part of culture but which are not conceptualized by those who follow them (1940a: 366).

Yet it is apparent from an examination of Murdock's material that he is concerned with much more than ideal patterns as these are commonly understood. For example, he discusses (1950b) the facilities for gaining divorce in a sample of 40 selected non-European societies or cultures and comes to the

32

conclusion that in only one society, the Crow, is a positive value placed on divorce. Divorce, it would seem, is thus part of Crow culture. Among the others, 'the general attitude is clearly that it is regrettable but often necessary'. Here culture includes actions which are not regarded as ideal but which, for people in at least some 19 of Murdock's sample cultures, are frequent throughout the life of the individual. Presumably Murdock means that individuals are frequently divorced and not that people believe that divorce ought to take place frequently. We are back in the world of actual behaviour.

The example is taken from a separate paper, and not from *Social structure* itself, where Murdock does not discuss divorce, referring to it as a 'non-structural' aspect of marriage, along with marriage ceremonial (1949a: 22). But even in the book real behaviour keeps creeping in. When discussing polygyny Murdock stresses that since there are a limited number of women available, one man's polygyny entails another man's celibacy. In most societies, whether or not polygyny is allowed, most men have to content themselves with one wife or none. Hence he plumps for a definition of a polygynous society which includes those societies where 'the culture permits, and public opinion encourages' polygyny, irrespective of how frequently polygyny actually occurs. Yet even this definition, with its distinction between culture and public opinion, is not entirely satisfactory; what sort of culture would it be that was opposed to public opinion? When he turns to consider the polygynous family, Murdock moves abruptly from the cultural to the behavioural level. He says: 'Here the issue is less what is culturally permitted or preferred than what is the normal social structure under which the majority of the population actually live' (1949a: 28). He sets an arbitrary dividing line at 20 per cent. If less than one marriage in five in any society is polygynous, the 'prevailing form of the family' is assumed to be monogamous. Hence in a society where only one marriage in four is polygynous, the prevailing family form is said to be polygynous. I think this is misleading.

The same mixture of ideal and actual behaviour enters into

33

Murdock's classification of marriage residence, with particular reference to the state of affairs when a couple are free to choose whether they will live with the bride's relatives or with the groom's. In discussing comments made by various writers on the attributes used for this characteristic in the 'World ethnographic sample', Murdock and his co-editors write 'We are not greatly concerned with distinguishing rules from practice in our definitions, since we assume that in integrated societies, for which our system is primarily designed, rules are ordinarily reasonably consistent with prevailing practice' (Murdock *et al.* 1962b: 117). Here he must have overlooked his earlier remarks about the rarity of integrated societies. Seven of the ten attributes he defines for this characteristic refer to the existence of cultural rules or norms prescribing a single mode of residence. Yet, despite the assumption of integration, the other three attributes, coded as B, C, and D, refer to the occurrence in the society concerned of one or other of three pairs of modes of residence, 'where neither alternative exceeds the other in actual frequency by a ratio greater than two to one' (cf. also Murdock 1967: 48). These three attributes must refer to behaviour, not to culture. Only in a society inhabited entirely by neurotic statisticians, or in one where all aspects of life have to confirm to a central diversified plan, would a cultural norm involving ratios be at all feasible, at least when we are dealing with marriage residence. It is true that in statistically sophisticated industrial societies it is possible for people to adopt a quantified cultural norm such as 'The level of unemployment ought to be about five per cent of the labour force', but I am sure that Murdock does not have this kind of norm in mind (nor I think does Lévi-Strauss; cf. p. 129 below).

Some attributes indicate the presence of both cultural rule and actual practice. Thus for example Murdock classifies societies as having the sororate only when the marriage of a widower to a sister of his deceased wife is 'common and genuinely preferential'. With some topics, it is clear that Murdock is dealing with ideals, with what people think ought to happen. His classification of kinship terminology is, I think we can

34

assume, entirely in terms of ideals. The *correct* term for a mother's brother is such-and-such, and the fact that in anomo-lous circumstances he may be called something else is irrelevant. Most ethnographic reports are written in this way and this alone would have limited Murdock's choice. In his discussion of incest, he is principally concerned with allowed or disallowed actions rather than with what is ideal or correct. When he discusses descent and social stratification he is interested in what actually happens most of the time.

The fact that these characteristics are abstracted from reality by different procedures, or, if you will, relate to different levels of abstraction, does not necessarily imply that they may not be correlated with one another. But Murdock does not discuss the way in which he has built up the ideal-real constellation to which he gives the name culture, nor is it likely that all the sources he uses for his evidence follow his or any other standard recipe. Most ethnographers have paid little attention to these matters because of the assumption that for the most part no significant differences exist between ideals, preferences, expectations, and actions. The concept of 'custom' embraces all these things, and it is easy to flit from one to the other without knowing it. In fact, a people's view of their own tradi-tional and distinctive behaviour may differ widely from their behaviour (cf. Barnes 1951a: 7–8; 1951b: 298) and people may often be unable to do that which they would prefer to do.

Another mixture of rules and practices is to be found with cross-cousin marriage. In *Social structure*, most of Murdock's discussion is in terms of rules of preferential marriage, not of frequent or prescribed marriage. He does however remark that in order to influence kinship terminology, such marriages must constitute a majority (1949a: 123). In the attributes used with the 'World ethnographic sample', marriage preferences and prohibitions are the relevant criteria. In the Atlas, however, Murdock distinguishes between relatives who cannot be married, those with whom marriage is merely permitted, and those with whom it is positively preferential or prescriptive

35

(Murdock *et al.* 1962b: 120). The rubrics for the various attributes are phrased in terms of preferences, not prescriptions, but it would seem that Murdock does not wish to distinguish between those two notions. However it has become abundantly clear from professional discussions during the last two decades that marriage preferences and marriage prescriptions are two distinct phenomena, even though there may still be argument about just what the differences are. In the present context it is sufficient merely to note that a preference for marriage with a certain type of relative is just as much a part of culture as a prescriptive rule; but it is a different part. A preference is not to be confounded with a frequent occurrence; this is the error of using pseudo-causal language against which Steiner complains (see below p. 40). A form of marriage may be preferential and yet rare. In my own culture, marriage to an heiress is preferential, but heiresses are hard to get and most of us have perforce to make other arrangements.

From this analysis we conclude that the scheme of attributes used by Murdock to classify cultures is designed, mainly but not entirely, for fully integrated cultures in which actual behaviour conforms broadly to cultural norms. This scheme is applied to societies which, in the majority of instances, are not fully integrated and in which behaviour and cultural norm cannot be assumed to coincide. Information about these imperfectly integrated societies reaches us via ethnographers who, in varying aspects and to varying degrees, have reported mixtures of norms and practices and have, or have not, distinguished between them. This, of course, is a rather gloomy view of the cross-cultural method; it may be that despite these imperfections, the method still works well enough and is the best we have at present. Naroll (1962) has at least made a start towards determining how seriously, if at all, these imperfections affect the results achieved by the method.

Although Murdock distinguishes formally between culture and behaviour, the close connexion he postulates between them enables him often to write as if they were the same. He does draw a distinction in discussing how changes come about.

Social change, he says, begins with innovation, 'the formation of a new habit by a single individual' and he distinguishes between different kinds of innovation – variation, invention, tentation, and cultural borrowing. The next stage comes with the process of social acceptance. 'So long as an innovation, whether original or borrowed, is practised by the innovator alone in his society, it is an individual habit and not an element of culture. To become the latter it must be accepted by others, it must be socially shared.' After acceptance, the shared habits that constitute a culture become 'progressively adapted to one another so that they tend to form an integrated whole' (Murdock 1956a: 250, 257–258, 259). I find it hard to fit a cultural change involving collective action, for example the adoption of parliamentary democracy in New Guinea, into this scheme although Murdock intends the scheme to apply not only to changes resulting from decisions by individuals, such as tattooing 'extended over a wider area of the body' and altered skirt lengths, but also to changes such as the adoption of patrilineal descent and, in the United States, the introduction of the New Deal.

With this notion of culture presumably in mind, Murdock writes that culture is learned, inculcated, ideational, and gratifying. More importantly for this stage in our discussion, rather than saying that behaviour is adaptive, which might be an ethologist's assertion, Murdock says that culture is adaptive. This assertion enables him to link culture directly with the process of learning by trial and error. For example, in a discussion of the ban on marriage and sexual intercourse between a man and his mother, sister, and daughter (prohibitions which are certainly part of culture in Murdock's terms), he writes: 'These universal prohibitions are understandable only as an adaptive provision, arrived at everywhere by a process of mass trial and error, by which sexual rivalry is inhibited . . .' (1950b: 200). This statement leaves unstated whether the mass trials are still continuing or whether now that incest taboos have become part of culture the trials have been discontinued. But the assertion that the taboos were

37

attained 'everywhere by a process of trial' suggests that Murdock envisages the taboos as the result of trials that took place everywhere, and presumably also all the time, rather than having been arrived at by trial and error in a few places and then spread everywhere else by diffusion.

A clear expression of culture as what one might term the summation of past behaviour is found in a comment Murdock makes on a statement by Leach. There is no space here to dissect Leach's views and my interpretation may well be wrong. As I understand, Leach on this occasion argues, in direct opposition to the view of Lévi-Strauss, that, at least for some societies, the concept 'social structure' is more usefully applied to a statistical model of actual behaviour than to a mechanical model of cultural ideas. With the Iban and Sinhalese in mind, Leach writes that 'social structures are sometimes best regarded as the statistical outcome of multiple individual choices rather than a direct reflection of jural rules' (Leach 1960a: 124). This statement indicates to me that Leach sees jural rules, i.e. consciously expressed culture, as being sometimes significantly different from the summation of actual behaviour (cf. below, pp. 55–56). Murdock, in my view, misunderstands Leach but makes his own position quite clear when he comments editorially: 'With this point of view I must register hearty and enthusiastic agreement . . . I would even go further and assert that social structures are always best regarded in the same light, and that jural rules themselves are the "outcome of multiple individual choices" in situations where one kind of choice is likely to be appreciably more strongly or regularly regarded than possible alternative choices.' He then goes on to attack 'certain British extreme structuralists who assert the opposite' (Murdock 1960a: 9). He extends the same doctrine to the whole of culture when he says:

> Whenever social behaviour persistently deviates from established cultural habits in any direction, it results in modifications first in social expectations, and then in customs, beliefs, and rules. Gradually, in this way, collective habits are altered

38

and the culture comes to accord better with the new norms of actual behavior (Murdock 1956a: 249).

We can draw the threads of our argument together at this point. According to Murdock there is operative in culture 'a selective process analogous to natural selection on the biological plane by which adaptations in culture are brought into being and perpetuated' (Murdock 1945: 136). Changes in culture are the consequence of multiple individual choices and are reached by a process of mass trial and error. The various aspects of the culture of society influence one another selectively and cause adaptive changes in culture to occur which result in greater cultural integration. If then our aim is to discover which attributes of culture influence, or have a functional relation to, which other attributes, and if we wish to measure the strength of these various relations and to determine their causal significance, it would seem that part of the evidence we must take into account are the processes of individual choice and mass trial and error.

5   Time and process

Given a sample of societies, and given an attribute A associated with characteristic X, and attribute B associated with characteristic Y, it is a simple matter to discover by counting in how many societies A and B occur together, and in how many they occur separately. It is then easy to calculate the probability that the co-occurrences are due to chance. If chance is an unlikely explanation, we then assume that there is some kind of systematic connexion between A and B. The statistical evidence may tell us nothing about the kind of causal connexion, if any, that exists between A and B. It cannot tell us anything at all about the mechanism that links them or about the chronological order in which A and B may first have appeared in the various societies, for we have evidence merely about their simultaneous presence at the time of inquiry. Yet Murdock,

39

like most of his readers, is interested in establishing directional causal relations and in postulating the socio-cultural mechanism through which they operate. More than many of his colleagues he is also interested in establishing temporal relations. The transition from synchronic evidence to diachronic causal inference is a crucial stage in his argument. Unfortunately this transition is clouded by his use of phrases which vaguely suggest causal connexions without asserting them unequivocally. When we say that A tends to be associated with B, the verb 'tend' does not necessarily imply any temporal sequence of action, and can if necessary be given a quantified meaning (e.g. Textor 1967: 36). But in ordinary speech tendencies may also be trends and it is easy to glide from synchronic to diachronic relationship. As Steiner (1951) points out, Murdock often uses 'a pseudo-chronological erudite colloquialism' – A tends to produce B, A is conducive to B, A favours B – when the only firm evidence is that A and B are simultaneously present. This manner of exposition sometimes leads Murdock into saying both that A causes B and that B causes A, as De Lint and Cohen (1960: 100) point out, as well as implying incompatible temporal relations.

But if at many places in his writings Murdock is merely using causal and temporal expressions rather loosely and figuratively, he is also elsewhere explicitly concerned with establishing an orderly temporal sequence of adaptive changes in various aspects of social organization. Murdock argues that external influences, i.e. famines, epidemics, wars, migrations, impinge more directly on some aspects of social organization than on others, and that adaptive changes in these aspects precede changes in the others. The key feature of social organization in setting in train the long sequence of cultural adjustment that leads from one stable integrated state to another is the rule of division of labour according to sex. This has a direct effect on the rule of post-marital residence, which is 'particularly vulnerable to external influences' (Murdock 1949a: 201). Murdock derives this view of the key part played by the rule of residence from the writings of Lowie (1949), though he notes

that Tylor also took changes in the rule as the starting point
for changes in other cultural characteristics. Changes in the
rule of residence lead to changes in the system of clans and
extended families, i.e. in the rule of descent. Changes in kinship
terminology begin after the localized clan system has changed,
but these changes are largely immune from direct outside
influences and may take place slowly, so that the final change
to a new system is sometimes not complete until long after a
new descent rule has been established. Thus a changing
society is continually altering itself so as to come nearer to
a new stable condition appropriate to its new external conditions. But before it achieves a stable condition, 'historical
and cultural influences originating outside the system' may
alter the rule of residence again, and the society sets off on a
new tack to a new stable goal (Murdock 1949a: 221–222).

This model of orderly adaptive sequential change, arbitrarily
interrupted by external influences, has been caricatured by De
Lint and Cohen (1960: 96) as 'one-factor magic'. They note
that although at various points in *Social structure* Murdock
attributes all changes in social organization to the effects,
direct or indirect, of an initial change in residence rule, elsewhere in the book and in other papers he argues *en passant* for
other modes and causes of adaptive change. For example, he
notes that a change in religion may bring about directly a
change in marriage rules, and that in Africa the introduction
of cattle has led to patrilocality (Murdock 1949a: 137n, 203;
1960b: 187). He still maintains the importance of the residence
rule in inducing major structural changes while admitting that
a shift in land tenure may determine which of two kinds of
bilateral organization are adopted (1959b: 140). However,
despite the force of this criticism, our attention here is directed
not at the notion of functional relations of some kind or other
between attributes, an idea few social scientists would reject,
but at the sampling and statistical procedures which are the
distinctive features of the cross-cultural method. We need note
merely that although these procedures are compatible with
the hypothesis of the existence of a single-factor stimulus to

c

adaptive or evolutionary change, they do not necessarily require one single factor such as a marriage residence rule, and only that, to trigger off a sequence of changes.

As might be expected from the criticism advanced by De Lint and Cohen, Murdock relies more on verbal argument and less on statistical evidence for his assertion of the causal primacy of changes in the rule of post-marital residence. A systematic attempt to educe statistical evidence for an orderly sequence of adaptive changes in certain cultural characteristics has been undertaken by Driver (1967). He tests Murdock's hypothesis that when societies shift from one stable structural type to another, the division of labour changes first, then residence after marriage, followed by the rule of descent, and finally by the kinship terminology. Driver inserts land tenure after residence and before descent, and shows that sister–cousin kinship terms change before mother–aunt terms. He confines his analysis to aboriginal North America, and his argument is based partly on the spatial distribution of cultural traits, exemplified in distribution maps, and partly on direct and indirect historical evidence. Thus, far, his method of analysis is broadly similar to that followed by Murdock himself in his book on *Africa* (1959a). However, by correlating all the variables, Driver seeks to show that correlations between pairs of cultural traits that are adjacent in this sequence of response to change are higher than those between non-adjacent pairs. His statistical evidence provides support for the validity of the sequence, or for a completely reversed sequence. Presumably he has other grounds for ruling out this latter interpretation.

Murdock's most ambitious attempt to make use of the notion of orderly adaptive change is contained in a chapter of *Social structure* entitled 'The evolution of social structure'. This is the longest chapter in the book, and the arguments advanced in it are given further support in a lengthy appendix. Murdock refers to adaptive changes in cultural characteristics as 'evolutionary' but it is clear that he has in mind what Service (1960: 748–749) describes as specific, rather than general, evolution. Murdock is not concerned with the irreversible evolutionary

42

changes that we presume must have occurred during the last ten millennia or so as societies based on hunting and collecting give way to agricultural tribes and modern industrial states. For the most part Murdock deals only with changes taking place within a given major stratum of general evolutionary development. Hence many of the changes he considers are reversible or cyclical.

The problem Murdock faces is simple. The evidence in the sample relates to the presence or absence of certain attributes in specified societies. The unit societies are all treated as timeless entities, existing in that twilight zone between warm reality and chilly model that we call the 'ethnographic present', even though they may be given a temporal label. No two units of the sample represent the 'same' society at two points of historical time, and the sample evidence is restricted to information on the presence or absence of the attributes in the several societies at a single instant of time, real or postulated. Yet from this evidence Murdock wishes to derive information about the way societies change their cultural characteristics, i.e. the presence or absence of the selected attributes, with the passage of time. He does help his argument with a few references to information not contained in the sample, as when he refers to the shift from matrilocality and matriliny to patrilocality and patriliny made by the Henga of Nyasaland under Ngoni influence (1949a: 209, 212); but these are incidental asides and do not form part of his main line of argument.

This argument may be summarized briefly. Some forms of society are stable, and are characterized by compatibility between the rule of residence, the rule of descent, and the terminology for cousins. For example, bilateral descent is compatible with neolocal or bilocal residence, and with a cousin terminology which does not discriminate between FZD and MBD, nor between FBD and MZD (i.e. Eskimo, Hawaiian, and Iroquois). Similarly, patrilineal descent is compatible with patrilocal residence. Ninety-seven of the 250 sample societies are classified as having compatible or stable forms, so that we cannot equate 'compatibility' with 'cultural integration', which

43

is said to be rare. Murdock does not discuss the difference between compatibility or stability and integration; maybe the compatible societies are perfectly integrated in respect of the three defining characteristics, but not necessarily in respect of others.

Other forms, defined by other combinations of attributes for these three characteristics, lack this compatibility and are to be regarded as transitional or incipient forms in which the full effect of a change in one characteristic has not yet manifested itself in the other characteristics. Initially, changes are caused by external factors, and 'quite different external influences are capable of producing an identical effect upon social organization, and . . . there are several series of multiple factors capable of producing different effects' (1949a: 200). The incompatibilities present in any society provide evidence of its probable antecedents.

At a formal level Murdock's working assumptions are not far removed from those held by the nineteenth century anthropologists who worked with a doctrine of survivals (Hodgen 1936), and there are fairly close parallels with the attempts to infer former marriage arrangements from present kinship terminologies exemplified in the work of Rivers (1914; cf. Firth 1968). The similarities are little more than formal, however, for the incompatibilities which Murdock makes use of in his technique of historical reconstruction are not survivals from some postulated earlier stage of general evolution but from a comparatively recent stage of 'specific' evolution. Furthermore Murdock does not rely on a vague notion of random survivals but on a precise, perhaps overprecise, model of orderly adaptive change based on the idea of 'cultural lag'. The sequences of cultural change he postulates are caused by internal interaction between characteristics of culture, rather than due to 'historical' influences from outside, and the changes are cyclical and sometimes reversible rather than progressive and always irreversible.

As we have seen, Murdock recognizes only a few different varieties of descent, residence rules, and kinship terminology.

He asserts that whereas some culture traits, such as myths, ceremonials and artefacts, are capable of very varied elaboration, the characteristics or traits of social organization possess only a strictly limited range of possibilities and can occur together in one society in only a limited number of combinations. This limitation on the range of possible forms of social organization makes scientific generalization possible, whereas no useful generalizations can be made about the way in which more variable aspects of culture change with time. In other words, Murdock argues in effect that the use of only a few attributes for the characteristics of social structure is not a limitation necessarily though unfortunately imposed by the mechanics of coding, but instead truly reflects the limited range of possibilities open to a society in real life. This view seems to conflict with his earlier statement that 'The true universals of culture, then, are not identities in habit, in definable behavior. They are similarities in classification, not in content' (1945: 125). I take this statement to mean that despite their differing content of customary behaviour, cultures can be classified satisfactorily in trans-cultural categories. The successive alterations Murdock has made in his analytical scheme demonstrate to me that there is not just one set of trans-cultural categories; use reveals that some sets are better than others, but they are all categories established by the analyst for his own convenience. The limitation on the range of possible variation in traits of social organization is merely a consequence of the limited number of alternative attributes used in classification, and a similar constraint applies when we classify myths, ceremonials, and the like. Yet in *Social structure* Murdock insists that cultural similarities occur only because of this limitation on the possible variations in social organization. I find this assertion both illogical and unnecessary, for Murdock does not claim that his analytical categories are anything more than convenient working tools. In subsequent chapters we shall comment on analogous statements made by Lévi-Strauss and Fortes about their own analytical schemes.

In *Social structure* Murdock distinguishes only four kinds of

45

rules of descent, five kinds of residence rule, and six types of kinship terminology, though in the Atlas more attributes are assigned to these characteristics. At several points in *Social structure* Murdock stresses the importance of changes in the division of labour according to sex in bringing about changes in the rule of residence, but he does not use the division of labour as a defining characteristic at this stage in his analysis. I presume that this is due to the greater number of possibilities of change in this characteristic which Murdock thought it necessary to recognize. In his article on the division of labour, which appeared before *Social structure*, he lists no less than 46 activities, with a five-point scale for the division of labour for each activity (1937a). Nevertheless it is curious that little use is made of this detailed information in the book, and that no information about the division of labour is included in the attributes listed for each society in the sample.

If the three chosen characteristics were independent of one another, there would be 120 possible combinations to consider. But some kinds of kinship terminology are never found with some kinds of descent rule; avunculocal and matrilocal residence rules do not occur with patrilineal descent; all societies with double descent have either a patrilocal (or matri-patrilocal) residence rule. Murdock arrives at a total of 47 possible combinations, of which 9 are held to be theoretically possible although there are no examples of these in the sample. These 47 'structural sub-types' are grouped into 11 primary types, with each type divided into 3, 4, 5, or 6 sub-types. Each type is defined by one or two rules of descent combined with one, two, or three kinds of cousin terminology. Sub-types of one type differ from one another in rule of residence or in rule of descent. Six types are described as stable, and the others are said to be incipient or transitional. For each type, one sub-type is designated as normal, and the others are named according to their defining rule of residence. All societies with double descent, however, are classified as if matriliny was dominant, so that in each of the three matrilineal types there is a sub-type defined by the presence of double descent. Murdock lists all the societies in his sample according to sub-type and gives coded information for each society in respect of seven other cultural characteristics. He shows that for most of the sub-types there is a good deal of similarity among all the member societies in these other characteristics, and draws the inference that his categories are not artificial and that his views about culture are corroborated.

There is nothing to prove or disprove in a scheme of static classification. It may be generally useful, or useful only for one purpose, but even if it is completely useless, it is not like a proposition and cannot be disproved. Whether or not Murdock's scheme is useful does not really matter, for he goes on to make statements that we can try to prove or disprove. He maintains that a society cannot change its culture so that it moves from any one of the 47 sub-types to any other; only certain moves are possible. If there were no restrictions, there would be 2,162 possible shifts. According to Murdock, only about 200 shifts are possible, and of these about half are improbable, leaving about 100 probable moves (1949a: 252–257). A puzzling minor feature of this scheme is that although the several sub-types of the Yuman and Fox types are said not to be connected in a diachronic or evolutionary sense, in contrast to the other nine sets of sub-types which are so related, shifts from one Yuman or Fox sub-type to another are listed as possible, consequential on a change of residence rule. In this respect, Yuman and Fox appear to be no different from the other types (1949a: 225, 253).

The scheme gives us 'a maze, in which a society can start at any given point and arrive at any other point whatsoever, but only by a limited number of possible routes' (1949a: 221). The 'maze' or digraph can be analysed into its three constituent parts, one for each of the three characteristics which define the structural sub-types. There are six attributes for cousin terminology, and each of the thirty shifts from one to the other is common in some appropriate context. For the other two characteristics the maze simile is more apt. Four rules of descent give a total of twelve shifts, of which eight are said to

47

be common, one rare (double to matrilineal), and three impossible (bilateral to double; patrilineal to matrilineal or double). Five attributes for rules of residence give a total of twenty shifts, of which fourteen are common and six impossible (avunculocal to bilocal or matrilocal; patrilocal to matrilocal; and bilocal, neolocal or patrilocal to avunculocal). However, when the three characteristics are taken together, the several constraints combine to reduce the number of possible shifts to about one tenth of the theoretical maximum.

Murdock uses the maze to trace out the 'social prehistory' of each sample society in turn. Thus, for example, the Tswana are in a transitional stage. They have patrilineal descent without exogamous kin groups. Residence is patrilocal, which is consistent with patrilineal descent, but their cousin terminology is of Iroquois type, in which father's sister's daughter and mother's brother's daughter are called by the same terms but are distinguished from sisters and parallel cousins. This kind of terminology is appropriate to either kind of unilineal descent, but the absence of patrilineal exogamy indicates that the Tswana are still moving towards a fully patrilineal system. Their present condition must therefore be seen as a transitional stage following a matrilineal, patrilocal condition, and that in turn was preceded by a bilocal, and before that by a matrilocal matrilineal state of society. This was a stable condition, though in this instance Murdock carries his projection one stage further back (1949a: 344–345). As with almost all the sample societies, this backward sequence is presented without the support of any kind of historical or archaeological evidence. With most of the societies in the sample, three or four steps backward suffice to arrive at a stable structural category from which the society concerned is said to have been derived. Exceptionally, with the Tanala of Madagascar, eight steps are required to reach a stable antecedent, though 'this reconstruction does no violence either to the reported ethnographic facts or to known Malayan distributions' (1949a: 343).

Murdock admits that his hypothesis in this chapter cannot be tested statistically and that 'the validation of the hypothesis must

48

rest on the extent to which the actual data as tabulated correspond to theoretical expectations' (1949a: 220). There are probably few critics who will quarrel with his contention that not all
kinds of transition from one structural subtype to another are
possible; but there are many who will hesitate to accept the sequences of changes set out for the prehistory of his sample societies.

Murdock's notion of a maze has been criticized by De Lint
and Cohen (1960), who argue that according to Murdock's list
of permissible changes, all 47 sub-types, after they have changed
not more than six times, reduce to a mere seven sub-types,
from each of which no further change is possible. This, they
say, does not make a maze. In fact Murdock's views on which
changes are possible and which are not are more complicated
than these authors suggest. A change from one sub-type to
another can be listed either according to the initial sub-type or
the sub-type reached after the change, which we may refer
to as the target sub-type. In *Social structure* there are four lists
of possible changes, two arranged by initial sub-type and two
by target sub-type. *Tables 61* to *71*, which nominate the societies
belonging to each sub-type, contain two lists of possible changes,
one arranged by initial sub-types and the other by target
sub-types. De Lint and Cohen make use of only the list arranged
by initial sub-types, and hence do not mention that although
54 changes appear in both lists, there are also 6 listed under
initial sub-type which are absent from the second list, and 14
that occur in the second list but not in the first. A third list,
arranged by initial sub-type, is given in *Table 73*, where the
changes are also classified as following from alterations in the
rule of residence, in the rule of descent, or in the terms used for
cousins. It transpires that all the 107 changes that follow from
a change in the rule of residence have been omitted from the
earlier tables, perhaps because they consist of changes from
one sub-type to another of the same type. Four of the changes
listed only by target sub-type in *Tables 61* to *71* are unaccount-
ably missing from *Table 73*, which does however contain 33
changes following alterations in descent rule or cousin terms
which are missing from the earlier tables. Finally, in *Appendix A*,

49

Table A, we have the fourth list, arranged by target sub-type. This contains only one new change not in any of the previous lists, but omits 21 of those included earlier. None of these inconsistencies is explained (Murdock 1949a: 228–247, 252–257, 324–326).

Discussing this system of possible changes, Murdock (1949a: 259) writes that 'The theory of social change propounded in this chapter, the associated typology, and the technique for historical reconstruction derived from them represent completely unanticipated products of the present study.' The unexplained inconsistencies in the four lists suggest that the technique was not fully worked out before being presented to the public. It is significant that in neither the 'World ethnographic sample' nor the *Atlas* are societies classified into the 47 sub-types, and that there is minimal reference to the results of the technique of historical reconstruction in Murdock's book on Africa (Murdock 1959a: 27, 40), despite the emphasis in that book on cultural history.

Even if the 'technique of historical reconstruction' has not been a great success, and even if the rule of post-marital residence does not always take the lead in adaptive change, we are still left with a useful model of culture as an aggregation of attributes between which there is a complex web of functional relations varying in strength and in temporal delay. We are more than adequately supplied with potential explanations for these relations; the next task is to discover where they are. In this task, Murdock employs statistics.

6   Statistical techniques

Murdock gives two main reasons why statistical methods are necessary in the study of culture. He says that because anthropologists cannot experiment with human beings, they have to fall back on quantitative comparative testing (1951b: 1). In other words, the anthropologist cannot rely on finding in nature the conditions he needs for decisively testing his hypothesis, conditions which, if he were working in some other discipline, he would hope to be able to establish in a laboratory. Instead, apart from happy accidents of the kind exploited by Mead and Holmberg, the anthropologist has to make do with the evidence thrust at him.

A more powerful reason, in my view, is given when Murdock asserts that in social science we cannot hope to discover laws which have no exceptions. In an early paper he says that 'cultures appear forever in a state of flux, always approaching but never achieving integration because of the numerous incomplete processes of readjustment which they invariably exhibit. Sociological "laws',' consequently, find expression only as tendencies, and "functions" can be discovered only with the aid of history . . .' (Murdock 1937c: 452–453). It is obvious that if sociological laws were of a kind that allowed of no exceptions, of the form 'Whenever A, then always B', most of the difficulties over sampling would disappear. If, for example, we were to assert that 'In all matrilineal societies, divorce is common', a single instance of a matrilineal society without common divorce would be sufficient to refute the assertion. There would be no need to count the number of confirmatory instances. It is only because we have to demonstrate merely a tendency, or imperfect correlation, that recourse to statistics is needed. Assertions that admit of no exceptions are notoriously hazardous to sustain in social science, partly because of the difficulty of determining the empirical facts and partly because of the similarity of effects produced by different causes (cf. Köbben 1967).

If we notice that in many societies, but not in all, two attributes appear together, there are two tactics we can adopt. Either we can merely state that one attribute tends to be associated with the other and go on to measure the strength of the association; or, by examining the contrary instances, we can progressively refine our generalization so as to reduce the number of instances that contradict it. For example, in their study of matrilateral cross-cousin marriage, Homans and Schneider (1955) follow the latter procedure.

On the whole Murdock follows the first of these alternatives.

51

He endeavours to demonstrate that one feature of social life tends to be, rather than always is, associated with another. In his 1940 article on the Cross-Cultural Survey, he says that he will undertake detailed examination of all 'exceptions or negative cases' (1940a: 370). However, in *Social structure* this procedure, although desirable, is said to be impracticable in view of the large number of contexts in which this would have to be done (1949a: ix). In fact, the procedure followed necessitates only occasional discussion of negative examples. Instead of an all-or-none attitude to correlation, Murdock seeks to show that the presence or absence of any one cultural attribute may be influenced by more than one factor. Indeed, at one point, he purports to demonstrate that one attribute, patrilocal residence (with or without an initial period of matrilocal residence) is correlated both with bifurcate collateral kinship terminology, in which a man calls his daughter and his brother's daughter by different terms, and also with bifurcate merging terminology, in which he calls them by the same term (1949a: 150–151, Theorems 9 and 10). This clear confrontation of statistically endorsed incompatibilities is rare. The usual form of argument can be seen, for example, in the demonstration that bifurcate merging terminology is associated with the presence of exogamous patrilineal kin groups (1949a: 164–165, Theorem 19), whereas bifurcate collateral terminology is associated with non-sororal polygyny (1949a: 146, Theorem 5). Yet non-sororal polygyny is very highly associated with patrilineal kin groups (1949a: 144). What kind of cousin terminology should we expect to find in a society with non-sororal polygyny and patrilineal kin groups, since bifurcate merging and bifurcate collateral terminologies are mutually exclusive? Murdock remarks that in patrilineal patrilocal societies 'The rules of residence and descent promote merging, whereas the associated phenomenon of general polygyny inhibits the tendency to extend terms from lineal to collateral relatives. Whether merging does or does not occur is therefore likely to depend upon such facts as which of the opposing influences has been longer established or possesses the greater relative efficacy' (1949a: 145).

In other words, we are dealing with tendencies and not with certainties. This seems to be implied by his 1940 statement that 'Only if one deals with a large number of cases can one expect to encompass all the significant causal factors, occurring in various permutations and combinations', estimate by statistical means their relative efficacy, and segregate by their quantitative preponderance the universal or cross-cultural factors from the local or historical ones' (1940a: 369).

Murdock's reliance on statistical support for the existence of functional relations between attributes inevitably channels his attention on attributes which are found in many societies rather than those that occur in only a few. His concentration on reaching generalizations 'of a universally human or cross-cultural character' (1940a: 364) also leads him to relegate to a subordinate explanatory status the evidence provided by cultures containing attributes that rarely occur. In a sense, the more often the more importance for a theory of culture. Yet he cannot entirely avoid some discussion of rare attributes, partly because other theorists have often paid particular attention to certain social institutions precisely because they are rare, and partly because he does acknowledge the intrinsic interest of exceptional or unique phenomena, as we shall see in his attitude to sampling. Thus for example polyandry is discussed in *Social structure*, but its influence on other attributes is not considered because there are only two sample societies where it is reported (1949a: 26, 140). Avunculocal residence is likewise discussed, but since there are only eight societies in the sample, its influence on other social phenomena is not assessed statistically (1949a: 35, 38, 70–71). Yet Murdock is able to state categorically that avunculocal residence can develop only out of matrilocal residence (1949a: 207–208). Likewise the significance of preferential marriage with a second cousin is not considered since it is reported only sporadically in the sample (1949a: 173–174).

Although he occasionally discusses exceptional societies one by one, Murdock seldom reaches the point at which he can assert that one attribute is either a necessary or a sufficient

53

condition for another. A significant number of contra-instances remains unexplained, and since all-or-none statements are inapplicable, the only kind of substantive assertion about the attributes that can be made must refer to the strength of the association between them. To measure this, Murdock has to use a delimited sample of societies or cultures, to which he can apply statistical indices. It is at this point that the cross-cultural method shows its distinctive features.

For Murdock, the principal reason why correlations between cultural elements are less than perfect appears to be that elements differ in the rate at which they respond and adjust themselves to changes in the external and internal social and natural environment. Köbben (1967) has discussed many of the practical considerations, such as inappropriate categorization, poor ethnographic sources, biased reporting, multicausality and the like, that lead to imperfect correlations. These are certainly important and have to be considered in executing any cross-cultural enquiry. But it is important to realize that, using Murdock's model of an adaptive culture, even if we had perfect ethnographic information and perfect ability to untangle causal chains, our analysis would still yield correlations that were less than perfect. According to Murdock's hypothesis, most societies at any time are not perfectly integrated, and the elements of their cultures will not all be in functional harmony with one another. All we can do is to see where between the two extremes of complete integration and complete random collocation the societies in our sample fall. The only landmarks between these two extremes are points on some scale of measurement, and to measure we have to count. This is where the difficulties begin. Having counted, we then have to apply statistical tests. Throughout his writings, Murdock is concerned with the composition of his sample, so that these tests may be valid. He and his co-editors write: '. . . the universe of human cultures has never been analysed and defined in such a manner as to make possible the drawing of any kind of a genuinely random sample. Under such circumstances, the use of probability statistics in comparative research is technically unwarranted.

Statistics is such a powerful scientific tool, however, that the adaptation of ethnographic data to its use is worth a heavy expenditure of effort' (Murdock *et al.* 1963: 249). The effort has certainly been heavy, but it has also been in vain unless there is a 'universe of human cultures', either existing as natural units or artificially constructed in accordance with some analytical definition arising out of the theory we hope to test. Murdock assumes that universe does exist, and his sampling and testing procedures are based on this assumption. In a later section I endeavour to challenge it.

In a review of *Social structure*, Leach (1950: 108) writes: 'I would advise the reader simply to ignore Professor Murdock's statistics and consider his verbal arguments on their own merits without regard for the alleged mathematical proof.' This advice has become harder to accept in the light of the publications that have appeared since *Social structure*, in which Murdock has devoted much more effort to improving the validity of his mathematical techniques than in strengthening his verbal arguments. The anti-diffusionist and pro-functional verbal emphasis in *Social structure* has attracted much less discussion than the reliance on statistical computations carried out on a sample of societies. His supporters have made constructive proposals for improving the mathematical basis of the cross-cultural method, while Murdock's critics have tended to assume that his verbal arguments contain nothing new and to concentrate their attention on his use of statistics.

It is important to be clear what kinds of data are subjected to statistical treatment in the cross-cultural method, particularly as Leach himself has not been clear on this point. Leach has drawn attention to the difference between, for instance, the statement that a given society has a legal or jural rule that a man may marry a cross-cousin and the statement that in this society there is a certain 'statistical frequency' of cross-cousin marriage (Leach 1957: 343). He argues that statistics are wholly irrelevant to the study of jural rules, while 'statistical phenomena' can be validated only by statistical demonstration. However, despite this preference for a statistically based concept

55

of social structure, Leach (1963) objects to the use of statistics in cross-cultural studies because in these studies jural rules are treated as if they were statistical phenomena. Leach's objection to the cross-cultural method is, I think, much the same as my own, as I hope to show later (pp. 91–92), but expressed in this way his objection misses the point. For in these studies the units which are subjected to statistical treatment are not jural rules or even 'statistical frequencies' of one or other kind of social behaviour, but unit societies or cultures. The use of statistics in cross-cultural studies has little in common with their use in describing the frequency of some mode of behaviour within a single society. In the former, the statistics relate to ethnic units, in the latter to individuals or to some specified class of social occasions. Indeed, I shall argue in the next section that what is wrong with the cross-cultural method is that it uses a sample of ethnic units whereas it might sometimes do better with a sample of individuals.

An objection to the use of ethnic units, as defined by Murdock, Naroll, or similar writers, for sampling purposes applies, or fails to apply, quite independently of how the units are sorted into categories, whether by reference to the presence or absence of some jural rule or by reference to the magnitude of the observed frequency of some specified mode of behaviour. For example, consider two sample societies used by Murdock, the Min Chinese and Tikopia. If we consider a jural rule like kinship terminology, we can add one to our list of societies with Hawaiian terminology on account of the Min Chinese, and another one for Tikopia. If we take an observed frequency like dependence on fishing, we can add one to the list of societies with between 6 and 15 per cent dependence for the Min Chinese, and one to the list of societies with between 46 and 55 per cent dependence for Tikopia (Murdock 1967: 86, 98, columns 3, 7, and 27). Either it is valid to treat Tikopia and the Chinese as statistically equivalent units in both contexts, as Murdock does, despite the enormous difference in population between the two societies; or it is invalid in both cases because of the population difference.

56

Although most of the characteristics used in the Atlas and similar sources have more than two attributes, the usual statistical technique used in *Social structure* and in many other cross-cultural studies calls for the construction of 2 × 2 tables. This is achieved by introducing additional lumping attributes, in many cases defined by the absence of some existing attribute. This process of dichotomizing characteristics is carried out formally in Textor's (1967) study, but the same procedure is followed in *Social structure*, as far as one can tell. Thus for example Murdock indicates in *Tables 61* and *71* the kind of kin groups present and the kind of terms used for aunts for each society in his sample. He distinguishes seven kinds of 'other kin groups' and four kinds of aunt terms. To construct the first line of *Table 36*, he groups the seven kin group attributes into two classes, those where exogamous unilineal kin groups are present and those where they are absent. Similarly the four aunt term attributes are divided into those where FZ and MZ are called by the same term and those where different terms are used for these two relatives. The intersection of these two dichotomies yields four categories and the number of societies in each cell is shown in the table (Murdock 1949a: 163, 226-247).

In *Social structure* Murdock calculates for the 2 × 2 tables chi square and Fisher's Coefficient of Association, Q (Murdock 1949a: 129; Snedecor 1946: 199; Yule and Kendall 1937: 44-45). These are nonparametric statistics, and their validity does not depend on normality of distribution. Driver (1961: 319) argues that it would have been better to use the combination of phi, coefficient of strength of association, and chi square, a method later followed by Textor, who also uses Fisher's exact test when the sample is small (Textor 1967: 14-16). Some other cross-cultural ethnologists have used tests which do assume normality of distribution (Whiting and Child 1953; cf. Naroll 1962: 40-42), an assumption that in many cases is likely to be not justified. I am not competent to add to the discussion of the relative merits of statistical tests (cf. Driver 1961; Cox 1961; Köbben 1967, with comments and references therein; Naroll 1967), nor are they relevant to the

57

argument of this chapter. All that needs to be stressed here is that the tests assume that the sample has been selected by a random procedure, whereas in fact no sample of societies is chosen in this way; thus, strictly speaking, the tests are invalid. Murdock is quite clear on this issue and his efforts for thirty years or more to improve his sampling procedures may be seen as a sustained attempt to overcome this inherent weakness.

One minor use of quantitative methods in *Social structure* deserves brief mention. Almost all the quantities in the book are either the number or proportion of societies in stated categories, or the values of the statistical indices Q and chi square. Exceptionally, Murdock gives a quantitative estimate for the relative efficacy of certain inherent distinctions in causing terminological differentiation. It will be remembered that when using the postulational method to develop several theorems about the determinants of kinship terminology, Murdock adopts a basic postulate which states more than is necessary to derive his theorems (see above, pp. 23–24). His postulate refers to the 'relative efficacy' of the inherent distinctions between pairs of kin-types, and of the social differentials and social equalizers affecting them. His eighth assumption (of thirteen) underlying the postulate is that the six inherent distinctions vary in their relative efficacy in producing differentiation in kinship terminology. In *Table 14*, Murdock gives the results of comparing, in 221 societies, the terms applied for various pairs of kin types differing from each other in respect of either generation, affinity, bifurcation, or collaterality. Kin types that differ only in generation are in over 97 per cent of instances known by different terms, whereas types differing only in collaterality are known by different terms in a mere 40 per cent of instances. Affinity and bifurcation occupy an intermediate position. Murdock interprets these percentages to imply that the relative efficacy is 'of the order of 25 for generation, 5 for affinity, 1 for bifurcation, and 1 for collaterality' (1949a: 134). The only use he makes of this index is to appeal to the large relative efficacy of the criterion of generation to explain why Crow and Omaha cousin terminologies, in which generation distinctions are

58

overridden, are found in only about a third of the exclusively matrilineal societies and a quarter of the patrilineal societies respectively. Murdock argues that 'it presumably requires both time and the full elaboration of unilinear institutions' to overcome the inherent distinction of generation (1949a: 168, 224). Murdock does not go on to measure the relative efficacy of the two other inherent distinctions, sex and polarity, and he says that 'A complete analysis of the relative efficacy of social equalizers and differentials . . . is probably not necessary.' He does however bring forward some statistical evidence to show that the rule of descent exerts a greater influence on kin terminology than does the form of marriage, while the rule of marriage residence has less influence than either of the other two factors. In this form of analysis we have the beginnings of an attempt to calibrate the model of functional relations. This aspect of the cross-cultural method has been taken much further by other writers who have used factor analysis and similar statistical techniques to measure the influence of one cultural attribute on another (cf. Ford 1967; Sawyer and LeVine 1966).

7 Coding

For the simpler forms of cross-cultural inquiry, the sequence of steps from ethnographic report to statistical correlation can be represented in the following paradigm. First the information in the report is translated into the coded attributes. The society concerned, in the form of a string of attributes, is added with others to form a sample. The sample societies are sorted according to two dichotomous characteristics and counted, the totals forming a 2 × 2 table. Statistical coefficients are calculated to measure the association between the characteristics. If the coefficients suggest the presence of a relation between the characteristics, this is taken as evidence for a functional relation already postulated or, alternatively, an explanation for the relation is sought from the theory of culture.

This procedure remains essentially unchanged in most of the

work that has followed the publication of *Social structure*. The sample has been enlarged and refined and statistical tests have been applied more relentlessly, until a terminus of this line of inquiry is reached in Textor's *Cross-cultural summary* (1967) in which 480 dichotomous characteristics are used and are correlated with one another to obtain some 20,000 statistically significant correlations. The reader may well feel, in the face of this massive analysis, that his brain is a computer of only modest size, incapable of digesting and synthesizing this deluge of coefficients, and be grateful for the attempt by Driver and Schuessler (1967) to reduce Murdock's categories to something he can comprehend. The underlying assumptions about the sample remain unchanged throughout this sequence of statistical treatments.

The use of a limited number of attributes for classifying ethnographic information, as a preliminary to the formation of contrasting pairs of cells, gives the cross-cultural method its special flavour. It is this requirement that has been the stimulus to the compilation of the lists in the World ethnographic sample and the Atlas, rather than the view of culture advanced by Murdock. His theory of culture has, presumably, had some influence on his choice of characteristics and attributes for inclusion in the Atlas even though, as I argue later, this influence has been too weak. But there is nothing to prevent the compilation of another Atlas with a different set of characteristics and/or attributes, reflecting a different view of what features of culture are significant. Similarly it is possible to agree with Murdock about the way in which cultures operate while disagreeing about the statistical techniques he uses to test hypotheses. Part of the criticism he has had to face, however, relates neither to his theory of culture nor to the statistical techniques as such, but to the first step in our paradigm, the simple process of classification by attributes. Two kinds of objection are raised. First, there are practical objections. Some commentators argue that even if we take the coding system as given, the encoding is not carried out as accurately as it should be (e.g. Pilling 1962; Patai 1965). Others say that the attributes are wrongly selected, either because they overlap or do not exhaust all the logical possibilities or because they group together what should be distinguished or make arbitrary and inappropriate discriminations (e.g. Leach 1964c). In particular, the application of the harsh alternatives, 'present' and 'absent', or the forced choice between saying that a society definitely has, or definitely does not have, a given cultural characteristic, demands in many instances a substantial loss of ethnographic information as well as the judicious use of the coder's discretion. This applies particularly to the coding of cultural forms that are present, if at all, only episodically or occasionally, as for example are kindreds in several societies (cf. Befu 1963: 351; Mitchell, W. E. 1963; Appell 1967; Murdock 1964b). The provision in the Atlas for recording alternative or secondary forms of certain characteristics meets part of this criticism, but in turn sometimes creates problems in deciding which of two attributes corresponds to the primary or dominant form and which to the secondary. These are all objections of practical importance, but do not raise any matters of principle, and we need say no more about them here. Murdock has sometimes defended particular published classifications as correct against the objections of critics, but in general his plea has been for better information about the ethnographic facts so that errors of coding may be avoided.

The second objection is theoretical rather than practical. Assuming correct classification, some loss of information is necessarily entailed when we replace paragraphs or pages of an ethnographic monograph by a single attribute which contains only three or four bits (binary digits) of information. Some critics argue that the loss of information in this step is so great that we are left with crude statements from which nothing very enlightening can be expected to emerge, however high-powered may be the statistical tests employed (e.g. Leach 1960b, 1964c: cf. Köbben 1952; 133–135). It is obvious that some kind of translation into a defined set of parameters, either digital or continuously variable, has to be carried out before any kind of quantitative statement can be made about a sample of societies, and in this process much of the information has to be discarded. Leach (1961b: 12–13) himself advocates just this kind of process as a means of escaping from the use of ethnographic categories with value-loaded names. Even if he sticks to words, an ethnographer cannot write a monograph without discarding a huge amount of the information contained in his field notebooks, and these in turn contain only a small fraction of what might have been recorded. Yet we do not insist that ethnographers publish only their raw field notes. I can see no real objection in principle to reducing further the stock of information recorded in the field, and also diminishing the additional information that has come to light through the synthesis achieved in writing the monograph, so that the modicum that remains can be tabulated easily on a punched card (cf. Kluckhohn 1939: 354–355). We accept and welcome the well-written well-organized descriptive monograph. The effort of producing it is justified if we can learn from it facts about the society as a whole which we could not glean, or would not have the time to glean, from reading through the author's field notes, and if these facts are more useful to us than are the details we miss because they appear only in the notes and not in the monograph. Similarly, the effort of reducing a monograph to a single line in the Atlas is justified if, in this form, the surviving information can be combined with similar statements about other societies to yield valuable results about societies in general which we could not gain from reading all the ethnographic sources on which the entries in the Atlas are based. Murdock asserts that these results are in fact worth the effort required to obtain them.

Murdock has drawn on an unusually wide range of ethnographic evidence in writing *Social structure* and compiling the Atlas, and he welcomes theoretical articles in the pages of *Ethnology* only if they are tied to ethnographic facts. Yet there seems to be an unbridgeable gulf, in his view, between ethnographic works on the one hand and theoretical or comparative works on the other. The ethnographic descriptions of single societies are seen as descriptions, and nothing more; they

62

provide raw material for the cross-cultural mill but do not generate any propositions on their own. Thus he says at the beginning of his introductory book on ethnography: 'Only facts, therefore, will appear in the text, – not broad generalizations, or speculative reconstructions, or romantic idealizations' (Murdock 1934b: viii).

This treatment of ethnography is in sharp contrast to that followed by many British writers who, from Malinowski on, have often used the intensive analysis of a single society as the basis for statements about the characteristics of human culture and social institutions in general. Murdock's relegation of ethnographic accounts of single societies to mere descriptions may explain the somewhat erratic selection of ethnographic sources in *Social structure* and subsequent publications, a fact to which several commentators have drawn attention (e.g. Köbben 1967: 9; Goody 1967), and which Murdock (1967: 2–6) has readily admitted, while defending himself against specific criticisms (e.g. Murdock *et al.* 1965: 114–115). The evaluation of ethnographic reports is an essential part of the cross-cultural method, and has been treated in a most sophisticated fashion by Naroll (1962; 1966). Murdock does not hesitate to rate as poor the ethnographic performance of even some of the most eminent anthropologists, as for example Boas on the Kwakiutl (1949a: xiv). The value of an ethnographic report appears to depend not on the theoretical insight achieved by the observer but rather on the range of topics covered (Murdock 1963: 541–542) and by the facility with which the factual information it contains allows the society or culture concerned to be categorized unequivocally by the available attributes.

In this way verbal qualitative statements in ethnographic monographs are reduced to digital form. The qualities that Murdock seeks in an ethnographic report are what we may call its codability and, provided it is adequately codable, its suitability, compared with codable reports of nearby societies, for inclusion in a sample of societies. Ethnography is essential but the ethnographer, so it seems, must stick to his last and not indulge in theorizing. Indeed the burden of Murdock's complaint against British social anthropologists for concentrating on the intensive description of one or a few societies is that the societies are selected 'without reference to their representativeness' (1951a: 469). Nothing much, it seems, can be learnt from these intensive parochial analyses.

On the other hand, the comparative theorist should leave the ethnographer alone and not try to re-write the ethnography of a society in the light of 'theoretical preconceptions'. Again, it is British social anthropologists who are the target for Murdock's criticism (Murdock *et al.* 1965: 115).

In fact the division between ethnographic description and scientific analysis, even cross-cultural analysis of the kind advocated by Murdock, is not an absolute gulf. The increasing sophistication of his categories with the passage of the years demonstrates how empirical facts reported in the descriptive vocabulary of contemporary ethnography have forced changes in his analytical scheme. Thus whereas in 1940, and still in 1949, Murdock recognized only four kinds of descent – matrilineal, patrilineal, double, and bilateral – in 1960 he recognized seven – quasi-matrilineal, quasi-patrilineal, and ambilineal, plus the previously mentioned four (Murdock 1940b: 555; 1949a: 15, 225; 1960a: 2, 7). Conversely, the lists of attributes used by Murdock have had suggestive value in ethnographic research. For example, the various proposals by Murdock and others for classifying rules and practices of post-marital residence (Murdock 1949a: 16–17, 225; 1957a: 670; Murdock *et al.* 1962b: 117–118 and references therein) have suggested to the ethnographer what he should look for in the field and what empirical distinctions his colleagues will expect him to make.

Cross-fertilization of this kind between ethnography and comparative scientific analysis occupies at best a subsidiary place in Murdock's paradigm, as seems to be indicated by his caution against using the *Outline of cultural materials* (Murdock *et al.* 1961) as a field guide. Indeed Naroll, whose writings certainly form part of the cross-cultural methodological corpus, elevates the distinction between ethnography and cross-cultural

64

analysis into a principle, Goodenough's rule: what we do as ethnographers is, and must be kept, independent of what we do as comparative ethnologists (Naroll 1964b: 306; cf. Goodenough 1956: 37). In my view, the dangers of adopting this principle are nowhere seen better than in the choice of characteristics and attributes used in *Social structure* and the Atlas. Attributes are selected because they can be applied unambiguously to the existing literature, and not because they are asserted to be important or significant in a theory or hypothesis which is to be tested. The inclusion in the Atlas of so much information about the shapes of houses, for example, seems to me quite unjustified in terms of its importance for theory testing; presumably the information was included merely because it was easy to get. Likewise the categories used in the classification of kinship terminologies are essentially categories of convenience, rather than of likely theoretical significance. Hence it can only be by good luck that a correlation between attributes, however statistically strong this may be, has any direct bearing on the truth or falsity of a theory. The criticism is sometimes made that Murdock's attributes and the correlations established between them, are meaningless because they are not 'structural'. But this criticism can be brought from the standpoint of any theory, whether 'structural' or not. Obviously Murdock had his own eclectic theory of human behaviour in mind when constructing his array of attributes, but this theory appears to have exerted only a very weak influence on the way the attributes were chosen. Yet an array of attributes which does not correspond to a set of natural categories, but which is intended for use with a wide range of possible mutually contradictory theories, is likely to be a quite imperfect instrument for testing any theory at all.

Murdock sees the matter differently. He says 'there can never be any generally valid science of man which is not specifically adapted to, and tested with reference to, the diverse manifestations of human behaviour encountered in the thousands of human societies differing from our own that are known to history and ethnography'. For this, the comparative method, as developed by Tylor and subsequently improved, is indispensable (Murdock 1957b: 249, 252). Evidence for these 'diverse manifestations' can be garnered from any reliable source, irrespective of whether the observer had in mind the propositions his information will help to test.

8   The sampling unit

In order to discuss the second step in our paradigm, the inclusion of an encoded society in the sample, we have to consider exactly what it is that we are sampling. Murdock, Naroll, and others have written at considerable length about how to construct a satisfactory sample, but the possibility of ever achieving this seems to me to rest on an assumption which never quite comes to the surface, though we get near it in the arguments about the distinction between society and culture. Murdock refers to 'the crucial problem; the delimitation of the sampling universe', and we shall look at the various answers he has proposed. He contrasts this with the problem of 'the definition of the sampling unit, which to me seems easily soluble' (1964a: 302). Murdock's remark is directed at Naroll, who considers the later problem difficult but soluble. Unlike both Murdock and Naroll, I think the problem is insoluble. In any case, the two problems are clearly inseparable, for until we decide what the units are, we cannot determine how to put them together in a sample. In my view, the crucial and most questionable step along the road of quantitative cross-cultural inquiry was taken long before the appearance of Textor's massive computer print-out and even of Murdock's *Social structure*. It was taken by Tylor and was queried, not by Galton, whose comments on Tylor's paper have been the inspiration of some of Naroll's papers, but by another member of Tylor's audience when he read his paper on 13 November 1888. W. H. Flower, at the time Director of the Natural History Museum in London, commented that 'such a method depended entirely upon the units of comparison being of equivalent value, and this seemed to him to be a very great difficulty when dealing with groups of mankind'. Tylor replied to this comment with a reference to the correspondences brought about by historical connexion but did not, I think, deal with Flower's objection (Tylor 1889: 270–272). It is essential for Tylor's argument to assume that it is meaningful to count cultures as if they are discrete homologous units. This assumption is taken for granted by Hobhouse, Wheeler, and Ginsberg as well as in *Social structure* and innumerable other cross-cultural studies. If this assumption is not justified, we cannot arrive any nearer the truth by doubling or trebling the size of the sample or by working out more sophisticated statistical coefficients. The statistical tests applied in *Social structure*, and even the simple statements about percentages, have no useful meaning unless the units that are added up are equivalent to one another. In addition, the units must be selected properly. But if the units are not comparable, there just is no proper way to select them and efforts to find one, however heroic, will necessarily be in vain. Murdock's own testimony shows the task of devising a proper procedure for choosing a sample has been difficult. I argue that the difficulties to arise because the units are not comparable in those respects required by the propositions which the sample is designed test.

A great deal of the discussion that has gone on about the appropriate units for comparative study is irrelevant to us here, for we are concerned with a method of analysis in which societies or cultures are compared in one particular way, by sorting them into sets and counting the number of members in each set. If we want to 'contrast and compare' societies by talking about how they are alike in some respects and different in others and about the reasons for this, then the units we contrast will vary with the task in hand. It is possible to talk interestingly about the similarities and differences of the Chinese and Roman empires, of Zulu and Swazi tribes, of the Tallensi and the Ashanti, and so on. The unit of comparison can be large or small and what is a perfectly satisfactory unit for one purpose may be useless in another context (cf. D'Andrade 1966: 151–152). In this view I follow Schapera (1953: 359–360), when he

67

advocates a plurality of levels of comparison for different purposes, though I do not agree with his argument that comparison
must only be made of societies within a given region, large or
small. For example, Evans-Pritchard's (1929) discussion of the
difference between Trobriand and Zande magic seems to me
an admirable example of an essay in comparison based on data
from two societies selected, at least in part, for idiosyncratic
reasons. But Evans-Pritchard (1963), Radcliffe-Brown (1951),
Eggan (1954), Redfield, and many others (cf. Singer 1953) who
have discussed or practised the comparative method, do not
count societies or cultures. For example, it makes no difference
to Evans-Pritchard's discussion whether we regard the Azande
as constituting one society or two or three. On the other hand,
if it is a matter of chance or arbitrary decision whether a particular constellation of human actions and thoughts is treated
as one culture or several, then statistics derived from comparing the number of units in one category with the number in
another are quite meaningless. For this reason, Naroll's (1964b:
283–286) discussion of how these and several other writers have
used terms like tribe, society, and culture, while interesting in
itself, is quite irrelevant to the cross-cultural method. The
writers he cites are comparativists, in that they have compared
several societies, but for them the process of comparison consists of an examination of similarities and differences discussed
seriatim. Only those writers who use that variety of comparison
that we label the cross-cultural method make statistical comparisons based on counting societies or cultures (cf. Lewis 1956).
Counting is the distinctive feature of the cross-cultural method,
and the way the counting is done is, in my view, its main
weakness.

Murdock has said a good deal about the conditions under
which two similar societies should not both be included in
a sample, and comparatively little about the definition of the
unit society or culture. But if we exclude one of a pair
of societies because they are close together and have similar
cultures, we are in effect treating the pair as if it was for
sampling purposes a single unit. We have already referred to
68

Murdock's use of the concept of 'nation' in classifying complex or stratified societies, and cited his formal definition of a culture (pp. 27–29). Naroll states his dissatisfaction with Murdock's definitions, and comments that the social unit constituting a 'society' for the purposes of the Files is nowhere defined (Naroll 1962: 15; 1963b: 307). He has overlooked an inadequate definition. Murdock writes:

> Every anthropologist who undertakes a regional or compara-
> tive study, as well as most of those who engage in field re-
> search, must make a decision as to the social groups which he
> will treat as cultural units, . . . The Human Relations Area
> Files faces this problem whenever it initiates work in a new
> area. It must, before processing begins, make a definitive
> decision as to which groups and cultures are to be segregated
> in separate files as essentially distinct and which are to be
> grouped in a single file as essentially only sub-groups or
> variants of the same larger culture (1953: 477).

Thus for the Files, and presumably therefore the samples as well, a culture seems to be defined operationally as a 'description of social life suitable for filing in one file'. For more informative statements about what in effect constitutes a sampling unit we have to look at Murdock's discussion about what societies or cultures should be excluded from the sample.

Looking back at his early attempts at sample construction, Murdock has been ready to admit their shortcomings (1957b: 253; 1964a: 302; 1968b: 305). In his early samples he aims at 'good descriptive coverage, wide geographical distribution, and the restriction of the number of cases selected from any particular culture area'. He stresses the need to include 'a representative selection of historical and modern civilizations' (1940a: 369; cf. 1947: 57). In *Social structure* his concern is, he says, 'to avoid any appreciable over-representation of particular culture areas' (1949: ix). In a 1950 article where he draws on data from 40 selected non-European societies, 8 from each of the world's major ethnographic regions, he claims that this method is 'as close to purely random sampling as is feasible today in comparative social science' (1950b: 195). A few years later, he discusses the possibility of using a random sample of cultures, and says that this would not be satisfactory, as it would entail the inclusion of many peoples whose social life has been described inadequately, and, more importantly, that it would yield a sample which did not take account of their distribution by types. Aboriginal Australia, because it contains many 'discrete but not notably divergent tribal cultures' would be over-represented in a random sample, while Europe and the Far East, because they contain large and homogeneous nations, would be under-represented, and 'truly unique cultures', like the Ainu, Tasmanians, and Todas, would be mainly omitted (1957a: 664–665; cf. 1957b: 252–253). It is not clear at first what criteria Murdock is using here to determine why a random sample would over-represent some societies and under-represent others. If the Ainu are 'truly unique', then presumably they are not very significant for making cross-cultural generalizations, just as in *Social structure* polyandry, second cousin marriage, and other phenomena are treated as unimportant because they are infrequent. At the same time, if European and Asian societies are under-represented because they are 'large and culturally homogeneous', this must be on account of their size, a criterion which in *Social structure* is excluded and which later receives explicit condemnation, as we shall see (see below, p. 93). Murdock goes on to say that in a truly satisfactory sample, cultures would be included 'approximately in proportion to their degree of cultural diversity' (1957a: 665). This remark can scarcely refer to the internal diversity of a culture, for our earlier discussion (pp. 27–31) on the concept of 'nation' suggests that the cross-cultural method does not recognize internal diversity as a significant cultural characteristic. The remark must refer to the diversity of the sample, the magnitude of the differences between one included culture and another, and the reference to 'approximately in proportion' might be taken to mean that the more a culture diverges from those already included in the sample, the greater the chances of it being selected. In fact,

70

Murdock's procedure here is to stratify for location, and then to adjust the number of cultures drawn from each area so as to 'reconcile differences in size and complexity'. Within each area cultures are chosen so as to represent as wide a range of variation as possible in type of economy, rule of descent, and linguistic affiliation. As Aberle (1961: 663) remarks, this method of selection 'maximizes "odd ball" systems, tending to produce a large list of "exceptions" to one or another items'. Essentially similar cultures are not duplicated.

One unexpected criterion appears in his comments on the societies selected for inclusion in his *Outline of world cultures*. He says he has leaned somewhat in favour of population rather than diversity because

> the societies with the largest populations and the most complex civilizations are presumably, by and large, those whose cultures have proved best adapted to the conditions of human existence and therefore deserve a slightly disproportionate representation in a sample which will be used primarily in the comparative study of man's cultural adaptation (Murdock 1958a: v).

Thus not only is the sample constructed as a compromise between two divergent principles; it is also slightly weighted in favour of successful rather than unsuccessful societies. We are to learn about human adaptation by studying successes rather than failures.

Even if we admit that cultures can be counted, we can hardly concede that they can be counted in only one way for every different purpose. If we are interested in finding out what most human beings have done, then we have to count heads and our sample cultures would have to be weighted by a factor of population times duration. If we are interested in looking at human behaviour under as many diverse conditions as possible, then the only reason for treating as different two otherwise similar societies from different parts of the world, or speaking different languages, would be that location and language were relevant conditions of diversity; and in Murdock's scheme of analysis these are not relevant criteria. The statements that large and complex societies are better adaptations to the conditions of human existence can easily be attacked; for most urban industrialized readers there is plenty of evidence close to hand. Even if we accept Murdock's statement, it does not follow that genuinely cross-cultural generalizations should be generalizations based more on adaptive successes than on adaptive failures. One plausible cross-cultural generalization might be that, more often than not, human beings have been less successful in their cultural adaptations than they might have been.

9   *Independent instances and independent trials*

From this long process of methodological development, Murdock emerges in the end with a sampling procedure that is clear and consistent and free of compromise in principle, even though the imperfection of the ethnographic record may force some compromise in practice. In his discussion of sampling procedures in the *Ethnographic atlas*, Murdock (1967: 3–6) lists five errors of method present in recent cross-cultural studies. Three errors are important but uncontroversial – the inclusion of societies inadequately described, the exclusion of any category of known and adequately described societies, and the biased selection of societies. Two other errors do call for comment. Murdock says that it is an error to include in a sample two or more societies 'whose cultures are very similar in consequence of derivation from a recent common source', or 'societies which are closely adjacent geographically, even though linguistic evidence does not suggest a genetic relationship between them' (1967: 3–4). In a more recent article, these criteria of linguistic and cultural similarity are quantified; no two societies should be included if their languages indicate a common origin within the past millennium or two, or if cultural borrowing seems to have gone on intensively over the same period. The criterion of proximity is taken to exclude from the sample any society whose geographical centre is less than 200 miles distant from

72

the geographical centre of any society already selected for the sample; this rule of thumb Murdock refers to as the 'three degree rule' (1966: 112–113; 1967: 4). All three criteria are introduced for the same purpose: to ensure that no two societies in the sample are 'contaminated by derivation from a common origin or by contact and cultural borrowing to such a degree that they might reasonably be suspected of being variants of a single case' (Murdock 1966: 97).

This statement, coming nearly thirty years after the publication of Murdock's first cross-cultural study, makes his final position plain. In this context he is interested only in establishing functional relations. The other two kinds of explanation for cultural similarities (see above, pp. 16–17), genetic connexion, and diffusion, are admitted as valid but irrelevant; the sample must be constructed so that the only admissible explanation for similarity is parallel adaptive change. Following Galton, Boas, and many others (cf. Murdock 1937c: 460–461; 1957b: 253; Naroll 1961: 17–18), he takes the view that we can speak of an independent instance of a functional relation between two cultural attributes simultaneously present in a society only when this conjunction of attributes has occurred in spatial, temporal, and genetic isolation. Presumably the restriction of isolation to two millennia and 200 miles is a quantitative concession to the view, as stated in one of Murdock's early papers, that 'even two separated branches of an originally homogeneous tribe will in a few generations develop divergent configurations in adjusting to their differing geographical and social environments . . . even historically connected cultures become in a very real sense independent units, at least to the extent that they have integrated their historically diverse components' (Murdock 1937c: 461; cf. 1957a: 667).

Most of the refinements introduced into his sampling technique by Murdock are aimed at eliminating the effects of diffusion, and stem from Galton's comment that Tylor should give full information 'as to the degree in which the customs of the tribes and races which are compared together are independent. It might be, that some of the tribes had derived

D

them from a common source, so that they were duplicate copies of the same original' (Galton in Tylor 1889: 270). Thus for Galton 'independence' means in this context 'independently invented, not copied', and Murdock seems to have accepted the force of Galton's criticism, referred to by Köbben (1952: 132) as the culture-historical objection. The ingenious techniques devised by Naroll (1961, 1964a) and D'Andrade (Naroll and D'Andrade 1963), which have earned Murdock's approval, are designed to measure the extent to which the presence of a cultural attribute may be due to copying the culture of an adjacent society. Murdock's revised sampling procedure aims at reducing or eliminating the possibility of diffusion from one sample society to another. These approaches assume that borrowing, or copying, a cultural attribute from a neighbouring society is an essentially different process from developing an attribute functionally by adaptive change so that the society moves to a more complete state of cultural integration. Borrowing or diffusion is seen as part of the accidents of history, and likely to be culturally disintegrative. Murdock's research goal is thus quite different from that of Kroeber and others who make statistical analyses of attribute (trait) distributions in order to determine to what extent diffusion has occurred (cf. Köbben 1952: 135–136). Driver (1966: 159) emphasizes the difference between adaptive change and changes due to diffusion when he contrasts the latter with 'the developmental cycle' of change by which residence, descent, and kinship terminology alter in response to economic changes or changes in habitat; he talks of 'historical changes which appear to have disrupted the slower-acting evolutionary processes' (Driver 1967: 271). But this seems to be a false contrast; as many commentators have pointed out (e.g. Collins 1966). The ethnographic evidence examined in the cross-cultural method is evidence of the simultaneous presence of attributes, whether the various attributes first appeared in the culture as a result of copying or of functional adaptation is irrelevant to a consideration of the maintenance of a functional relation between them. Whichever way they arrived, attributes that are functionally related

74

tend to persist together through time, whereas combinations of attributes that happen to occur together for other reasons tend to break up with the passage of time.

Murdock seeks to count the number of times that specified attributes appear together in historically isolated cultures, rather than in all cultures. His aim is clearly the detection of adaptive cultural change, for he argues that 'the integrative tendency in the process of cultural change justifies the treatment of individual cultures as independent units for statistical purposes' although some historical anthropologists think that the fact of diffusion invalidates this assumption (1949a: ix–x). In a later article, discussing the effects of diffusion, he asserts that 'borrowed like invented and pre-existing traits undergo a process of integrative modification' (1957b: 253). It seems, therefore, that it is because of 'integration' that the units in his sample can be treated as independent. But what justification is there for restricting his attention to adaptive changes that use locally-manufactured cultural attributes and for excluding those changes making use of important cultural material? How does this procedure relate to the hypothesis of functional relations between attributes which he is endeavouring to prove? If social structures are the outcome of multiple individual choices, if cultural adaptation is behaviour learned as the result of trial and error, then why do we exclude from our calculations those outcomes of adaptation which occur not in isolation but in temporal and spatial association with parallel series of trials and choices going on in adjacent societies? If, as Murdock maintains, culture is learned rather than inherited, does it not have to be learned afresh by each generation? Each generation has the choice of continuing the existing social structure unchanged or of altering it, so that in some sense a culture that remains unchanged through time does so only because it is chosen by each successive generation. If therefore we wish to determine how many times a specified combination of cultural attributes occurs in nature, so that we can test the strength of functional relation between them, surely we ought to treat each generation's experience as an independent trial.

75

The presence or absence of the required combination in one generation does not determine whether it will be present or absent in the next. The stronger the functional relation, the greater the likelihood that the combination would persist through time. If we do not allow in our calculations for temporal persistence, then a short-lived occurrence of the combination of attributes is given the same statistical weight as an occurrence that persists for millennia. I do not wish to argue that each generation starts with a clean slate, or that its choice is entirely independent of that made by the previous generation, for obviously the process of cultural socialization, if successful, ensures that the odds are loaded in favour of cultural continuity through time. But it seems to follow from Murdock's theory that the socialization process is more likely to be successful if there is a functional relation between the attributes that are being learned by the rising generation; the traits then form stable combinations, indicative of cultural integration, in contrast to the unstable combinations found in inadequately integrated, transitional societies. Hence cultural persistence, even though it is achieved in part by successful socialization, is still indicative of the existence of a functional relation. If this argument is accepted, it follows that we should weight the units appearing in our sample by a factor proportional to the number of generations, or length of time, that the society or culture concerned has persisted essentially unchanged. The notion of discontinuous generations exposed in succession to the socialization process, and making a once-and-for-all choice is, of course, quite artificial, but provides a first approximation to what happens in fact. Some error would be introduced by treating alike those cultures no longer extant, i.e., where a series of trials had been completed, and cultures still persisting unchanged, where the trials are still in progress; but there might be ways of allowing for this (cf. Barnes 1967e: 73–83).

Yet if we admit that we should take into account the length of time that a culture has persisted, we find that we have to take account of population as well. For if we are to treat as independent for statistical purposes the choices made by individuals at different points of time in successive generations, must we not also treat as independent the choices made by different individuals, or groups of individuals, at the same time? If, for instance, the cultural presence of poker and chess (Code P, column 35, in the *Atlas*) at two points of time a generation or more apart is to be treated as two independent instances, should we not also treat the presence of these games in two related tribes as two independent instances, for a tribe is no more forced to play chess merely because its neighbour does than one generation is forced to follow the chess-playing habits of its predecessors. Yet if we are to treat related tribes as independent in this sense, why stop there? Why not treat villages, hamlets, and even individuals as independent? It becomes clear that what is required is some measure of the extent to which similar cultural choices have been made throughout an area at a particular time. We admit that individuals and groups do not make cultural choices in isolation or in ignorance of the choices made by their neighbours. But as with socialization, so with cultural conformity and copying. Cultural attributes do not possess any mobility of their own, despite the reified way in which we so often talk about them. As Murdock (1941: 144) himself says, culture is not 'a closed system, self-perpetuating and self-propagating'. An attribute found in one social group is more likely to be copied by members of a neighbouring group if the latter feel a need for it (1957b: 253). As Naroll (1961:20; 1966: 155) points out, it is probably true that combinations of functionally related attributes are more likely to diffuse together than are functionally unrelated combinations, though he does not regard this as proven. Hence the extent to which a combination has diffused should provide a measure of the strength of the functional relation between its component cultural attribute. How far we can treat contemporaneous tribes, or villages, or hamlets, or individuals as making effectively independent choices to accept or reject a specified cultural trait, will vary enormously from one context to another. But if we need a simple and widely applicable measure of the extent to which an attribute has diffused, the size of the population

77

accepting the attribute as part of its culture is the obvious parameter to use. Following this argument then, to measure correctly the strength of functional relations between attributes we
should weight each of our ethnic units by a factor proportional
to the product of its population and the time it has persisted.
In other words we should abandon the various procedures
worked out by Murdock to eliminate the effects of diffusion;
instead we should include in our universe all societies however
similar they may be, taking care to weight each society by the
appropriate population–time factor. If we do this, we no longer
have to worry about appropriate boundaries for our ethnic
units. For example, whether we treat China as a single society
with a certain weight x, or as 500 separate societies each with
weight x/500, makes no difference.

Whiting (1954: 527–528) points out that although many
ethnographers write their monographs as if they were describing
the culture of a whole tribe, the field observations they make
on many aspects of culture may be confined to a single hamlet,
or may be based on a single informant. Whiting advises the
comparative ethnologist to choose his sample according to the
group from which material was actually gathered in the field
rather than according to the title of the monograph. Applying
Whiting's advice to our own argument, if cultural norms and
practices differ from one small group to another within an
ethnic unit, we may say that we are not justified in weighting
the reported cultural characteristics of the unit by a factor
proportional to the population of the whole sampling unit; we
should use instead the population of the group actually observed by the ethnographer. I think there would be a case for
this alternative procedure, for we would then be using a weight
indicative of the number of cultural trials reliably known to
have taken place within the sampling unit. But if we did this,
then we would have no reason to exclude from our sample
reports from other ethnographers writing about the same
sampling unit, provided their field observations had been
carried out in different villages or hamlets, or with different
informants. These parallel reports would have to be weighted

according to the same formula. Whichever way we went about the matter, our aim would be to estimate how widely a particular cultural profile is distributed and to apply a weight proportional to the population concerned. We would break up our existing ethnic units into as many smaller units as there are independent ethnographic reports, and weight each new unit according to that fraction of the total population thought to bear the culture reported by the ethnographer concerned. We would in effect reject the concept of a discrete culture with boundaries and replace it by the concept of the culture at a datum point, defined in space and time.

For most cultures, we can scarcely guess how long they have persisted. Populations of sampling units are often quite unknown, and we are frequently in the dark about the range of observations made by ethnographers whose reports on what is ostensibly the same culture differ from one another. Hence on three counts it may be argued that proposals I have advanced are quite impracticable. I accept this objection. But in this study my object is not to devise feasible alternative methods of inquiry but to come to grips with the assumptions and principles embedded in the cross-cultural method as it is now practised.

There are two other arguments against the proposals that we should consider. The first is that I have simply ignored all the refinements Murdock has introduced into his sampling procedure. From his earliest papers he has made a firm distinction between similarities due to parallel adjustive adaptation resulting from the 'strain towards consistency' mentioned earlier (p. 17) and those caused by diffusion or genetic connexion. How then can we hope to measure and detect adaptive adjustment if we simply ignore these distinctions?

My reply would be that when Murdock discusses the kinds of changes which upset the cultural equilibrium of a society and make it imperfectly integrated, he is usually not talking about diffusion. He writes:

The conditions of existence in any society are always undergoing change – sometimes rapidly, sometimes slowly – in

79

consequence of natural events such as famines and epidemics, of social events such as wars and revolutions, of biological influences such as increasing population density, of internal adaptations such as technological inventions, and of external contacts which may stimulate cultural borrowing (1949a: 203).

Diffusion here appears last in the list of the kinds of causes of change. Furthermore, if we restrict our attention to functional relations between attributes of social organization rather than between cultural attributes of all kinds, diffusion becomes even less important, according to Murdock. He writes that the evolution of social organization 'rarely involves cultural borrowing except as a short-cut to an internal reorganization which is already under way' and that 'rules of descent, forms of familial and kin groupings, and kinship systems, under conditions of contact with other cultures do not ordinarily change by direct diffusion but rather by a process of internal adjustment to altered conditions of life' (1949a: 198, 199). Again in a later paper he argues that diffusion, at least where it concerns social organization, is less like migration and more like parallel adaptation (1960b: 186).

Thus Murdock presents us with a model of society in which cultural attributes are imperfectly integrated because of their differential rates of adaptation to internal and external changes rather than because they have copied attributes arbitrarily from neighbouring societies. If attributes of social organization that do not increase the degree of integration are copied only rarely, there seems to be no justification for treating the process of diffusion of these attributes as essentially different and distinct from their attainment by a process of purely internal adjustment.

Driver (1966), in a study contrasting geographical-historical and psycho-functional explanations of kin avoidances, presents evidence that Jorgensen (1966: 162) interprets as implying that 'the diffusion of avoidances does not depend upon the presence of the psycho-functional correlatives'. This conclusion contradicts Murdock's assertion about cultural borrowing. However, both Jorgensen and Driver remain dissatisfied with the samples they have used and, as might be expected, both call for further testing, using larger samples, containing one or two thousand societies. On a broader canvas, Naroll (1965: 434–438) has called attention to the abundant evidence provided by diffusion studies for correlations between attributes that cannot plausibly be thought to have a direct functional relationship. He notes, for instance, that in northeastern Peru there is a high correlation between tribes with exogamous clans and tribes whose men wear narrow G-strings, who beat on wooden drums, and who use thin spears with pointed, poisoned tips. Naroll's response is to advocate methods for eliminating from his sample those cultures whose members might have copied from one another or from a common source, a procedure which I think is unsound. On the contrary, the evidence from diffusion studies demonstrates to me the inadequacy of searching for valid functional relations merely by looking at the distribution of the attributes of a pair of characteristics. If, to take an example used by Naroll (1968: 259), societies may adopt matrilocal residence and matrilineal descent not only because there is a functional relation between these two attributes, but also because they are both already present in some source of diffusion, then surely we should try to measure the strength of both of the forces making for cultural change. One of the factors presumably influencing the speed and direction of institutional change is the range of possible alternative attributes known to members of a society from their experience of the social institutions of their neighbours in other societies near and far. To take this into account, more sophisticated techniques are required; path analysis, for instance, might provide part of the answer. Whatever multifactorial technique may prove suitable, my argument is simply that the postulated 'strain towards consistency' underlying functional relations cannot be thought of as ceasing to operate as soon as there is a possibility of copying the social institutions of neighbouring societies. In this context diffusion is interesting not because it sometimes happens but because most of the time it fails to happen. People are not always copying the social institutions of their neighbours and we assume, following Murdock's model, that this is partly

81

because their own social institutions interact on one another to inhibit wholesale copying. To measure the strength of this interaction we have to include in the evidence those instances where copying occurs as well as those where it does not.

The first counter-argument against weighting and ignoring diffusion may thus be refuted, but the second strikes home. Consider the assumption we have made about the independence of contemporaneous and intergenerational choices. We may be willing to admit that, within limits, each individual is free to make his own choice whether, for example, to follow his father in playing chess, or to introduce chess to his household by copying the game from strangers, or to throw his father's chessboard on the fire. He may, in some circumstances, be equally free in deciding what to do about cross-cousin marriage. But can we plausibly assume that each individual is free to make an independent choice whether or not to continue or adopt a system of moieties, or a jurisdictional hierarchy of eight levels? The first two examples are of cultural attributes dependent, by and large, on individual decisions, the second two on decisions taken by a group. If individuals are not free to alter cultural features independently of the decisions of their fellows, then we can scarcely treat the collective decision as equivalent to the sum of the postulated individual decisions taken by each member of the group. Consider a correlation given by Textor (1967: statement 84/390). He divides the societies in his sample into those where the level of political integration is the large state, and those where it is not. He also divides them into those 'where premarital sex relations are strongly punished and in fact rare' and those where this is not the case. If we wished to adopt the weighting system proposed above, we could argue plausibly that the rarity or lack of rarity of premarital sex relations in the various societies is the result of ostensibly independent decisions taken, one way or the other, by successive generations of unmarried individuals. Therefore we should weight each society by a factor based on its population and on the length of time it has persisted. But the decision to punish strongly, or not to punish strongly, those who indulge in premarital relations can be seen as likely to be taken not by every individual but by only certain leaders in each community, and the ratio of leaders to population may vary from society to society; hence a weight based on population does not necessarily reflect the number of independent decisions that have been taken. Even more to the point, the 'decision' to integrate the society at the level of the large state (i.e. at least 100,000 in population) cannot be thought of as taken independently by each member of the society. The effective decision may perhaps be taken by only a few people, and the majority of the population may be firmly opposed to this decision but lack the power to alter it. The significant decision may even be taken outside the society and duly introduced into it by officials whose acquiescence or obedience has no specific reference to the particular decision. Köbben (1967: 15) provides the example of the absence of slavery in Surinam after 1863; the effective decision was taken in the Netherlands and implemented in the Dutch colony by government officials in the face of protests from local slave-owners. At the other end of the political spectrum we have societies where there is an 'absence of any political integration even at the local level, e.g. where family heads acknowledge no higher political authority (Murdock 1957a: 674). Hence it seems that whatever weighting formula we adopt, it would not be uniform throughout the range of societies at the various levels of political integration. The same variation applies to the choices made by successive generations. Some cultural attributes can be easily rejected or modified by the rising generation, while others are harder to alter. Language, because it is learned while very young and is used for inter-generational communication is, in general, much more resistant to change than, say, items of material culture. There may be greater compulsion to persist with a descent rule, where individuals belonging to several generations are simultaneously involved, than, say, with a customary division of labour where only one generation is mainly concerned. Hence the weighting for persistence through time would have to vary according to the various cultural attributes being considered.

83

Even a flexible weighting scheme of this kind would break down as soon as we attempt to correlate two cultural attributes such as, for example, level of political integration and sexual behaviour, which call for radically different kinds of weighting. We then have to abandon any attempt to construct a simple two-by-two table using weighted sampling units. In brief, even if we were miraculously supplied with all the ethnographic information required, the proposed weighting system applied to cultures-at-a-point does not offer any real solution to the quest for a satisfactory basis for sample construction unless it is combined with much more sophisticated statistical techniques than are usually found in the cross-cultural method.

10 Discrete or skinless cultures?

Any procedure for counting cultures presupposes that there are discrete cultures ready to be counted. We have to conceive of the whole world, at any given moment of time, as divided into a finite number of non-overlapping, though not necessarily consolidated, regions, each region inhabited by all those, and only those, who bear the culture of the region. My impression that Murdock conceives of discrete cultures as existing as units in nature, waiting to be discovered, is strengthened not only by the unsatisfactory quality of his attempts at analytic definitions of a culture, but also by his readiness to guess at the total number of cultures and culture areas in the world, including those at present unknown to scientists. He guesses that there are at least 3,000 distinct cultures, and somewhat more than 430 culture areas (1956a: 247; 1967: 7). These guesses about unknown entities are quite meaningless without an assumption that there are real boundaries between cultures and culture areas that have to be discovered and approximated to, and which therefore cannot be drawn at will merely to suit the convenience of the comparative ethnologist. Rules of thumb proposed by Murdock, like those based on similarity of language and common membership of a political organization, may be necessary in our imperfect state of ethnographic knowledge in order to reach a working approximation to cultural boundaries and cultural content; but we cannot positively assert that our information is incomplete without assuming that the facts we seek do exist and that we are not chasing a conceptual will-o'-the-wisp. The point I wish to stress is not that Naroll's or Murdock's or somebody else's rules of thumb are better or worse, but that no criteria can be applied at all unless we assume either (1) that discrete cultures exist in nature, in which case we can do our best to identify them, or (2) that discrete cultures are analytical constructs, in accordance with some definition found to be heuristically useful. If we make assumption (2), then we have to make sure that the nominal definition of a culture – as Willer (1967: 87–88) puts it, some specified kind of constellation of attributes in functional relation to one another – corresponds with the operational definition used for determining from the ethnographic evidence where the limits of a specified culture lie. Unless we make one or other of these assumptions, then I cannot see how we can choose between alternative rules for defining the unit.

Assumption (2) could lead to a logically defensible form of cross-cultural analysis based on counting cultures; whether this would yield useful results remains to be seen. I doubt if it would be feasible in practice, and it is clear that this is not the assumption made by Murdock or by other practitioners of the cross-cultural method. As Naroll (1968: 253) says, 'The sampling universe of most cross-cultural surveys has not been defined with much care or precision.' The discrete culture as an analytical construct has not been defined, and Naroll's own efforts seem to be directed towards establishing a convenient, unequivocally delimited unit rather than a unit whose definition is derived from the theoretical assumptions about the nature of society and culture that are, or should be, under test. Most current users of the cross-cultural method seem to make assumption (1), that there are naturally occurring discrete cultures, and they adopt a variety of procedures aimed at making as close as possible an approximation to these cultures using the limited available ethnographic evidence.

Cultures are said to be 'borne' by individuals, so that they may be said to be located in time and space by the temporal and spatial distribution of the individuals bearing them. Some anthropologists might be inclined to argue that a culture in some sense exists in its own right independently of its imperfect manifestations in the thoughts and actions of its bearers, but this seems not to be Murdock's view, and would be contrary to the strong empirical emphasis found in most of his work. We can say of him, with much more confidence than of the other two writers we discuss, that he is not what Popper (1961: 28–29) would call a methodological essentialist. Even though he appears to believe that discrete cultures exist, Murdock's readiness to offer new operational definitions whenever he thinks them necessary puts him firmly in the nominalist camp. The manifest similarities in the behaviour of many individuals enable the observer to lump them together as bearers of a common culture and sometimes enable the actors themselves to conceptualize this similarity. But just how similar must behaviour be before we can say that here is one culture? If we could completely specify the cultural behaviour of every person in the world at a given moment of time, there would, of course, be some lines of discontinuity on the resulting distribution maps that would enable us to say that on these lines there is a cultural break. There breaks would be seen wherever two sets of people with distinctive ways of life live in spatial proximity. But these lines of discontinuity would not form a connected set of boundaries dividing the world into discrete areas each with its own distinctive culture. For most of the world, the division of the surface into areas of common culture would be a matter of judgement or convenience. If we introduce the time dimension, it is even clearer that although there are many instances of an indisputable cultural break in a given locality between one generation and the next, at most times and in most places we have to exercise our discretion in deciding when one culture is replaced by another. There are far too few 'natural

86

breaks' in the multidimensional continuum of space, time, and culture, and we therefore draw boundaries so as to convert the continuum into a collection of dated and located discrete cultures (cf. Mukherjee 1964). My contention is that these boundaries are drawn essentially for convenience, so that the procedure may be operationally feasible, as Naroll puts it, and so that the established routines of the cross-cultural method may be retained. Only a limited amount of these boundaries corresponds to discontinuities in the real world of space-time.

More significantly, the point of transition from one culture to the next has little bearing on the functional theory that the statistics obtained by sorting cultures into categories are intended to prove. The theory of functional relations between various cultural features that Murdock, along with most other anthropologists and sociologists, advocates and that he and his followers have sought to establish by the application of the cross-cultural method, seems to stand or fall quite irrespective of whether culture is a continuum or is divided into discrete units. When Lowie writes: 'In defiance of the dogma that any one culture forms a closed system, we must insist that such a culture is invariably an artificial unit segregated for purposes of expediency' (Lowie 1937: 235), he is attacking the assumption of complete cultural integration he found in the writings of Malinowski. As mentioned earlier (p. 26) this comment brought a sharp response from Murdock who argued that Lowie was here denying that culture was shared by members of a group and was refusing to recognize that 'cultures and subcultures are organically related to the structured social groups and subgroups that carry them' (Murdock 1940a: 365; 1954b: 20). Lowie's comment seems to me not to bear the construction Murdock puts upon it. Rather, Lowie is here raising the same point as Leach and others about the size of the culture-bearing unit, the unit which contributes a score of one when the sample is counted. Lowie writes:

Social tradition varies demonstrably from village to village, even from family to family. Are we to treat as bearers of such a closed system the chief's family in Omarakana, his village, the district of Kiriwina, the island of Boyowa, the Trobriand archipelago, the North Massim province, New Guinea, or perchance Melanesia? The attempt to adhere rigorously to any one of these demarkations precipitates absurdities (1937: 235–236).

We could add that from Disraeli to C. P. Snow the same question has been asked of British culture and no single answer has found acceptance. Lowie, of course, is here concerned not with the requirements of the statistical methods used in cross-cultural analysis but with Malinowski's functional integration. Yet the question he asks concerns the definition of the unit to be analysed, and has nothing to do with the assertions that culture is shared among group members and is related to the structure of the group, which Murdock would have him deny. Lowie was as firmly committed as Murdock to the view that the several aspects of the culture of a group exercise an influence upon one another, despite his much misunderstood quotation from 'The Mikado' about our civilization as 'that planless hodgepodge, that thing of shreds and patches' (Lowie 1946: 119; 1949: viii, 428; Murdock 1943: 443; 1949a: 322). The 'fundamental characteristics of culture', as seen by Murdock (1940a; 1965a: 80) are that it is learned, inculcated, social, ideational, gratifying, adaptive, and integrative. The first six of these seven characteristics involve no assumptions at all about the existence or absence of cultural boundaries. Only the last entails a consideration of the possible existence of discrete cultures with boundaries.

Let us make another attempt to retain the notion of a discrete culture. If culture is everywhere and always fully integrated (this is the view attributed to Malinowski that Lowie attacks), then is not the whole world necessarily divided into discrete groups bearing distinctive cultures? If so, we would be able to count them. To prove this, suppose that we have one set of fully integrated attributes, one distinctive cultural profile, present at a given moment of time at a point X, and another different but equally fully integrated set at point Y. Then as we move along any line drawn from X to Y, the state of culture we encounter at points on the line must change. The changes from one set to another, we might argue, cannot happen gradually, for the assumption of complete integration rules out the possibility of a change first in one aspect of culture and then in another. Hence the changes must be abrupt. At the point on the line at which we change abruptly from the culture of X to the culture of Y (or to some geographically intervening culture), here we have the boundary of the area to which X belongs. Since this applies to any route whatever from X to Y there must be a cultural boundary all round X, and similarly another boundary all round Y. In other words, we have discrete non-overlapping cultures.

There are two objections to this line of argument. Some cultural characteristics, as described by Murdock, can only change abruptly; for example, either there are patrilineal moieties in a given culture, or there are not, and there is no halfway house. The encoding procedure, which allows only the two possibilities, in this case reflects accurately the state of the culture itself. But other cultural characteristics can vary continuously, and with these the use of a limited number of codes necessarily provides us with only an approximation to the true state of affairs. Thus, for example, the mean size of local communities, the length of the post-mortem sexual taboo, and the relative dependence on the various major types of subsistence activity (Columns 31, 36, and 7 in the Atlas) are all characteristics that can vary continuously between certain limits. It would be compatible with the maintenance of complete integration for the transition from the culture of X to the culture of Y to occur gradually, with no discontinuities, provided that the two cultures differ only in respect of characteristics that are of this continuously variable kind. The relevant characteristics could thus vary gradually and concomitantly as we move from X to Y and there would be no point at which we could unequivocally say we had left the area of the culture of X. In other words, even with perfect integration, culture discontinuities

89

are necessary only in respect of those cultural characteristics which vary discontinuously.

More importantly, the theory of cultural integration and functional relationship that we are examining does not postulate any such condition of universal integration. As we have already noted, Murdock holds the view that integration is rare or never actually achieved. Since the other fundamental qualities of culture do not entail discrete countable cultures, there seems to be no need for the concept at all, except that it appears to open the way to statistical analysis. To me, this seems to be a case of the tail wagging the dog.

A physical analogy may help to make clear my notion of culture. A culture is similar to an horizon. A man standing at a given point on the earth's surface sees an horizon, and can describe what he sees in terms of distance, colour, shape, and other characteristics. If necessary the description can be reduced to coded attributes associated with several characteristics. The attributes of the horizon may change with the time of day, the seasons of the year, the erection and destruction of buildings; the changes of the 'horizon associated with a given point' may be cyclical or progressive. As our observer moves from one point to another, the horizon he sees may change slowly or quickly, gradually or abruptly. We can generalize and even make quantitative statements about the horizons seen from points in a given area during a given period of time, but it is quite meaningless to ask how many horizons there are.

Murdock's theory of social structure does not call for the construction of some arbitrarily-defined ethnic unit comprised of individuals bearing cultures falling within, say, some specified degree of similarity or whose level of interaction exceeds some threshold value, as Chapple (1964) suggests. There is therefore no reason to see these attempts to define satisfactory cultural units as a step towards the replacement of assumption (1), that cultures are natural units, by assumption (2), that cultures are analytic or etic units (cf. p. 85). Indeed, there would be very serious difficulties in specifying a generally applicable standard of similarity, quite apart from the fact that

90

a significant feature of any cultural environment is the extent to which diversity in behaviour and belief is prevented, tolerated, or encouraged.

The most comprehensive attempt, apart from Murdock's own efforts over the years, to formalize and standardize the units used in cross-cultural analysis has been made by Naroll. At the beginning of his article he quotes a query raised by a biologist: 'Exactly where is the *skin* of a culture?' The article is a sustained attempt to define cultural skin, or the limits of a single culture, in an objective and uniform manner. Unfortunately Naroll overlooks the more important question: does a culture have a skin at all? However, the notion of skinless culture, as it were, does have to be considered, not only because it is a closer approximation to what happens in the real world, as I have argued, but also because it can be used to explain Murdock's own attitude to the criticism raised by Leach and others, the 'population of China' objection. The eighty columns of the Ethnographic atlas provide a great deal of information about the societies or cultures listed, but give no indication about population. Column 31 indicates the mean size of local communities, but not the number of communities in the society. The omission of information on population may be due to a judgement by Murdock that, with only eighty columns at his disposal, this statistic must be excluded in favour of other more important cultural characteristics; presumably this is why the Ethnographic atlas does not include any information on, for instance, divorce frequency, attitudes to suicide, beliefs about witchcraft, and so on. However, the persistence of some of Murdock's critics that population is relevant to cross-cultural sampling has brought, somewhat belatedly, a clear statement of Murdock's opposition to this view.

As mentioned earlier, one of the objections brought by Leach against the cross-cultural method is that populous societies like China and societies with small populations like Tikopia are treated as units of the same order (Leach 1950: 108; 1960b; McEwen 1963: 162; Köbben 1963; Levy 1963; cf. Naroll 1964b and comments therein). One of the sample societies used in *Social Structure* is simply labelled 'Chinese'. In later samples the cultures of several groups in China appear separately, even though we are told that China is a single society (cf. pp. 29–30). Tikopia, with a population of 1,300 in 1929, appears as a single unit in all Murdock's world-wide samples. An analysis of Murdock's response to this criticism reveals the assumptions underlying his final solution to the sampling problem.

There are two aspects to Leach's objection. First, Leach may be arguing that a complex society such as China has some specialized institutions which have no analogue at all in Tikopia; in other words, China and Tikopia differ not only in the attributes they display in respect of common characteristics, but also in the range of characteristics needed to give an adequate picture of the culture. We have already touched on this part of the objection, when we referred to Murdock's concept of 'nation' (above, pp. 27–28). Second, Leach is also arguing, so I understand him, that the difference in population makes the two units not comparable. Murdock deals explicitly with this criticism in an editorial statement (Murdock *et al.* 1963: 249–250), stressing that the sample is a sample of cultures, not of societies or populations. He makes his point by comparing China and Aboriginal Australia. China has long been a single society, but its population is some 10,000 times that of Aboriginal Australia, which was divided into over 500 distinct societies. The two areas contain approximately the same number of distinct cultural types, six in China and five in Australia according to the Atlas (Murdock 1967: 22, 27). In a random sample of societies, Australia would be represented over 500 times as heavily as China, while in a random sample of equal populations China would be represented over 10,000 times as heavily as Australia. In a random sample of cultural types, China and Australia are about equally represented.

Murdock's earlier statements have not been so clear, as we have already seen in his shifts from samples of cultures to samples of societies and back again. In the 'World ethnographic sample' the first of the desiderata for the inclusion of a society is that it should be the most populous in its area or occupy

92

the greatest expanse of territory (1957a: 667). As mentioned earlier, in his *Outline of world cultures* he says that the choice of societies for his sample 'represents the best compromise of which the author is capable between the sociological point of view which would emphasize population and the anthropological point of view which would emphasize cultural diversity'. He leans somewhat towards the sociological viewpoint (1958a: v). Yet a few years later he refers to population size as one of the 'irrelevant or adventitious facts' to be ignored in constructing a sample. This change of view may explain why population estimates are given for some societies but not for all in the notes that accompany the tables of the Atlas (Murdock 1966: 99; 1697: 8; Murdock *et al.* 1962b: 124).

The assertion in Murdock's later scheme of analysis that population size is irrelevant must be seen as the end result of a long process of analytical clarification. In his earlier works, Murdock writes of a sample of cultures chosen 'to represent as adequately as possible the whole range of known civilizations' (1937c: 460). Cultures are grouped into culture areas, and the same number of tribes chosen from each area. In 1963 Murdock formalized his quest for 'the whole range of known civilizations' by introducing the concept of 'cultural type', defined as 'either a single unquestionably distinctive culture or a group of cultures which differ from one another to a degree not significantly greater than the local variations to be expected in a culture of any homogeneous society of substantial geographical extent' (Murdock *et al.* 1963: 249).

This definition looks circular or infinitely regressive, for just how homogeneous does a society have to be to be labelled homogeneous? Presumably, as homogeneous as is to be expected. With this definition, Murdock assumed that the total number of known cultural types would prove to be about 400. This prediction was borne out three years later when a complete list of these cultural types, renamed cultural clusters, was published (Murdock 1966: 99–100; 1967: 7–45). The 412 cultural clusters have now been grouped into 200 'sampling provinces', clusters being placed in a single province if there are particularly

93

close linguistic relationships or particularly close cultural resemblances between them, or if they are spatially close; 'Two or more clusters whose principal members are separated from each other by less than 200 miles are automatically grouped together, regardless of linguistic or cultural dissimilarity, on the assumption that over such short distances an appreciable measure of reciprocal cultural borrowing is inevitable.'

The third criterion is particularly baffling. It is an adaption to clusters of the 'three degree rule', applied originally to societies. As far as I can tell, Murdock does not define what societies are the 'principal members' of a cultural cluster, and presumably we cannot identify them by appeal to the irrelevant and adventitious criteria of population or territorial extent. It is apparent if we happen to choose as 'principal members' societies which are located strategically on the periphery of the area occupied by each cultural cluster, then by judicious use of the Behring Strait and the Sinai Desert the whole world, except perhaps for a few oceanic islands, reduces to a single sampling province. This is not how Murdock applies this criterion, and some additional working rule must be used, though it is not stated.

Be that as it may, Murdock arrives at a total of exactly 200 sampling provinces, and he proposes the use of a 'standard world sample' consisting of one society, specified tentatively, from each province. If we take this to be Murdock's final solution to the sampling problem, then we can see why the population size of the separate encoded societies is 'irrelevant' and 'adventitious', and why Murdock is not concerned with arguments about the definition of the cultural unit. For in the standard world sample the cultural characteristics of each selected society is in effect taken to be representative of the sampling province as a whole. If then we wished to adopt the line of argument advanced earlier in this chapter and applied a population–time weighting factor, the relevant population to consider would be that of the sampling province, and not of the selected society.

Whether or not we apply weighting factors it becomes irrelevant, following Murdock's latest procedure, to argue about

94

the number of ethnic units constituted by, for example, Min China. If it is taken as a single unit or as 500 ethnic units, the answer is the same. In either case we have only a single sampling province, contributing a single society, weighted or unweighted, to the standard world sample. From Murdock's latest point of view it does not matter whether we regard the boundaries between ethnic units within a single province as representing discontinuities occurring in reality or as entirely arbitrary and artificial divisions, for the composition of the sample is not affected. On the other hand, the validity of the sample does depend on the validity of the boundaries between sampling provinces. If two contiguous ethnic units are divided by a provincial boundary, then there is a chance of both appearing in either the standard or an alternative world sample, whereas if they are in the same province, they cannot both appear in a sample.

In brief, Murdock's latest sampling procedure calls for a sample of discrete countable cultures borne by people who are not genetically connected, do not live near one another, and who have not copied cultural attributes from one another. Against this I maintain that there are no naturally occurring discrete cultures; that if we wish to test for the presence of adaptive functional relations established by trial and error, we should use the notion of 'culture at a point' and should include, not exclude, the cultures borne by individuals who are genetically connected, who live near one another, and who copy one another; and that the rough and ready formula for weighting each 'culture at a point' by population and duration applies only when the relation under test is between attributes whose presence is the result of decision-making processes of similar scale.

II *Assessment*

If the criticisms I have raised against the cross-cultural tradition are valid, what value is there in Murdock's work?

Something may be inferred even from the unweighted statistical tables themselves. Although the presence of an apparent statistical association in these tables is not conclusive evidence of the existence of a functional relation between the relevant variables, the converse of this statement does not hold. If there is a true functional relation between, say, the extensiveness of menstrual taboos and the intensity of castration anxiety (Stephens 1961), or between the custom whereby a man avoids his wife's parents and a cultural emphasis on unilineal kin groups (Sweetser 1966), then this relationship should manifest itself in Tikopia and in all the five hundred parts of China. Whatever sort of weighting or lack of weighting we use, and whatever kind of sampling procedure we follow, unless this gives a definite bias in favour of 'misses' rather than 'hits' (Naroll 1961: 20, 22), the relationship should show itself statistically. Hence, if there is no statistical association, it is unlikely that a strong functional relation exists. In other words, the statistical tables can be used to provide useful evidence for the absence of any strong functional relation between two cultural elements but they are only poor evidence for the presence of this relation (cf. Naroll 1967: 104; Lévi-Strauss 1963a: 306).

Apart from this negative use of statistical evidence, it seems best to follow Leach's advice and to consider Murdock's verbal arguments on their own merits. His views on the importance of the family, his mixture of norm and practice, his heuristic use of fantastic anecdotes, all these are easy to criticize. But at least he has seen the need to make the theories and results of social anthropology compatible with those of other social sciences like psychology, and he has not been inhibited from crossing those arbitrary boundaries between disciplines which are really often nothing more than the relics of interdisciplinary battles fought long ago and which long ago should have been forgotten. There is a great deal of circularity in his hypothesis of functional relationship, just as for example there is in Radcliffe-Brown's functionalism. But whereas the circularity in Radcliffe-Brown's views appears to stem from his definitions, Murdock's circularity appears to me to reflect a real situation in which there is

96

a multiplicity of feedback effects between different aspects of culture and of behaviour. Murdock's main achievement as a functionalist has been his grasp of the necessity for a theory with a temporal dimension, and for a model of society that is rarely in equilibrium, with its various parts changing simultaneously in different directions and at different rates. Murdock may have produced far too simple a model, and assigned far too prominent a place to changes in the rule of post-marital residence, but at least it is a model with the right ingredients.

Without accepting Murdock's rigid distinction between ethnography and theory, we can recognize the value that his attempt to encompass all societies, throughout the world and throughout time, has had for ethnographic inquiry. Ethnographic fieldwork involves its practitioners in such considerable intellectual and affective investment in a restricted geographical area that it is not surprising that, despite its pretensions to scientific status, anthropology as taught in most universities remains a kind of natural history, organized regionally as well as by topic and oriented as much towards description as to nomothetic explanation. Murdock's work has operated to modify this professional regionalism (cf. Erasmus and Smith 1967: 116, 130–132). The assumptions that go unchallenged in unilineal Africa about the way societies 'naturally' operate are challenged by the evidence from South America, and Aboriginal Australian societies are seen to be not *sui generis* but variants of a common pattern.

The holes that encode on cards the information included in the *Ethnographic atlas* may well have been made with sledge-hammers, and the classifications of the Human Relations Area Files may not always be reliable, but they do provide a first point of entry into a bibliographic jungle where any guide, however imperfect, is welcome. Needham can scarcely be classed as a protégé of Murdock, and his style of analysis has nothing in common with Murdock's cross-cultural methodology. Yet he acclaims (Needham 1964: 238) the value of Murdock's work in pointing out where to begin to look in the ethnographic corpus.

97

The continuing discussions about the identification of ethnic units, and about how to sample them, indicate a determination to retain an accepted method of analysis, namely counting and the application of statistical techniques suitable for use with discrete units, rather than to examine the theory which the method was originally developed to test and then to devise better tests. The intellectual and material investment in the method is considerable and this determination can well be understood. Murdock began the cross-cultural survey in order to have 'access to a dependable and objective sample of the ethnographic evidence' from which 'scientific generalizations of a universally human or cross-cultural character' (1940a: 361, 364) could be made. But the enterprise has acquired a momentum of its own, and generated 'curiosity about what one could do with the Human Relations Area Files' (Udy 1964: 161). Altschuler (1967) comments that the Files have 'made it too easy to engage in superficial statistical "research"'. Given the constant pressure to undertake research which is characteristic of contemporary academic life, and similar pressure to utilize an expensive bibliographic investment, it is not surprising that cross-cultural studies have increased and became a recognized specialized form of anthropological inquiry. Comparable instances of the routinization of techniques of analysis and of increasing elaborations designed to meet continuing criticism are to be found in other scientific disciplines (cf. Kuhn 1964). An appreciation of the cross-cultural method in historical perspective may facilitate a change to something better.

A last point concerns Murdock's style of debate. He has been outstandingly forthright in expressing his opinion of the work of his colleagues, and outspoken in the claims he has made for the importance and value of his own methods of inquiry. It is typical of his approach to understanding that he should preface his book on Africa with the observation that he had visited the continent only three times and never for more than a fortnight. His book is avowedly iconoclastic, but although its mistakes have been seized on by the experts, the value of its fresh look has been recognized (Murdock 1959a: vii; Wrigley 1960; Fage 1961).

His *obiter dicta* are fired in all directions and range from specu-
lating whether the persistence of the Soviet Union may be due
to the inclusion of Julius Lippert's work in communist reading
lists to classifying the League of Nations and the United Nations
as gigantic hoaxes (1931: xxv–xxvi; 1956b: 146). He has pro-
voked others to attack him and, while some heat has been
generated, much light has also resulted from these interchanges.
The gusto with which he has gone into battle has been matched
by his readiness to admit the limitations in his own work, and
by the constructiveness of the suggestions he has made for
improving it. Even the attempt to find 'safety in numbers' may
have been worth while if the efforts at improvement now being
made bring to the surface the inherent limitations of present
methods.

2 Real models

In my mind, models are reality and I would even say that they are the only reality.

Lévi-Strauss (1953b: 115)

2 Real models

1 Introduction

It is not my intention in this chapter to discuss the whole of the work of Claude Lévi-Strauss. Although *Les Structures élémentaires de la parenté* (1949a) was his first major theoretical work, and although he foreshadowed in that book the publication of further studies in kinship (on complex structures and on Ambrym) which are now unlikely to appear (1969: xxxvi, 125 f.n. 6, 465), his recent work, apart from the Huxley memorial lecture (1966c) has been mainly in other fields. There is an essential continuity of method and interest between this early thesis and what he has written in the last few years on myth and the structure of thought. Questions of kinship are discussed at numerous points throughout his work. It would be easy to show that many of the themes prominent in *La Pensée sauvage* (1962a) and later works are already present in *Les Structures*. But I am concerned here with these later publications only for the light they throw on *Les Structures* and on his articles specifically dealing with kinship. In fact they throw a great deal of light, for they make explicit many assumptions and preferences that are left unstated in *Les Structures*. Much of the bewilderment that in Britain and America greeted the publication of his book arose from a failure to appreciate that here was an essay in a different and unfamiliar tradition, and not merely an Anglo-Saxon work that happened to be written in French (cf. Scholte 1966). The volume, brilliance, and popularity of Lévi-Strauss's writings published in the last ten or fifteen years have ensured a wider understanding, though not necessarily wider approval, of his work even among anthropologists with objectives and techniques quite dissimilar from his. Yet *Les Structures* still tends to be judged by criteria that are more relevant to a tribal monograph or a report of a social survey than to an attempt to synthesize a large body of data from what was then an original and unexpected point of view. This is perhaps because *Les Structures*, much more than its successors, is written essentially for a technical audience. It is true that the book was reviewed by Simone de Beauvoir (1949) and won for its author the Prix Paul-Pelliot, and that Lévi-Strauss himself admits that some of his readers may not be able to follow at first reading his discussion of Murinbata Kinship (1969: 153 f.n. 5). Nevertheless this is a professional enunciation of a professional argument, a doctoral thesis in a mandarin system, whereas his later works are aimed at and have reached an audience much wider than the anthropological profession and have to be assessed differently. It is not its size alone that has so long delayed the translation into English of *Les Structures*.

My aim, then, is to look at what Lévi-Strauss has to say about kinship from the point of view of anthropology, and not from those of philosophy or literature or the battle of ideas in Paris (cf. Barnes 1971). It may well be that Lévi-Strauss's most enduring achievement will be his success in disengaging anthropology in France from the ruins of French colonialism (cf. Guiart 1965; Lévi-Strauss 1966b: 126), but questions of that sort cannot concern us here. I shall not be directly concerned with his views on myth or thought or with his statements about 'distanciation' and authenticity. For this reason my remarks will follow lines that diverge considerably from those chosen by most of his other commentators (for bibliographies, see *Arc* 1965b; Simonis 1968: 363–370).

Some of Lévi-Strauss's works were written in English while several articles first published in French appear in translation in *Structural anthropology* (1963a). Some of his books have been translated but much of his writing on kinship and cognate topics is not available in translation and I have worked from the French originals. The caveat that Lévi-Strauss enters for himself about the difficulties of using a language not one's mother tongue (1958a: i–ii) must be mine too, in reverse and in much greater measure. Leach (1965: 26–27) notes the 'harmonic ambiguities' in Lévi-Strauss's French, and I am aware that in several places I have sought to resolve ambiguities that are intentional and not accidental. I have tried therefore to cover as wide a range of his writings as feasible, hoping to minimize the risk of misunderstanding by seeking as many instances as possible of the statement of each point of view.

In trying to interpret a book written in the late 1940s in the light of books and articles written during the ensuing fifteen years or more, it is easy to read into *Les Structures* a mature system of concepts and analytical procedures that in fact are present only in nascent form. Yet it is certainly right to expect some continuity. Lévi-Strauss has commented that, both in *Les Structures* and in the later studies of myth, his aim is to reduce an apparently arbitrary and inchoate domain to a very small number of significant propositions. But in the field of kinship, he says, the structure of the mind does not operate alone; the domain is also constrained by the exigences of social life. His experience in this first inquiry did not satisfy him. By contrast, in the field of mythology, the mind seems most free to give rein to its creative spontaneity, and its laws may there be elucidated (Lévi-Strauss *et al.* 1963: 630). We may assume therefore that in *Les Structures* we have to deal with both 'the laws of the mind' and 'the exigences of social life', and that the author's interest veers towards the former rather than the latter. The 'exigences of social life' are not entirely neglected but we should not be surprised if it is here that we find the least satisfactory parts of his analysis. Perhaps this expression of preference, implicit in the shift of emphasis from kinship to mythology during the 1950s, makes sense of a remarkable statement made in 1952, only three years after *Les Structures* first appeared, while his paper on 'Social structure' was being discussed. He said: 'When I was assigned this paper, I discovered to my surprise that I had no idea whatsoever of what social structure was, and that I had written quite a deal on social structure without knowing what

E

it was' (1953b: 116). This delightfully disarming remark has to be set against his thesis that we all can and do make significant statements about the social structure of our own society without necessarily realizing exactly what that structure is. What is sauce for M. Jourdain the citizen is presumably also sauce for M. Jourdain the anthropologist.

2 Objectives

Our first task is to determine what Lévi-Strauss is writing about, for he does not address himself in college textbook style to first-year students; his aim and scope manifest themselves gradually and progressively. What soon emerges is that he is much concerned with the special place of social anthropology among the disciplines, and with the special advantages of structural analysis over other kinds of inquiry. Social anthropology and structural studies overlap, neither completely containing the other, and it is the overlapping area that is our concern, more particularly that portion of it which falls under the rubric of kinship. But to understand Lévi-Strauss on kinship, we have to discuss as well his notion of structure. It is true that, despite its size, *Les Structures* is not a general treatise on kinship, and still less on the concept of structure; it is an exhaustive discussion of only a delimited aspect of kinship. Nevertheless, the aim of the book is to demonstrate that the origin and regulating function of kinship is to be found in exchange in all its forms (1969: 233). This proposition about exchange, already latent in his earlier assertion that warfare among Amazonian tribes establishes an unconscious bond of exchange between them (1943b: 124), became in a somewhat broader form the dominant theme of most of Lévi-Strauss's work during the 1950s, whether dealing with kinship or with other forms of social interchange. In these later works the view of structure largely tacitly assumed in *Les Structures* is enunciated and developed. Here I endeavour to analyse this notion and its application to kinship in general terms. Elsewhere, in a monograph dealing with the
106

Murngin kinship system, I examine this application in a particular instance, along with the contribution of other writers towards the elucidation of the same empirical data (Barnes 1967c). I shall not discuss in detail Lévi-Strauss's propositions relating to other societies or ethnographic regions.

Everyone would agree that no science can study everything; the investigator has to select from the range of possible observations those that are relevant to his own interest and his own scheme of analysis. Lévi-Strauss attacks those critics who seem to think that structural anthropologists aim 'at acquiring an exhaustive knowledge of societies'. On the contrary, they 'simply wish to derive constants which are found at various times and in various places from an empirical richness and diversity that will always transcend our efforts at observation and description' (1963a: 82–83). We cannot tell in advance where these constants are to be found. 'Our experience of the concrete has taught us that it is often the most fluid and the most transient aspects of a culture which provide access to structure. That is why we pay such intense, almost compulsive attention to details' (1963a: 327). In fact, Lévi-Strauss has been criticized for inadequate attention to detail, as to his handling of certain ethnographic data in *Les Structures* (cf. Leach 1961b: 77–78; 1964b: 1110; 1969). Yet we cannot ignore his close attention to those details of culture that catch his attention, whether it is strangers offering one another wine in southern France (1969: 58–60), or the Hopi classification of natural objects and phenomena (1962a: 56). Indeed, his remarkable paper on the use of wild plants in South America (1950b) demonstrates this admirably (cf. Steward 1950: xii).

Structural studies, then, are firmly based on detailed empirical observation. His rule is that '. . . all the facts should be carefully observed and described, without allowing any theoretical preconception to decide whether some are more important than others' (1963a: 280). This sounds like a recipe for kleptomaniacal phenomenologism, and even if this advice relates only to the preliminary observation and not to the subsequent analysis, it cannot be taken literally, for facts are innumerable and it is impossible to record them all. Even before he begins to observe, the ethnographer has to have some preferences; his dilemma is that when later he has thought about his observations, it is then too late to go back in space and time to make those observations which he now sees would have been relevant. Lévi-Strauss's advice has to be understood as an appeal for accurate, unprejudiced, and free-ranging observation.

Empirical observations may be of many kinds: where people live, what they say to one another, their actions in a ceremony, the names they give to flowers and animals, their beliefs about how the world began, and so on. Social relations have been treated by most writers as first-order abstractions from empirical reality, not immediately apparent to the camera or the uninformed eye but fairly easily derivable from observed behaviour. The social relations present in a community interact on one another, change, or persist, and it is possible to describe the salient or invariant or enduring properties of the network of relations as a social structure. Few anthropologists would quarrel with Lévi-Strauss's statement that 'The object of social-structure studies is to understand social relations with the aid of models' (1963a: 289). Yet for Lévi-Strauss, social relations belong to concrete reality, 'they are truly observed' (1953b: 116), and he attacks Radcliffe-Brown for making social structure appear to be nothing else than the network of social relations (1963a: 303). Social relations, and other empirical observations in this sense, are to be seen as merely raw material. He does not quite say that social structures are built up of social relations but rather that 'social relations consist of the raw materials out of which the models making up social structure are built' (1963a: 279), which is not quite the same. But the weight of emphasis is clear. Marriage rules, and presumably other parts of social structure, belong to that social world that Mauss saw as 'a world of symbolic relationships' and where, says Lévi-Strauss, the symbols are more real than the things they symbolize (1950a: xv, xxxii). Social structure is a model; models are not abstractions and they alone are truly real (1953b: 115). On the other hand, 'the term "social

108

structure" has nothing whatever to do with empirical reality but with models that are built up after it' (1963a: 279).

These uncompromising statements about reality, and in particular the sentence last quoted which was repeated unchanged ten years after first publication, have puzzled many anthropologists. It is easy for those whose interest is chiefly in understanding how societies work to dismiss these remarks as metaphysical asides that are irrelevant to the main argument. Thus when Lévi-Strauss's paper 'Social structure' (1953a), in which he first puts forward a comprehensive statement of his views on models, was discussed by his colleagues, Nadel (1953: 113) suggested that discussions on the nature of reality belong to religion, and implied that anthropologists could make better use of their time. In his reply, Lévi-Strauss argued that 'this is also mostly a linguistic problem, because in English it is difficult to distinguish between reality and concrete reality' (1953b: 115). But there is more at stake here than the mere naming of metaphysical concepts.

First, there is a value judgement: concrete reality is something that has to be transcended, and if structure 'has nothing whatever to do with empirical reality' it becomes easy to say of any item of empirical evidence that it 'has nothing whatever to do with' structure. In another passage Lévi-Strauss states his position more fully, using the language of Marxism. Although the infrastructure is primary and, as it were, provides the unalterable preconditions for human life and thought, it does no more than this; it supplies the pack of cards, and deals the hands, but the rules of the game and the way the hands are played are left to the players to decide. Lévi-Strauss is concerned primarily with the invented rules of the game, to a lesser extent with what happens in particular games, and, according to his declared intent, not at all in how the pack gets assembled or dealt. He writes: 'It is to this theory of superstructures, scarcely sketched by Marx, that we wish to contribute, leaving to history – assisted by demography, technology, historical geography and ethnography – the task of developing the study of infrastructures properly so called; this is not primarily our own task, for

109

the ethnologist is first of all a psychologist' (1962a: 124, 126, 173, 174).

Second, all models, whether home-made by the actors or constructed by the anthropologist, tend to be treated as equally real. The proposition that social structure has nothing whatever to do with empirical reality leads to uncertainty about the criteria whereby models may properly be rejected, as I hope to show; the proposition that social structure has to do with models that are built up after empirical reality leads the investigator to attribute to indigenous notions properties they do not always have. On the other hand, his assertion that social relations belong to concrete reality and are truly observed indicates that Lévi-Strauss does not need a concept at an intermediate level of abstraction, somewhere between empirical reality and social structure. This is because he is not greatly interested in systems of action. It will become clear that, despite a distinction between 'lived-in' and 'thought-of' orders (1963a: 312–313), his models of social structure are essentially models of systems of thought. As Leach notes, Lévi-Strauss asks 'How does man conceive of himself in relation to the world of society?' and not as do most British anthropologists 'How does society work?' (Leach 1964b: 1110). If he were to ask the latter question, he might have to promote social relations to a higher conceptual level.

Lévi-Strauss lists anthropology as a 'human' rather than a 'social' science, since its aim is to 'apprehend some reality immanent in Man'. It is not primarily concerned with the individual man or the individual society (1964: 549). The phenomena of kinship, or at least some of them, are universal phenomena, and hence any explanation, to be satisfactory, must draw on universal human characteristics (cf. Josselin de Jong 1952: 1). Consequently, he declares himself not primarily interested in historical and geographical problems. *Les Structures* is a typological analysis, not a historical reconstruction or a geographical description (1969: 358). Like Mauss, he is concerned with primitive societies because they exhibit social phenomena under simpler forms. He cites Mauss's comment that 'it is easier to study the digestive process in the oyster than in man; but this does not mean that the higher vertebrates were formerly shell-fishes' (1945b: 527). He is reported to have said in oral discussion that kinship terminology does not evolve progressively; on the contrary, kinship systems shift violently from one form to its opposite (1950c: 409). This must surely be an oversimplification of what was intended, but it is consonant with a renunciation of historical problems. He refers to one system of kinship being genetically related to another, but this is to be understood in a purely logical and not in an historical sense (1953b: 114). In fact, as Josselin de Jong (1952: 35) points out, *Les Structures* does contain what are in effect historical arguments. His discussion of the concept of archaism (1952; cf. 1969: 62) is among other things a plea for better historical understanding, and he discusses his data on kinship in eastern Asia from a geographical standpoint, even if mainly to show the inadequacy of purely historical and geographical explanations (1969: 388, 460–463). He suggests how the present kinship system of the Dieri and Wikmunkan may be built up through a series of steps which can be read as easily historically as didactically (1969: 206, 211, 499–500). Indeed, in an article (1949b) written at about the same time as *Les Structures*, Lévi-Strauss argues cogently for the indispensability of cooperation between historian and anthropologist. He does not aim to state merely what is common to all mankind, a highest common factor of human society as it were. Rather, the main, if not the sole, aim of anthropology is 'to analyze and interpret differences' (1963a: 14). Only history can provide the 'individualized and concrete knowledge of social groups localized in time and space' which are needed to elucidate these differences. A little history is better than no history at all (1963a: 11, 12). Later he asserts: 'As with linguistics, it is the discontinuities which constitute the true subject matter of anthropology' (1963a: 328; cf. 1961b: 17). At first sight these statements may seem hard to reconcile with his contention (1953a) that the ultimate aim of social anthropology is to construct 'mechanical' models, using reversible and non-cumulative time, whereas historical time is 'statistical' and always appears as an oriented and non-reversible process (1963a: 285–286). I have commented elsewhere on Lévi-Strauss's view of history and time (Barnes 1971) and here need note only that in the study of what he calls 'elementary structures' of kinship, history plays a minor formal role. Only with the development of more complicated kinship systems, with which Lévi-Strauss has not yet dealt at length, does history, along with politics and economics, have to be taken seriously into account in the analysis of kinship (cf. 1966c: 20).

History and time are separate notions, and several kinds of time have nothing to do with history. In *Les Structures*, which is devoted to a study of unhistorical elementary kinship structures, there is very little discussion of time. Subsequent publications by Lévi-Strauss have demonstrated the need for non-historical concepts of time in the study of even elementary structures, and their absence from *Les Structures* may be the reason for these unresolved contradictions between typological and historical analysis. The notion of diachronic models, those in which the passage of time is a significant dimension, is only latent in *Les Structures* and seems to have been first stated explicitly many years later (1962b: 42). Even so, he appears to mistrust the use of diachronic models, at least at this stage in the development of anthropological inquiries, and confines them to those situations where, as in the familiar developmental cycle of domestic groups (Fortes 1958a; see below pp. 200–201), repetitive cyclical non-cumulative processes appear as structural or invariant features (cf. Vogt 1960: 21). Lévi-Strauss seems to regard repetitive changes of this kind as not properly processes at all. If I understand his references to the French Revolution correctly, diachronic structures (models) cannot be used to explain changes or 'processes' that are irreversible or historically unique. Yet whether or not a process is seen as unique depends partly, and perhaps wholly, on the scale of the model of which it forms a part. For example, in his analysis of Highland Burma, Leach develops a model of political structure which embodies as a repetitive and non-cumulative process transitions from a state policy to comparative statelessness and back again, transitions which simpler political models had treated as irreversible pro-

cesses. Furthermore, this model is held to be consciously present
in the minds of the members of the society as a set of verbal categories and not merely an analytical construct (Leach 1964a: xiii).

Left with only unique and irreversible changes under the
heading of 'process'; Lévi-Strauss is able to say that there is a
relationship of uncertainty (in Heisenberg's sense) between
structure and process; 'the one can be perceived only by ignoring the other' (1964: 546; cf. 1962b: 44–45). In *Les Structures* he
deals mainly with synchronic models but suggests (Radcliffe-
Brown would presumably say 'conjectures') how societies may
move from one model to another. Historical factors, such as the
fortunes of war, seem to be treated as random events, external
to the facts being analysed (1969: 73). In his own terms, process
is ignored so that structure may be perceived.

Lévi-Strauss cites with approval (1963a: 308) Lowie's comment (1929) that 'Sometimes the very essence of a social fabric
may be demonstrably connected with the mode of classifying
kin.' Lowrie was writing at a time when kinship studies were
still dominated by what Malinowski used to call contemptuously
'kinship algebra' (Fortes 1957a: 159), but it is significant that
Lévi-Strauss goes back to this remark. For in what is perhaps
his earliest published theoretical statement of the nature of
kinship (1945a), he draws a distinction between kinship as a
system of terminology and as a system of attitudes (1963a: 37).
In other words, terminology is important; so are 'attitudes';
kinship as a system of action is not mentioned. It is true that
'attitudes' include marriage rules and are social as well as
psychological in nature, but even these are seen as forming,
along with language, economic relations, art, science, and
religion, a collection of symbolic systems which aim to express
certain aspects of physical and social reality and their interrelations (1950a: xix). Social anthropology may consist exclusively of a study of rules (1963a: 298), but it seems that these
rules are to be studied for their symbolic function, rather than
to see how they are enforced, what happens when they are
broken, and the like; they are, as it were, rules of the spirit
rather than rules of the police court.

3   Fundamental elements

Before we can understand the taxonomies and propositions put forward by Lévi-Strauss we have to learn his terminology; in learning the terminology we begin to come to grips with the relations between the terms. As good a point of departure as any is his notion of limited possibilities, for this is the notion he sees as distinctive of his own work (cf. 1962d: 144).

He says that:

> . . . in its social undertakings mankind keeps manoeuvering within narrow limits. Social types are not isolated creations, wholly independent of each other, and each one an original entity, but rather the result of an endless play of combination and re-combination, for ever seeking to solve the same problems by manipulating the same fundamental elements (1963c: 10).

The same idea is expressed in several places: 'the spectrum of institutional possibilities, whose range is probably not unlimited' (1963a: 133); and 'human societies . . . chose certain combinations from a repertory of ideas which it should be possible to reconstitute' (1961a: 160). In *Les Structures* he says that the rules of kinship and marriage are reducible to a small number; there are only three possible elementary kinship structures, formed with the help of two forms of exchange, which in turn depend on whether the society is harmonic or disharmonic (1969: 493). All these terms have specialized meanings which we shall examine presently; here my point is merely that Lévi-Strauss works with a strictly limited set of contrasts. It is not just that the 'empirical richness and diversity' mentioned earlier can for convenience be sorted into one or other of a limited number of analytical categories because the analyst does not wish to discriminate more finely. Instead, we have the proposition that certain categories are given and are few in number; they are fundamental elements, not tools invented for analytical convenience. There is, as he might say, a privileged level of analysis, and this is the level of fundamental reality. The argument

114

with Nadel about reality is not just an instance of Anglo-French misunderstanding, for without some notion corresponding to that of 'elementary particles' in physics the uniqueness of structural analysis fades away. It is true that at the beginning of the revised version of 'Social structure' Lévi-Strauss (1963a: 277) quotes from Rousseau's (1952: 334) 'On the origin of inequality' that 'The investigations we may enter into . . . must not be considered as historical truths, but only as mere conditional and hypothetical reasonings', but in the heat of battle this venerable disclaimer gets forgotten. For practical purposes we have to deal not with hypotheses about pragmatically useful ways of analysing empirical observations but rather with structural analysis aimed at discovering underlying reality.

The notion of fundamental elements is closely linked in Lévi-Strauss's thought with the concept of the phoneme in linguistics (cf. Jakobson and Halle 1956). His use of linguistic concepts has been criticized as ambiguous or meaningless (Moore and Olmstead 1952; cf. Oliver 1959: 511) but his admiration for the achievements of linguistics remains. He writes that in about 1944 he became convinced that the rules of marriage and descent were not fundamentally different from those of linguistics (1954: 585), and throughout this work linguistics is held up as the exemplar for anthropology (1969: 492–493). Just as the rules of grammar are obeyed without being consciously known, so the model of marriage rules explains what happens even though it remains unknown to those who arrange marriages. More importantly, the phoneme provides from linguistics a well-tested example of a privileged level of analysis. Sounds can be analysed into their phonetic components with as great a degree of specificity as required; the only limit is the sensitivity of the linguist's oscilloscopes and other equipment. At the other extreme we have words and sentences, loaded with meaning that has to be learnt and is not intrinsic to the words themselves. In between these levels every known language is found to make use of a set of phonemes, varying from a dozen to about eighty in number. Each phoneme corresponds to one or more delimited portions of the sound spectrum. Phonemes are combined to make words. Where-abouts in the sound spectrum the limits are drawn between one phoneme and the next varies from one language to another. Phonemes have no meaning in themselves; it is only ordered combinations of phonemes that have culturally ascribed meaning. The specificity of phonemes is not something arbitrarily set by the phonetician, nor is it consciously set by society. They 'explain' language, even though men using language have not known about them consciously until linguists discovered them. Lévi-Strauss's fundamental elements, as I understand them, are postulated as the analogues of phonemes, just as he postulates 'gustemes' as the analogous constituent elements of a system of cuisine (1958a: 99).

Whereas many modern descriptions of a language begin with a list of its phonemes, Lévi-Strauss never enumerates exhaustively the fundamental elements used in structural models. He merely describes duality, alternation, opposition, and symmetry as 'basic and immediate data of mental and social reality' (1969: 136; cf. 1949a: 175) and in a later statement refers to thought that 'proceeds by successive dichotomies and by pairs of oppositions' as constituting the lowest common denominator of all thought (1962c: 218). He mentions three 'fundamental mental structures' which nevertheless seem to be elements rather than structures built up out of elements. These three are discernible even in the thought processes of children and are: the requirements of the Rule as Rule, by which I understand him to mean recognition of the fact that there are binding rules additional to natural constraints (cf. 1969: 32), the rule of incest being the fundamental instance of cultural intervention and interdiction; the notion of reciprocity; and the synthetic character of the gift, the fact that the act of giving makes partners of the donor and the recipient and imparts a new quality to the gift (1969: 84–85; cf. 1950a: xlv).

These elements are not specifically concerned with kinship and are presumably to be found as components in models of all kinds. All kinship systems, that is, models of kinship systems, are built up out of a single type of 'elementary structure' con-
116

sisting of a woman, her brother, her husband, and their son. This constitutes the unit or atom of kinship (1963a: 46, 48 72; cf. Flament 1963: 125–126; Atkins 1966). Lévi-Strauss takes this as his elementary building-block rather than the so-called elementary family favoured by all his predecessors in kinship studies, in order to include at this fundamental level the relationship between brothers-in-law, that is, between the man who gives a sister and the man who receives her as his wife. He also includes, at the sub-atomic level, as it were, the relationship between a man and his mother's brother, since this is always present, in contrast to the relationship between a man and his father. The relationship with the mother's brother is truly elementary, and not secondary, as Radcliffe-Brown and others would have it, for the essence of human kinship is to require the establishment of relations *between* elementary families (1963a: 51).

Although Lévi-Strauss refers to the atom of kinship as an elementary structure, this usage in an article published in 1945 (but apparently written before the war. Cf. Simonis 1968: 18) should not be confounded with that followed in *Les Structures* where the name 'elementary structure' is applied to a larger entity, embodying a plurality of atoms of kinship and contrasted with 'complex structure'. These larger structures will be discussed later (pp. 138–140).

4   Models, structures, and time

Granted the notion of fundamental elements, the way is open to use these elements to construct an array of models that would exhaust the whole range of possible social structures, whether or not they have, or have yet had, any historical counterparts. Indeed, Lévi-Strauss maintains that the use of computers should enable us to escape from the limitations of historical availability and to explore in the laboratory the full range of logically possible structures (1966a).

Lévi-Strauss makes great use of the notion of 'model' but I

think that nowhere does he give an explicit definition of what he means by this much abused term. He is almost entirely concerned with models that are also structures, and these he does define. Nutini (1965: 725–726) has tried to give some precision to Lévi-Strauss's use of models, but while it might be convenient if Lévi-Strauss by 'model' always meant some 'supra-empirical explanatory construct', as Nutini would have him do, he does not, in my view, restrict himself in this way. Attempts by philosophers of science to clarify what may be meant by a 'model' have usually been aimed at models in the natural sciences (e.g. Braithwaite 1953: 88–114) and these attempts are relevant for social science only if the dichotomy between the scientist and his objects of investigation is preserved (cf. Willer 1967: 15–66). As we shall see, models for Lévi-Strauss are not always supra-empirical constructs built by the anthropologist, but are sometimes part of the empirical data that he observes. Some of these 'home-made' models, as he calls them, explain very little, and it is perhaps for this reason that we find Lévi-Strauss sometimes using the term model to refer to constructs made by the anthropologist which also explain very little and which merely summarize aggregations of similar empirical data. His use of the term can best be understood if we outline seriatim the various kinds of model he distinguishes. For the moment we may regard a model as a mental replica or analogue corresponding in certain respects but not in all with some segment of the empirical or perceptual world.

For Lévi-Strauss, a structure is a special kind of model. He echoes the work of Von Neumann and Morgenstern (1953: 32–33) on the theory of games in saying that a structural model must be systematic, i.e. a change in one part must affect all the other parts; it must be transformable, so as to generate a series of models of the same type; and it should 'make immediately intelligible all the observed facts' (1963a: 279–280). This definition is reminiscent of Radcliffe-Brown's (1952: 5–6, 9) concept of system, despite the fact that Lévi-Strauss sees Radcliffe-Brown as the heir to the views of Montesquieu, Comte, Durkheim, and Spencer, while Lévi-Strauss, so he

118

claims, derives his own view from Marxism and *Gestalttheorie* (1962d: 143). Radcliffe-Brown certainly saw himself as holding views very different from Lévi-Strauss, and wrote to him 'I use the term "social structure" in a sense so different from yours as to make discussion so difficult as to be unlikely to be profitable' (Radcliffe-Brown 1953). Yet even though the end-products of their analyses are indeed very different, the definitions from which they begin are not so far apart. Indeed, Lévi-Strauss's definition is not particularly close to Von Neumann's ideas, as Lévi-Strauss's own footnote citing *The theory of games* shows. Von Neumann and Morgenstern are careful to restrict the similarity required between model and reality to 'a few traits deemed "essential" *pro tempore*'. Lévi-Strauss announces that he seeks to explain all the observed facts, but actually, like Radcliffe-Brown, he is concerned with partial explanations. They differ in the part they seek to explain. By and large, Radcliffe-Brown saw himself as making his own choice, whereas for Lévi-Strauss there is no choice, for structural explanations apply at the level of fundamental reality. Historical factors which may explain the details of the empirical world lie outside his main target of inquiry, though as we have seen he turns to them from time to time.

We hear very little about those models that are not structures. He does however introduce the term 'reduced model' to refer to a skeleton genealogical kinship diagram showing as economically as possible the way in which relationship terms are used in any given system, with 'the greatest possible number of applications corresponding to the least possible number of positions' on the chart. Although he calls this a structure, it does not satisfy the definition just cited, which appeared three years later. A similar diagram that does provide a complete representation of a kinship system he calls a 'developed model' (1949a: 331; 1969: 274). Lévi-Strauss categorizes the structural models with which he is concerned by a variety of criteria which we may summarize under six headings. A structural model may be distinguished by (1) the kind of time it uses, (2) its scale, (3) its content, (4) whether it is conscious or unconscious, (5) whether it is home-made or constructed by the anthropologist, and (6) whether it is true or false. We shall deal with these headings in order, though our discussion of (3) content will take us further than Lévi-Strauss's comments under this heading and will include an examination of what he means by a 'rule'.

Time must be a parameter in a kinship model, not because marriage, birth, ageing, and other activities have temporal duration but because the relationships expressed in the model between one generation and another, and between older and younger siblings, are relationships with an intrinsic temporal component. The time dimension in a model may be either reversible or irreversible; it may be straight, circular, progressive, empty, non-cumulative, or statistical; there is also micro-time and macro-time. The significance of different kinds of time in indigenous thinking and in social analysis has been familiar to anthropologists from the work of Evans-Pritchard (1939), as Lévi-Strauss acknowledges, and of Fortes (1949c). Lévi-Strauss's distinctions follow in this tradition.

In one sense it might seem foolish to expect to be able to use kinship models in reversible time, for the basic relationships of kinship between parent and child are essentially ordered in time. The parent begets the child, is older than the child, and rears the child. It is not accidental or insignificant that a man is always older than his son. Hence at this level we cannot expect the same sort of reversible time as is exemplified by a model of a pendulum swinging to and fro for ever in a vacuum in a steady gravitational field. This model is the same whether we measure the passage of time or of 'minus-time'. There is no beginning, no end, no progress. If we are to find a meaning for 'reversible' in the domain of kinship we have to look not at relationships but at shifts from one configuration of relationships to another. As I understand him, a model in reversible time is for Lévi-Strauss one in which, if A and B are any two states of the model, it is impossible to tell whether A precedes B in time or B precedes A. If time is irreversible, then either A can only follow B or B must follow A; in other words, if B follows A, then after B we never get back to A however long we wait. Lévi-Strauss has also referred to cyclical time (1963a: 301) or to a circular framework of time (1963a: 74), and this seems a more accurate way of expressing what he has in mind than reversible time. Thus for example the system of eight subsections found among the northern Aranda is said to be a model in reversible time, but in fact the sequence of subsections in either of its two matrilineal cycles is never reversed; it merely repeats itself indefinitely down the generations. Lévi-Strauss also refers to this sequence as its 'oscillatory structure' (1969: 179) but the most appropriate nomenclature is to call this a model in cyclical time.

The notion of empty time is used to describe one part of the Hopi kinship system. Both in Ego's father's mother's matrilineage and in his mother's father's matrilineage, the same term is used to refer to lineage members, irrespective of their generational level. In other words, the terminology is indifferent or non-specific for generation. This property Lévi-Strauss describes by speaking of 'empty' time, stable and reversible. In female Ego's own lineage, members of each of the five generations centred on Ego are referred to by a distinctive term; this calls for 'progressive, non-reversible time'. In male Ego's matrilineage, female members are referred to by two terms only, one for each set of alternating generations. This needs 'undulating, cyclical, reversible' time (1963a: 301). In another description of the Hopi system (1953c), the time used in female Ego's lineage is described as 'progressive and continuative' (1963a: 74). 'Non-cumulative' appears to be a synonym for 'reversible'; 'statistical', 'oriented', 'non-reversible', and 'progressive' for 'irreversible' (1963a: 286). All three kinds of time used in the Hopi system are characterized as 'straight' or 'linear', in contrast to the Zuñi system, which uses a 'circular' framework or structure (1963a: 74, 302). The adjective 'circular' refers to a system of nomenclature in which one term is used for members of female Ego's matrilineage in both the first ascending and the first descending generation, and another term is used for members in the second ascending and second descending

121

generations. Thus a woman calls her mother and her daughter by the same term, and both her grandmother and her grand-daughter by another term. This is not a happy choice of adjective, for Lévi-Strauss speaks also of 'circular' marriage systems, with a closed circuit of women clearly in mind; in the Zuñi terminology there is nothing analogous to this. Many of these adjectives describing different kinds of time add colour only and are analytically redundant, for they are not used to make additional contrasts. The distinction between micro-time and macro-time (1963a: 290) is one of degree only and is not discussed; no specific qualitative contrast seems to be intended; For the rest, the important distinction is simple enough; it is between irreversible and reversible, i.e. cyclical, time.

We can now look at the second way models are distinguished, for these two kinds of time are typically associated with two kinds of model, statistical and mechanical (1960a: 23), which differ in scale. In a mechanical model phenomena and model have the same scale, while in a statistical model they differ (1963a: 283). For illustration, Lévi-Strauss refers to classical mechanics, which deals with the relations between a few bodies and uses a mechanical model to state how one body acts on the others; on the other hand thermodynamics uses a statistical model to express the regularities in the movement of millions of particles in a gas. Likewise in social science suicide can be studied with a mechanical model, in which one takes into account 'the personality of the victim, his or her life history, the characteristics of the primary and secondary groups in which he or she developed'; alternatively suicide can be studied with a statistical model by looking at suicide rates at various times and places and in different kinds of groups (1963a: 284-285).

At this point we can ask two questions that will need careful discussion. Given the two kinds of model, why does one require reversible time and the other irreversible time? Do the models describe or explain the same phenomena? It is obvious that classical mechanics is largely, if not wholly, a system using reversible time; in the Newtonian scheme we can reverse the direction of the planets and make them run backwards, without violating the laws of motion, whereas the second law of thermodynamics provides the crucial instance of an irreversible process; entropy is always increasing. But Lévi-Strauss clearly does not intend to hang his own scheme of analysis on to a contrast in physics; these references to mechanics are made by way of analogy only. He makes a contrast between societies like those of the industrialized modern world, whose marriage systems are determined or described by statistical models, and those primitive societies which use mechanical models, with positive rules about who shall marry whom. Now it is true that the mechanical models of primitive marriage systems which Lévi-Strauss uses, particularly in *Les Structures*, are in reversible time; they are the same now as they were a generation ago and will be the same a generation hence. Likewise, modern industrial society is in fact a rapidly and irreversibly changing society. But there seems to be nothing intrinsic in the notion of a statistical model of modern marriage that is incompatible with stable conditions extending over an indefinite span of generations. Indeed, the analyses of modern marriage systems cited by Lévi-Strauss do not use irreversible time, nor does his own statistical sketch of the range of husbands available to the average Parisian girl (1955b: 1208). He cites Forde's study of Yakö marriage (1941) as providing both a mechanical and a statistical model for the same society. Forde describes the exogamic rules that limit a man's choice of wife among the Yakö, and this description is mechanical rather than statistical, in that it relates to what happens in particular marriages and not to characteristics of an assemblage of many marriages. Forde also gives statistical evidence of non-cyclical change in Yakö marriage patterns, and this we may regard as a statistical model. Time appears in this model in the same way as in the work by Sutter and Tabah (1951) on consanguineous marriage in France, and the studies that have followed (cf. Sutter and Goux 1962). These works contrast a statistical description of affairs at one point of time with similar descriptions at other points of time. Forde does the same when he contrasts the marital experience of members of one age-set with the experiences of other sets. This type of presentation enables us to see what is happening through time, and we can summarize this by speaking of a trend through the years towards, say, less consanguineous marriage or more polygyny. We have a composite diachronic account rather than a simple synchronic statement. Yet clearly these are not models in irreversible time in the sense in which the second law of thermodynamics posits an irreversible process. For there is nothing in the description of the number of men in a given age-set who have married polygynously which entails that the number of polygynists in a later age-set shall be more, or less, than in the earlier set. Likewise, in the work of Sutter and Tabah, the percentage of cousin marriages in one year does not determine that the percentage a decade later shall be greater, or smaller, or the same. In these examples, to explain an observed secular trend towards less polygyny or less cousin marriage we have to appeal to factors like the spread of Christianity, the growth of opportunities for investment, and increasing urbanization and spatial mobility. By bringing in these factors we may well introduce irreversible processes, but until we do this, all we have are a number of descriptions in reversible time that can be arranged chronologically.

The distinction between models in reversible, cyclical, and irreversible time is pertinent to much that has been written about lineages and segmentary societies, and should not be confounded with the difference between models of stationary and changing societies. Two contrasting examples illustrate the difference. A model of a maximal lineage in which segmentation occurs regularly in each generation is a mechanical model in irreversible time and implies a steadily increasing population, even though the processes of segmentation do not alter from one generation to the next. On the other hand, Christian's model of an island society with only four members in each generation, two men each with one sister, always practising cross-cousin marriage (Blackstone 1800: 205, cited in Freeman 1961: 206–207) is a mechanical model in reversible time. The more sophisticated models of segmentary societies, embodying processes of the telescoping of generation and of fusion as well as segmentation, represent efforts to build models in cyclical time that are compatible with a constant population.

Uncertainty about the correlation between kinds of model and kinds of time is less serious than it might be since Lévi-Strauss has almost entirely confined his work to the construction of mechanical models. Indeed, this predilection for mechanical models is seen as a diagnostic feature of anthropology. In a table he has published twice (1963a: 286; 1964: 542), social anthropology and ethnography are contrasted with history and sociology, the former pair being associated with mechanical, and the latter with statistical models. Presumably the study of complex structures, foreshadowed in *Les Structures*, would have to deal mainly with statistical models and some elaboration of his views on this matter would be necessary, but in the present context we have to deal principally with mechanical models using reversible time. Indeed, Lévi-Strauss's later statements on the incompatibility of studies of structure and process, and his comment that there does not exist any 'meta-process' that would subsume the disparate 'processes' experienced in the French revolution by aristocrat and sans-culotte (1962b: 45), seem to imply that he now regards structural models in irreversible time as impossibilities, whether they be mechanical or statistical.

5 Kinship structures

We can now turn to the third way in which Lévi-Strauss distinguishes models, by content or domain. In his view, the structural method can be applied to many broad classes of phenomena: myths, languages, cooking, music. Everywhere we can expect to find the same 'combination and re-combination' of the same 'fundamental elements'. In the life of any society there are several forms of communication, and we can analyse these forms by building various kinds of communication structures. There are three principal 'levels' of communication: women, goods and services, and messages. Hence we have a kinship structure, showing how women are communicated or circulated; there is an economic structure, giving the rules for the provision of goods and services; and there is linguistic structure, the set of rules whereby messages are encoded and decoded. There are also, it seems, other structures, such as subordination structures, by which is meant what others would call political structures, which are not communication structures (1963a: 310). These lie outside the scope of this chapter and Lévi-Strauss says little about them. The 'fundamental mental structures', which are really elements rather than structures, have already been mentioned, along with the elementary kinship structure (see pp. 116f. above).

If for the moment we confine our attention to communication structures, we find we have among others a structure of kinship and marriage, consisting of the rules of kinship and marriage of the society concerned. A consistent and unambiguous set of rules can easily be seen as a mechanical model. For example, to return to the northern Aranda example mentioned above, we start with eight homologous classes, such that every member of the society belongs to one and only one of these classes. The classes are approximately equal in size, each contains men and women, and members of any one class may marry only members of one other specified class, while their children are assigned to another specified class. In one sense the model may be thought of as made up of the atoms of kinship already described, connected by rules, though the classes in the model do not correspond simply to collections of these atoms; a formal transformation would be needed to re-write the Aranda system in atomic terms. Using the rules discovered empirically to be in use among the Aranda, we soon find that we have a model that repeats itself indefinitely. The model is clearly mechanical; its rules are about individual marriages, not about the mean direction of myriad marriages. Also the model is a model of rules, and social anthropology, we have already learnt, is exclusively a study of rules. But the word 'rule' has many

126

meanings, and we have to be careful that we do not shift unknowingly from one meaning to another. The Aranda rule we translate as stating that a man of A1 shall marry a woman of B1 and that their children shall belong to D2 (1969: 163) is certainly a rule in the sense that it is an instruction to a computer, part of the programme required if the computer is to print out the Aranda cycle of matrilineal descent entailed by the rules. It is also a rule in the sense that it is an instruction to a certain Aranda man who is in A1 and who wants to marry about where he should look for a wife; or if not an instruction to him, it is at least an idea in his mind about how he should behave, or how people in A1 do behave when they are acting in conformity with the system. But it is not necessarily a summary description of what happened when, say, Aranda Alfred married Betty and had a child Donald; for we do not know whether Alfred and Betty kept the rules of the system.

What sort of rules are to be found in statistical models? From the examples Lévi-Strauss cites, and from his association of statistical models with history and sociology, it is hard to escape the conclusion that statistical models deal only with what actually happens, or with attempts to mirror what actually happens as accurately as possible. He cites (1963a: 284) Forde's study of Yakö marriage, Elwin in the Muria, and Suttar and Tabah (1951) on part of France. The statistical analyses in all these studies are concerned with describing what actually happens. Suttar and Tabar base their inquiries on a sample of marriages, and are concerned to construct a model which would represent patterns of marriage in a wider community. They also construct or enunciate rules, in the sense of 'instructions to a computer'. But they are not rules about how people *should* marry or even how French people, other than professional demographers, think Frenchmen in general marry. Forde (1941: Tables) and Elwin (1947: 699–700) are much less ambitious and merely publish tables summarizing information about many marriages. Their analyses can be considered as models only in a very broad sense, but in as much as they are models at all, they are clearly statistical rather than mechanical. They consist of statements about the properties of aggregates of marriages, not about single marriages. As such they meet the scale requirement for statistical models.

Lévi-Strauss refers to these 'descriptions' as 'models', but we should be clear that they are not models in the sense of 'supra-empirical explanatory constructs'. Hence it seems to me that Nutini's (1965) account of Lévi-Strauss's use of models does not tally with the evidence. These 'models' explain nothing or very little; they are statistical summaries that need to be explained.

A better example to take, had it been available, would have been Zelditch's study of Navaho marriage. In later publications Lévi-Strauss (1960b: 200) notes this study with approval. Zelditch explicitly constructs what is certainly a model. It is a statistical model in that its 'rules', i.e. the instructions to the model-maker or computer, are statements about aggregates of marriages and not about any one marriage. For example, Zelditch's first rule states that

> If a generation G_1 of clan C_i marries significantly into a clan C_j, then a generation G_2 of C_i tends to avoid C_j in allocating its proportion of marriages and marries significantly into some clan C_k (Zelditch 1959: 480).

The rules are stated partly qualitatively, as with the rule just cited, and partly quantitatively, though it would appear that the data could in principle be used to generate a model that was fully specified quantitatively. Zelditch's model explains or describes relations between generations, and the time direction is significant; what happens in G_1 influences events in G_2 and G_3, and not the other way round. But although the model is not in reversible time, it is also not cumulative, for the effect of the pattern of marriages in any one generation on patterns in successive generations is quickly damped down. On the other hand there is no regular sequence to ensure that after a lapse of n generations, the distribution of inter-clan marriages in $G_n + 1$ is the same as in G_1. Hence the model may be said to be in irreversible, non-cumulative, non-cyclical time. It is a model which simulates as accurately as possible how Navaho actually marry, and only secondarily does it explain the somewhat conflicting statements Navaho make about their own marriage system.

My argument is then that statistical models are attempts to summarize and explain what actually happens in fact, and that, apart from some hypothetical society consisting of professional statisticians or demographers (cf p. 34 above), we are unlikely to find regulations or perceptions that can be expressed in, or are thought about in, statistical form. Mechanical models can be used to express the interconnexions and implications of rules or ideal types, and they can also be used as a first approximation to what happens in actual fact. I should make it clear that this is my view, and not that of Lévi-Strauss. Nutini (1965: 720, 730, f.n. 5) argues that when Lévi-Strauss says that a society with cross-cousin marriage that is recommended but infrequent requires both a mechanical and a statistical model, it is clear that mechanical models stand for ideal behaviour and statistical models for actual behaviour. But this interpretation does not fit Lévi-Strauss's statement that in our own society we have a mechanical model to determine prohibited marriages and rely on a statistical model for those that are permissible, or that the same data may often, and presumably therefore not always, be used to construct a mechanical and a statistical model (1963a: 284). Ideal behaviour and actual behaviour are different data, and Nutini's argument fits well the example he cites, but Lévi-Strauss's view is not so simple. If Nutini is right, then the kind of model to be examined depends only on whether we are interested in ideal or actual behaviour; the choice is always there and it is ours. But in Lévi-Strauss's view, it seems that societies themselves also make a choice. It is our own society, and not its anthropologists, that 'has' a mechanical model and 'relies' on a statistical model. He writes that, in modern society, the social contacts made by each individual are sufficiently numerous to enable a marriage rule allowing the greatest possible freedom of choice of mate, provided only that the choice made is outside the restricted family, to produce a continuous mixing, making for a homogeneous and well-blended social fabric (1956a: 279). He refers to 'our loosely organized and highly statistical marriage system' (1963a: 299) implying that the kind of model to be used is inherent in the system. In other words, just as there is a privileged level at which the structural analyst tries to work, at which indeed he must work, so there is a preferable kind of model that he has to construct or discover. The thesis that the investigator does not have a free hand, and that the models he deals with are waiting to be discovered, not invented for his analytical convenience, is critical in understanding Lévi-Strauss's work.

It would be possible to rephrase Lévi-Strauss's statements on Western marriage as follows. The homogeneous and well-blended social fabric of modern society is maintained by a marriage system in which few marriages are explicitly prohibited and each individual is free to choose his mate from a wide range of alternatives. The working of this system can be best described by a statistical model, together with a mechanical statement of a few marriage prohibitions. However, this reformulation eliminates the notion that each society has some shared idea or collective representation of what is its marriage system. This notion is expressed in the next two ways in which he classifies models, as conscious or unconscious and as 'home-made' or constructed by the anthropologist (1963a: 282). This cross-classification gives four cells, but Lévi-Strauss uses only three of them, since normally anthropologists fabricate only conscious models (cf. Barnes 1967c for some examples of unconscious models by Murdock, Lévi-Strauss, and others). Every society, he says, uses models to resolve or conceal its inherent contradictions (Lévi-Strauss 1963a: 334). Native or home-made models may be either conscious or unconscious, and he cites Boas (1911: 70–71) in support of the view that conscious home-made models are inaccurate, for they justify or rationalize social facts but do not explain them. An exception from this condemnation is made for the inhabitants of Ambrym (1969: 125–126) and the Australian Aborigines, some of whom, he says, have made more satisfactory models of their kinship systems than have the anthropologists who have studied them. They have developed logically a conscious theory to set out their own problems (1969: 108, 110, 133). In his Huxley memorial lecture, Lévi-Strauss seems to broaden this exception and suggests that 'plenty of theoretical thinking of the highest order has been carried on all the time . . . among a small minority of learned individuals . . . Elegant solutions such as the rules of . . . marriage . . . far from being the recent outcome of unconscious processes, now appear to me as true discoveries, the legacy of an age-old wisdom . . .' (1966c: 15).

But in general the sociological representations of the natives, just as those of more advanced societies, may contradict their actual social organization or omit certain elements (1963a: 130–131). '. . . conscious models are by definition very poor ones, since they are not intended to explain phenomena but to perpetuate them' (1963a: 281). Indeed it is not at the conscious but at the unconscious level that we are most easily able to transcend the cultural barriers that divide us from the peoples we study. At this level, where the fundamental phenomena of the mind are to be found, we have to deal with forms of activity that are common to all men and all times (1963a: 21). The unconscious will become 'the mediating term between myself and others' (1950a: xxxi).

The home-made conscious model may give a false picture of social phenomena (1950a: xxxix), and the anthropologist must guard against the mistake of interpreting primary phenomena, the unconscious foundations of social life, by conscious or semi-conscious superstructures, which are secondary and derived (1969: 184). We do not need to know the laws of grammar to talk, nor the laws of logic to think; nevertheless these laws exist and it is right to try to discover them. A modernistic melody may be related to a classical piece of music by a purely mathemetical transformation, even though the composer may be entirely unaware of it (1953b: 62). Likewise the rules of a marriage system are not necessarily known consciously or accurately by those who live subject to the rules;

yet it is these rules that explain the system (1969: 177). If we find that the same criteria are used in many different areas of social life to distinguish similar though not identical phenomena, then we 'have the right to conclude that we have reached a significant knowledge of the unconscious attitudes of the society or societies under consideration' (1963a: 87).

Lastly, a model may be true or false. '. . . the best model will always be that which is *true*, that is, the simplest possible model which, while being derived exclusively from the facts under consideration, also makes it possible to account for all of them' (1963a: 281). Lévi-Strauss criticizes Mrs Seligman (1927, 1928) for postulating the existence of certain rules of descent, for which no evidence can be found, to explain marriage rules in parts of Melanesia. He argues that a model based on double unilineal descent, particularly when there is no firm evidence for the existence of two kinds of unilineal groups, is a 'lazy explanation' for the existence of cross-cousin marriage (1967: 131: cf. 1969: 112). Yet to me Mrs Seligman's constructions seem to be no more contrived than, for instance, the hypothetical six-stage sequence Lévi-Strauss himself proposes to explain present-day Sherente social structure (1963a: 126).

Mrs Seligman's models were constructed by her, and may perhaps be false; but home-made models also may be untrue, in that they may rationalize rather than explain. Thus Lévi-Strauss even suggests in one cryptic sentence that possibly restricted exchange 'is never found empirically other than in the form of an imperfect rationalization of systems which remain irreducible to a dualism, in which guise they vainly try to masquerade' (1963a: 151), restricted exchange being, as we shall see, an arrangement whereby pairs of groups interchange women in marriage. This view is advanced only as a tentative conclusion or working hypothesis, and was proposed in 1956, several years after the publication of *Les Structures*, in which restricted exchange is given solid ethnographic backing. Yet even if this particular hypothesis cannot be sustained, the possibility that a home-made model may be a 'masquerade' remains. Perhaps it cannot be entirely false either, for, writing of religious models, Lévi-Strauss asserts that

... the imagery with which a society pictures to itself the relations between the dead and the living can always be broken down in terms of an attempt to hide, embellish or justify, on the religious level, the relations prevailing in that society among the living (1961a: 231).

6 Data for the model to explain

We can summarize our exposition of Lévi-Strauss's scheme so far. We begin with fundamental elements common to all human thought. These are combined unconsciously to form models which somehow are related to the way people behave. People remain only partly aware of these models and they are also imperfectly informed about what actually happens. They construct conscious models which constitute their perception of what happens. The anthropologist has to penetrate past these home-made models to arrive at the unconscious models that really explain things.

But our question about the kinds of phenomena or data explained by the two kinds of model remains unresolved. It seems that Lévi-Strauss, like many of his colleagues, begins with a view of human society in which the discrepancies between what ought to happen and what actually happens are comparatively small and can be neglected in making a first approximation. For instance, given a rule of marriage or a rule of descent, at least in the first step of our analysis we assume that all marriages take place according to the marriage rule and that all children are correctly assigned according to the rule of descent. In his Huxley memorial lecture he states explicitly that a society in which MBD marriage is advocated, but where few such marriages occur, can best be understood as an approximation to a society where all marriages are with an MBD (1966c: 17–18; 1969: xxx). The fact that some people

133

speak ungrammatically does not destroy the notion of grammar, whether this is thought of normatively or consensually; indeed, it entails the notion of grammar. Likewise, the fact that a few people marry in the wrong way, or join their mother's group rather than their father's, does not undermine the notion of rules of marriage and descent; the 'wrong' cannot exist except in contrast to the 'right'. The danger comes when many people marry wrongly, or worse still, when they start to disagree about how people ought to marry. For if we accept the view that what is really important, the only things that are truly real, are models made up of fundamental elements which are understood only unconsciously, then it is easy to assume that whatever people actually do, the model persists unchanged. The events of concrete reality 'have nothing to do with' or, more accurately, are several orders removed from, the structural model, and hence there is no easy way of finding out whether or not the anthropologist's model is identical with the natives' unconscious model.

There is no easy operationally defined procedure for linking the two, and yet the link has to be made. For Lévi-Strauss is not merely dealing with 'real' mental models, and he cannot ignore completely the ephemeral and comparatively insignificant world of concrete events. On the contrary he states that 'the assertion that the most parsimonious explanation also comes closest to the truth rests, in the final analysis, upon the identity postulated between the laws of the universe and those of the human mind' (1963a: 89). The relationship between model and concrete reality is crucial to our understanding of his work and is manifestly a matter of importance to Lévi-Strauss himself. At one extreme he criticizes Gifford's attempt to deduce a kinship system from genealogies, because 'native thought is interested more in the objective order of the system than the subjective order of the genealogies, and secondly, because a system described by informants or deduced from questions is rarely reflected in concrete situations, and this leads to the appearance of lacunas and contradictions' (1969: 365). Here we have the model or system as objective and the object of interest of native and anthropologist alike, while the concrete situation, what actually happens, is only subjective (cf. 1959a: xxx). Elsewhere in *Les Structures* he takes a slightly more empirical view. He writes:

> Now a certain latitude always exists in this respect, a marriage system never being able to function rigorously because that would require a mathematical equality of the sexes, constant life-span of individuals, and an equal stability of marriages, all things that cannot exist except as a limit. This latitude is turned to account to achieve by the marriages, the best possible integration of the local group, without endangering that which is sought as a more essential goal, the integration of the two types of complementary local groups (1949a: 549; cf. 1969: 442).

In this view, the system is clearly a system of rules, but they are rules that are not applied rigorously; presumably this means that they are usually followed in practice but are occasionally broken. However, in later statements he goes even further and appears to suggest that the system that the anthropologist's model should explain is the system of actual marriages. Thus in his paper on 'Social structure' he mentions the various ways in which the Murngin kinship system has been treated by different authors. In the earlier version of this paper he goes on to say: 'By getting a good statistical run of actual marriage choices among other excluded possibilities one could get at a "true" solution' (1953a: 538). This statement can mean only that the 'facts' that the 'true' model explains are what actually happens, who marries whom, and not who should marry whom in conformity with some agreed rule. Elsewhere he writes: 'These are the hypotheses which should be tested in the field by computing the actual rate of optional marriages and their rhythm of alternation' (1961c). He refers (1960b: 200; 1962b: 42) with approval to Zelditch's study of Navaho marriage choices, mentioned earlier. He suggests that Goodenough's study (1956: 25–27) of marriage among the Nakani and Fortes's (1949c) study of Ashanti marriage, both of which reveal order in an apparently disorderly synchronic picture by introducing explanatory temporal processes, do not present us with a conflict between the structural and the empirical orders but rather with situations where the structure is diachronic, and where age, residence, and status enter as structural factors (1962b: 42). Lastly, he contrasts the 'lived-in' orders, of which kinship is one, with the 'thought-of' orders of myth and religion. Unlike the latter, the 'lived-in' orders can be checked against the experience to which they refer (1963a: 313). These may all be seen as attempts to bring the model closer to explaining what actually happens.

Yet these attempts are hard to reconcile with the doctrine that social anthropology is exclusively concerned with rules, unless we restrict the concept of rule to 'instructions to the computer'. This is stretching and narrowing the concept quite radically. The plot thickens when we note that in the revised version of 'Social structure' published in 1958 the reference to 'a good statistical run of actual marriage choices' is deleted (cf. 1963a: 299). Furthermore, as already noted (p. 112), he restricts the notion of diachronic structure to take account of only repetitive variations in empirical reality, and excludes structural explanations of unique changes or cumulative variations.

Lévi-Strauss carries further the contrast between 'empirical concrete reality' and the model made of rules in his discussion of dual organizations. In *Les Structures* he argues that the dual form of organization, in which a society is divided into two halves, which are usually exogamous and often matrilineal, is not a single 'institution'. As Lowie noted, it is a term applied to a heterogeneous set of institutions that have little in common with one another. It is rather 'a method for the solution of diverse problems', flexible rather than crystallized (1969: 69, 74–75, 82, 102–103). In a subsequent paper (1956b) he discusses several societies said to have dual organizations, and draws a distinction between what he calls diametric and concentric dualism, the latter forming a middle term between asymmetric triadism and symmetric dualism (1963a: 151). I find this article hard to understand. Maybury-Lewis attacks this paper on many grounds, including the correctness of Lévi-Strauss's ethnographic data, and argues that the triskelion diagram used by Lévi-Strauss to illustrate the social structure of several disparate societies shows nothing more than 'that disparate elements drawn from these societies can be represented in identical patterns. But this formal identity of the models has no sociological implications' (Maybury-Lewis 1960: 35). In his reply, Lévi-Strauss rejects this, and goes on to label Maybury-Lewis as

> still a structuralist in Radcliffe-Brown's terms, namely, he believes the structure to lie at the level of empirical reality, and to be a part of it. Therefore, when he is presented a structural model which departs from empirical reality, he feels cheated in some devious way. To him, social structure is like a kind of jig-saw puzzle . . . if the pieces have been arbitrarily cut, there is no structure at all. But if, as is sometimes done, the pieces are automatically cut in different shapes by a mechanical saw, the movements of which are regularly modified by a cam-shaft, the structure of the puzzle exists, not at the empirical level . . . : its key lies in the mathematical formula expressing the cams and their speed of rotation: something very remote from the puzzle as it appears to the player, although it 'explains' the puzzle in the one and only intelligible way (1960d: 52; cf. Schneider 1965: 25–26).

In this last clause, the 'puzzle' is social structure, not empirical reality; the mathematical formula, i.e. the unconscious model, explains only the conscious home-made structural model, not empirical reality. On the other hand, Lévi-Strauss draws a distinction between Bororo dual organization, i.e. symmetrical diametrical dualism, which belongs only to the domain of symbolic representations, i.e. as a home-made model, and Bororo concentric dualism, which exists 'on both the religious and the social levels', i.e. both as home-made model and in empirical reality.

F

It would seem then that for Lévi-Strauss structure is where it can be found; it may be there or it may not be, and we cannot tell until we have looked. Parts of the domains of both symbolic fundamental reality and empirical concrete reality are ordered and structured, particularly the former, while other parts are unstructured, particularly the latter. This doctrine of 'limited order' may save the investigator from forcing a false explanation on data he does not fully comprehend, but it diverts attention from the task of understanding why empirical reality does so often appear disorderly and unstructured. Lévi-Strauss avoids the Aristotelian mistake of confounding orderliness or 'lawfulness' with frequency, as Lewin puts it, but fails here to achieve the homogenization or extension of the validity of law to all phenomena, which is an essential feature of the Galileian scientific approach which he advocates (cf. Lewin 1933: 5–10). In some instances, it seems, there can be 'no structure at all'. Indeed when commenting on Radcliffe-Brown in his inaugural lecture, Lévi-Strauss implies that structure is never to be found at the empirical level (cf. 1960a: 24, 26).

We shall return later to the question of what it is that the structural model explains, noting only that the question is unresolved. We now turn to Lévi-Strauss's classification of kinship models.

7 Restricted and generalized exchange

The notions of incest and the sexual division of labour lie behind the systems of marriage rules. In *Les Structures* more attention is given to the implications of incest, whereas in the article on 'The family' we read that 'what makes marriage a fundamental need in tribal societies is the division of labor between the sexes' (1956a: 274). Lévi-Strauss argues that the prohibition of incest is 'on the threshold of culture, in culture, and in one sense, . . . culture itself'. 'It is the fundamental step because of which, by which, but above all in which, the transition from nature to culture is accomplished' (1969: xxviii–xxiv,

138

12, 24). In more prosaic terms, it 'establishes a mutual dependency between families, compelling them, in order to perpetuate themselves, to give rise to new families' (1956a: 277). It follows that, contrary to what Fortes (1957a: 177–178, 186–187) has argued, incest and exogamy are two complementary aspects of the same reality (1958c: 371). It is less a rule prohibiting marriage with a mother, sister, or daughter than a rule requiring them to be given to others. Incest is socially absurd before being morally wrong (1969: 481, 485). Thus the prohibition of incest links families and the sexual division of labour is 'nothing else than a device to institute a reciprocal state of dependency between the sexes' (1956a: 276). Given the need for women to bear children and to do women's work, and the illegitimacy of providing them from within the group, the stage is set for the game of matrimony to begin. There is also a 'maternal instinct' linking a mother to her child and 'psychological drives' making a man feel warmly towards the offspring of a woman with whom he is living (1956a: 270–271). Hence we have not only marriages but families as well.

Kinship systems manifest themselves in many areas of social life: in the organization of activities as diverse as cooking, eating, copulating, sleeping and gardening; in the procedure for transmitting knowledge, values, positions, and property from one generation to the next; in the way in which people address and refer to one another; in how they perpetuate the memory of the dead. Lévi-Strauss's salient interest in these systems lies in the marriages they require or prohibit and his classification of kinship systems is in this light. We have 'to interpret kinship systems and marriage rules as embodying the rule of that very special kind of game which consists for consanguineous groups of men in exchanging women among themselves' (1956a: 283). Exchange is the universal form of marriage, and although relations between the sexes are not symmetrical, marriage itself is a bilateral act, a symmetrical institution involving two groups (1969: 114, 129–130, 143).

In a marriage system, women are exchanged or communicated. Because of the universally recognized prohibition of incest, a woman cannot find a husband within her family of orientation. She has to seek a husband from outside this group, and likewise her brother has to look for a wife elsewhere. In all societies men control the destinies of women in marriage rather than the other way round, though even, if the position was reversed, the structural form would not be changed (cf. 1969: 132; 1963a: 47). Hence we may look upon the marriages entered into by members of a society as generating a flow of women within the society. There are two ways of explaining or describing or ensuring this circulation. Either it can be left to non-structural factors, such as preferences based on social class, beauty, brains, or religious persuasion, that are not directly associated with kinship and which therefore can be regarded as chance for purposes of this analysis; or else there can be positive rules included in the kinship system specifying who shall marry whom (1969: xxxiii–xxxiv). The negative rules of incest operate in either case. If marriage choice is, in this sense, left to chance, we speak of a complex kinship structure (1969: 465). Where there are positive rules we are dealing with an elementary kinship structure. *Les Structures* is an analysis of these elementary structures. In his Huxley memorial lecture Lévi-Strauss places marriage systems with Crow–Omaha type kinship terminologies in a position intermediate between elementary and complex kinship structures; these Crow–Omaha systems are characterized by negative rules stating which of his relatives a man may not marry. These rules are more restrictive than the few incest prohibitions found in complex, as in all other, systems, but are less restrictive of marriage choice than the positive marriage rules found in elementary systems (1969: xxxv–xxxix). It is typical of Lévi-Strauss's style of argument that even in the act of establishing this three-stage morphological scale he destroys it. He writes that the notions of 'elementary structures' and 'complex structures' are 'purely heuristic' and that all systems of kinship and marriage contain an elementary core and a complex aspect (1966c: 18).

In some elementary structures, the rules are such that if

there is one rule requiring a man of group A to marry a woman of group B, there is always another rule requiring a man of group B to marry a woman of group A. These structures Lévi-Strauss refers to as systems of restricted exchange (1969: 146). They are characterized by a division of society into an even number of groups, constituting intermarrying pairs. Typically the groups aggregate into two moieties, with one member of each intermarrying pair belonging to each moiety. In his later work, he distinguishes between societies where dualism is applied to natural phenomena and ideas as well as to social groups, and those where there is merely a division of society into moieties, or halves of moieties (1963b: 48). These latter, though they display a dual organization, may not be dualist societies. Thus it seems that Lévi-Strauss sees reciprocity as the principle underlying dualism (1963a: 162), although in fact the notion of binary opposition, which characterizes much of his later work on primitive thinking, seems more relevant.

In *Les Structures* restricted exchange is contrasted with generalized exchange, though later (1956b) he comments that 'Today this distinction appears to me naïve, because it is still too close to the natives' classifications. From a logical point of view, it is more reasonable and more efficient to treat restricted exchange as a special case of generalized exchange' (1963a: 150–151). In *Les Structures* (1969: 69–70, 72), he stresses the fundamental role of the principle of reciprocity, which may be codified in a dual organization. Some commentators have taken his remarks to imply that reciprocity is the distinguishing characteristic of restricted exchange. In his Huxley memorial lecture he corrects this interpretation. He emphasizes that in this contrast restricted exchange is distinguished by the fact that it entails a division of society into an even number of inter-marrying units, whereas generalized exchange can 'organize within an unchanging structure any number of participating units' (1966c: 21 f.n. 2). The first definition of generalized exchange in *Les Structures* (1969: 177–178) refers only to a man of A marrying a woman of B and a man of B marrying a woman of C. Lévi-Strauss states that the appellation 'system of

THREE STYLES IN THE STUDY OF KINSHIP

generalized exchange' indicates 'thereby that they can establish reciprocal relationships between any number of partners'. Yet he does not discuss further how many groups there may be in the system as a whole and the reader may well be misled by his reference to 'the division, formulated or unformulated, into moieties' and by the fact that the system of generalized exchange that he provides as an illustration happens to have four groups. In a later formulation (1956b) he stresses that the fundamental distinction between restricted and generalized exchange lies in the number of groups involved.

There is another source of confusion about generalized exchange. The groups referred to in the first definition are Australian-style marriage classes, such that a child belongs to a class different from those of both his parents, whereas most of the discussion of generalized exchange in *Les Structures* relates to unilineal groups, such that a child belongs to the same group as a designated parent. In a system of marriage classes the rules of marriage choice remain unaltered over the generations and the single specification of choice in the definition is adequate for all varieties of exchange system. Several varieties of generalized exchange are theoretically possible, though in *Les Structures* only two are discussed at length. In a system of unilineal groups the rules of marriage choice remain unchanged in one of the varieties but not in the other, which calls for the specification of two sets of marriage choices, operative in alternate generations; in this case the definition given in *Les Structures* is inadequate. The two varieties of generalized exchange are those in which marriage is allowed with a matrilateral, or with a patrilateral, cross-cousin. We use the adjectives 'matrilateral' and 'patrilateral' with reference to the groom, not the bride, so that in matrilateral cross-cousin marriage a man marries his mother's brother's daughter (MBD), while in patrilateral cross-cousin marriage he marries his father's sister's daughter (FZD). These two varieties are of unequal status. The ethnographic evidence for patrilateral cross-cousin marriage in *Les Structures* is poor, while good evidence is provided for the existence of matrilateral systems.

142

Formally, the two modes are different in that patrilateral cross-cousin marriage is said to be 'not a system, but a procedure' (1969: 446) and only a 'borderline' form of reciprocity (1963a: 122). As we shall see, under the patrilateral rule, if a man of unilineal group A marries a woman of group B, then in the next generation, whichever rule of descent applies, a man of group B marries a woman of group A. Lévi-Strauss's initial definition of generalized exchange has therefore to be read strictly as referring only to marriage classes, and cannot be extended to refer to unilineal groups without excluding patrilateral marriage from the category of generalized exchange.

Most of the time when Lévi-Strauss talks of generalized exchange, he has only the matrilateral version, or some transformation of this, in mind (cf. 1969: 440). Thus in his discussion of the external limits of this kind of exchange, the conditions under which it breaks down with the continued fission of intermarrying groups and the increased inequalities in wealth, he is dealing with only matrilateral systems (1969: 269–291: cf. Josselin de Jong 1952: 21–22). On the other hand, his notion of the internal limits of generalized exchange is based on a postulated antagonism among the Gilyak between two marriage systems, matrilateral cross-cousin marriage, which is allowed, and patrilateral cross-cousin marriage, which is forbidden (1969: 309).

Restricted exchange is possible only in a system containing an even number of groups, whereas generalized exchange is compatible with any number of groups (1963a: 150). Yet though, as we have just noted, in the Huxley lecture this seems to be the defining contrast between the two systems, in *Les Structures* it is easy to get the impression that the two types of exchange system are definitively contrasted by reference to two different types of marriage rule, and that the contrast between the possible number of participating groups follows merely as a consequence of the difference between the marriage rules. In fact there are three interrelated characteristics: the rule of marriage, specified in genealogical terms; the number of groups in the exchange system; and the contrast between what has come to be called symmetry and asymmetry. Lévi-Strauss has little to say about the difference between specifying a man's permissible wife in strictly genealogical terms, e.g. as a man's mother's brother's daughter, and making the specification in indigenous terms, by saying for instance that a man must marry a woman whom he calls by a vernacular term (e.g. *galle* among the Murngin) which he also applies to his own mother's brother's daughter. Clearly there is a difference, and this difference has been the subject of much controversy in recent years, but it is not a matter with which Lévi-Strauss has been concerned. His attention is on models of marriage systems, not the application of systems of rules to concrete situations; therefore he can afford to discuss the entailments of these systems as if every man married his own mother's own brother's own daughter, or whatever relative happens to be required. By a symmetrical relation between two groups is meant in this context that each gives women in marriage to the other, whereas if the relation is asymmetrical wives are given in one direction but not in the other. If the relation is symmetrical, sister-exchange marriage, in which a man and his sister marry a woman and her brother respectively, is possible, whereas if the relation is asymmetrical, sister-exchange marriage is impossible. If there are n groups, then certain combinations of symmetrical or asymmetrical relations and certain kinds of marriageable relative are logically possible and others are not, depending in part on whether n is even or odd.

It is simpler to discuss these logical possibilities and logical entailments in terms of the genealogically closest possible relative who satisfies the specification for a wife in the system concerned. The most important of these relatives are a man's cross-cousins. However, Lévi-Strauss stresses that it is the notion of exchange or reciprocity which is fundamental and which determines the 'universal form' of marriage, whereas the marriage of cross-cousins is merely a 'special case' of this universal form which enables us to see particularly clearly the ubiquity of reciprocity (1969: 143). In his models, he assumes that a classificatory system of kinship terminology assigns a

144

single term to all individuals of the same sex and generation within a wife-exchanging group (cf. 1969: 119), so that for most purposes it is sufficient to describe the operation of the model as if each group contains in each generation only two individuals, a man and his sister. The groups are exogamous, and in the simpler models each group is a matrimonial class (1969: 72–73) (unilineal rather than Australian), in that it may give to only one other group and may receive from only one group. The rules of the model are expressed in two ways, in terms of the genealogical relation required between the spouses and in

FIGURE I Restricted exchange

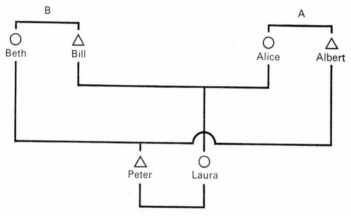

terms of the groups to which they must belong. The discussion turns on how these two kinds of rule are connected, and whether the choice of unilineal rule of descent is relevant.

In restricted exchange, groups A and B interchange women. The woman Alice of group A marries the man Bill of group B and his sister Beth, also of group B, marries Albert the brother of Alice. Sister-exchange marriage is possible, and when Peter, the son of Beth and Albert, marries Laura, the daughter of Alice and Bill, he is marrying a woman who is both his MBD (mother's brother's daughter) and his FZD (father's sister's daughter). This arrangement works with either rule of unilineal descent. If A and B are patrilineal groups, Peter is in group A and Laura in B, whereas if there is matrilineal descent, Peter

145

is in B and Laura is in A. In either case, Peter and Laura are in different groups. We can see that double (or symmetrical or bilateral) cross-cousin marriage is compatible with the rule that the two groups must exchange women.

In matrilateral cross-cousin marriage, the rule is that a man must marry a woman who is his MBD and not his FZD. There must therefore be more than two groups in the model for, as we have just seen, with only two groups, the same woman is MBD and FZD simultaneously. Three groups are sufficient for

FIGURE 2   Matrilateral cross-cousin marriage
First-generation rule: women of A marry men of B
women of B marry men of C

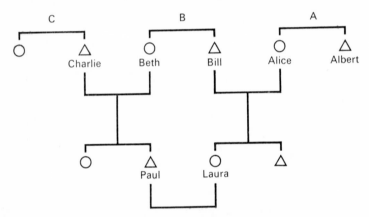

a workable model, though there is nothing in the form of the rules restricting the number of groups to three. Let the rules be that women of A marry men of B, and women of B marry men of C. If these rules apply in one generation, then we have Alice of A marrying Bill of B, while Bill's sister Beth marries a man Charlie of group C. Alice and Bill have a daughter Laura, and Beth and Charlie have a son Paul. Laura is MBD to Paul and is not his FZD, so that he can marry her. If descent is patrilineal, Paul is in C and Laura in B, so that we have a woman of B marrying a man of C, whereas if descent is matrilineal, Paul is in B and Laura in A, so that a woman of A marries a man of B. In either case, the marriage in the second generation is in conformity with the rules specified for the first generation, so that the model will work in the way required if the same inter-group rules apply in all generations. The model can be completed by a rule that women of C marry men of A, or other groups may be introduced into the chain of exchanges.

In patrilateral cross-cousin marriage, a man marries a FZD who is not his MBD. Again at least three groups are required. Suppose that the same rules apply as before in the first generation, that Alice and Bill have a son Len and that Beth and

FIGURE 3   Patrilateral cross-cousin marriage

First-generation rule: women of A marry men of B
women of B marry men of C

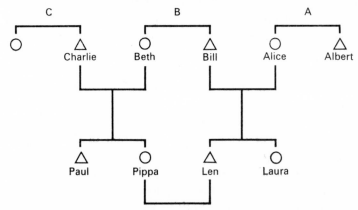

Charlie have a daughter Pippa. Then in the second generation Pippa is the FZD of Len and is not his MBD, so that he marries her. With patrilineal descent, Len is in B and Pippa in C, whereas with matrilineal descent Len is in A and Pippa in B. In either case the second-generation marriage conflicts with the marriage rules applied in the first generation. Lévi-Strauss argues that patrilateral cross-cousin marriage requires a reversal of marriage rules with each successive generation. If the system is closed in the first generation by women cf C marrying men of A, then in the second generation men of C marry women of A, but as before additional groups can be added to the chain.

The distinctions between restricted and generalized exchange, and between the two versions of generalized exchange, are thus seen to be matched by a difference in the types of cross-cousin marriage possible. Lévi-Strauss discusses the many theories that have been advanced to explain the custom of cousin marriage, and argues that cross-cousin marriage, as the most universal of all institutions except the prohibition of incest (1969: 124), must be explained in universal terms. It is the 'elementary formula of exchange', the simplest conceivable expression of the law of reciprocity (1969: 129, 144). He rejects convincingly the thesis that a rule of cross-cousin marriage depends on a double unilineal dichotomy (1969: 106–107, 112), but his demonstration that parallel cousin marriage cannot take place without upsetting the exchange process is hard to follow. It is clear that if there are exogamous patrilineal descent groups, a man will be in the same group as his father's brother's daughter and hence cannot marry her. Similarly with matrilineal descent, a man cannot marry his mother's sister's daughter. The problem is to explain why frequently both kinds of parallel cousin are forbidden as wives, irrespective of the mode of unilineal descent. In explanation of this empirical fact, Lévi-Strauss develops a strange calculus in which a man who receives a wife from another group is given a debtor or negative sign, while his children, because of his marriage, are therefore given creditor or positive values. He says:

> Thus, the notion of reciprocity allows the dichotomy of cousins to be immediately deduced. In other words, two male cousins who are both in the credit position towards their father's group (and in the debit position with regard to their mother's group) cannot exchange their sisters any more than could two male cousins in a credit position with regard to their mother's group (and debit position with regard to the father's group!). This intimate arrangement would leave somewhere outside not only groups which did not make restitution, but also groups which did not receive anything, and marriage in both would be a unilateral transfer (1969: 131).

148

The difficult style of exposition seems to be due to Lévi-Strauss's reluctance to attach importance to a specific rule of descent. Josselin de Jong's gloss on this passage (1952: 13) is no better, and Lévi-Strauss's diagram (Figure 6) does not help. But it is clear that any marriage may be seen as establishing a debtor/creditor relation between the wife-receiving and wife-giving groups which carries over into the next generation, when either the relation must be reinforced or the debt repaid. Parallel-cousin marriage is a diversion of women from both of these tasks. In fact the existence of parallel cousins cannot be accommodated in the simple models with which Les Structures is concerned. To have parallel cousins we must have more than one sibling of the same sex. Lévi-Strauss' arguments, like those of most of his forerunners in this field, relate to what he calls palaeolithic models (1966c: 16), in which each married couple have only two children, a son and a daughter. Once we begin to allow more than this, and thus to use 'neolithic' models, we have to consider not merely whether a son shall marry into the same group as a daughter (i.e. whether there shall be restricted or generalized exchange) but also whether two sons, or two daughters, shall marry into the same group. These questions are implicit in the discussion of the circumstances in which a single group participates in more than one exchange cycle (1969: 266) but they are nowhere fully discussed in Les Structures. Elsewhere (1966a) Lévi-Strauss examines at length the significance of these questions in myth.

Cross-cousin marriage is classified as a preferential union, in contrast to the levirate, sororate, and avuncular marriage, which are privileged unions (1969: 120). In making this arrangement, Lévi-Strauss is concerned not with the distinction stressed by Needham and others between a preference and a prescription for a given kind of marriage, but rather with the fact that it is impossible to have a marriage system in which all marriages are leviritic, or all to a dead wife's sister. Marriages of this kind can occur only in company with marriages of other kinds and may even, as with dead wife's sister marriage, entail a previous marriage of another kind. These privileged unions, or prerogative marriages as Josselin de Jong (1952: 12) calls them, are presumably explained by the transfer of rights from one individual to another. This is how various forms of marriage with relatives in the filial generation are to be understood. Marriage with a sister's daughter is seen as a substitute for FZD marriage, for in a particular instance a man had taken as wife the woman normally taken by his son. Similarly, in a system of matrilateral cross-cousin marriage, a man may choose to marry his wife's brother's daughter, who would normally be married by his son (1969: 368, 434). The global structure of the system is not affected by these anomalies, and for purposes of model-building we confine ourselves to cross-cousin marriage.

The contrast between preferential and prescribed marriages just mentioned does not emerge in *Les Structures*, for although he writes of '*unions préférentielles*', his whole discussion turns on the rule, and not on the frequency or desirability, of cross-cousin marriage. In reply to criticism by Homans and Schneider, Lévi-Strauss uses the word '*prescrit*' (1958a: 345 f.n.), translated as 'prescribed' (1963a: 322), thus making it clear that the systems he discusses in *Les Structures* are characterized by prescriptive rules rather than by statistical preferences. On the other hand, he contrasts rules of cross-cousin marriage with the dual form of organization and seems to imply that the rules of the latter, which constitute a global structure, can be observed in practice more readily or more often than can the rules of cross-cousin marriage, which constitute less of a system than a tendency (1969: 101–103).

In his Huxley memorial lecture, and in the preface to the second edition of *Les Structures*, Lévi-Strauss refers to the distinction drawn by Leach and Needham between preference and prescription, and says that he cannot regard it as important as they would have it. He associates prescription with mechanical models and preference with statistical models (1969: xxxv), associations which certainly follow simply from the definitions of these two contrasted types of model. But with typical preference for the dialectical prescription, Lévi-Strauss

150

dazzles us with the italicized statement that 'even a preferential system is prescriptive at the level of the model, while even a prescriptive system cannot but be preferential at the level of the reality' (1966c: 17; cf. 1969: xxxiii). This makes pedestrian sense only if we assume both that models are always mechanical and never statistical, and that preferences are always statistical tendencies and never cultural norms. The first assumption is obviously wrong, even on Lévi-Strauss's own terms. The second is nevertheless in accord with his definition: '. . . the term preferential does not suggest a subjective inclination toward a certain degree of kinship . . . I call "preferential" a system in which, notwithstanding the lack of any "prescriptive" constraints, the rate of marriage with a given type of kin is higher than would be case if all marriages were made at random' (1966c: 18).

Marriage is viewed as an exchange of women between groups of men, and a series of marriages as constituting a cycle of reciprocity by which several groups are linked together (1969: 115–116). These cycles may be long or short, and any cycle may either stand on its own or embrace all the groups in the society, in which case we have a global structure of reciprocity. At least in restricted exchange, where men can exchange sisters in marriage, the global structure of reciprocity is 'immediately and intuitively apprehended by social man' (1969: 137). In a matrilateral generalized exchange, the chain of wife-giving goes from A to B to C and so on back to A, and in Lévi-Strauss's model, it includes in its path all the groups in the society; we therefore have a long cycle of exchange and a global structure of reciprocity. In restricted exchange with only two groups which exchange women, we also have a global structure, but with a short cycle. Now Lévi-Strauss ascribes a short cycle and a global structure to all restricted exchange systems, whether or not they have more than a single pair of groups. In fact, a multiple-pair system has only short cycles of exchange, each group simply exchanging women with the opposite group of its own pair. But these cycles remain discrete and the structure is not global unless the pairs are linked to one another in some way. The only multiple-pair systems dealt with at length by Lévi-Strauss in *Les Structures* are the Australian systems with four or eight groups (sections or sub-sections), and with these the intermarrying pairs are all linked to one another by rules of descent; there are relations of child-giving as well as wife-giving in the global structure. With this additional requirement for restricted exchange, Lévi-Strauss's assertion holds. On the other hand, in patrilateral generalized exchange the cycle is short, from A to B in one generation and from B back to A in the next. This may be satisfactory from the point of view of each single family, but 'a total structure of reciprocity never emerges from the juxtaposition of these local structures'. The cycle of reciprocity 'will never exceed the stunted form of so many precocious plants'. Furthermore, some cultural elements that appear to be evidence for restricted exchange are really due to the simultaneous presence of the patrilateral formula of generalized exchange alongside the more manifest matrilateral formula. Human societies 'have always thought of generalized exchange in contrast with – and therefore, at the same time, in association with – the patrilateral formula', so that in some areas 'bilaterality is a secondary result, a product of the convergence of two forms of unilaterality which are always present and given' (1969: xxxii, 445, 448, 453).

Lévi-Strauss's ethnographic evidence for patrilateral generalized exchange is much weaker than for other types of exchange. Although he classifies the Mara and Aluridja as having patrilateral generalized exchange, the classification is based on inferences from the marriage class system that can be challenged (cf. Needham 1962: 108). Radcliffe-Brown (1930–1931: 325, 332) claimed that both these tribes had a rule of marriage with MMBDD like the Aranda. Many writers have raised objections to treating patrilateral cross-cousin marriage as formally homologous with the matrilateral version, while others have denied that a patrilateral system has ever, or could have ever, worked in practice. This last objection seems not to trouble Lévi-Strauss, for he writes of patrilateral cross-cousin marriage that 'The model of such a system does undoubtedly exist, not only in the mind of the anthropologist who can represent it in diagram form, but also in that of most of the natives who advocate, permit or *reject* this formula' (1966c: 16, his emphasis; cf. 1969: xxxii).

Here we are back at the basic ambiguity in Lévi-Strauss's work, the extent to which evidence from the world of action (that the system will not actually work) has any relevance to the world of thought. We can all think about systems that do not work; indeed, perhaps most of the systems we think about would not work if we tried to put them into practice. Leaving this issue aside, we can still ask in this context whether it is valid to argue that the simple reversal of the flow of women in successive generations under a patrilateral rule prevents the appearance of a global structure. If a woman of A is given to a man of B in a patrilateral system, then that man's sister must go as wife to a man in C and his sister to a man in D, and so on exactly as in a matrilateral system (Homans and Schneider 1955: 13; Wouden 1956: 206; Maybury-Lewis 1965: 216) and to this extent there is a global structure. The difference between the two models lies only in the next generation, for in a matrilateral system the same sequence is repeated whereas in the patrilateral system it is reversed. Lévi-Strauss's non-ascription of global structure makes sense only if we require the structure to remain unaltered from one generation to the next.

I think he would reject this line of argument. For him, it is an optical illusion to imagine that in the model of a patrilateral system there is a long cycle of exchange in one generation. The only cycles present in the model are the short cycles, from A to B in one generation and from B back to A in the next. The long cycles, he insists, belong only to the diagram drawn by the anthropologist, not to the model in the mind of the native. Indeed, the fact that few, if any, patrilateral systems are to be found in the world is evidence that these systems are perceived as containing only short unsatisfactory cycles, and that they are rejected for this reason (1969: xxxiv, f.n.1). To this I can reply only that if the patrilateral long cycle is an illusion, we have to ask whether the long cycle in matrilateral systems is also illusory, a mere fiction of the anthropologist.

Types of marriage exchange are also classified as direct or indirect, and the exchange may be continuous or discontinuous. In restricted exchange women are exchanged directly, as between A and B, so that sister-exchange marriage is possible. In generalized exchange this is prohibited, and the exchange of women takes place indirectly, either from A to B to C to D and so on until finally back to A; or from A to B in one generation and from B back to A in the next. In the matrilateral version of generalized exchange, exchange is continuous, in that the flow of women as wives is always from A to B, whereas with patrilateral cross-cousin marriage the flow is discontinuous or alternating, first in one direction and then in the opposite direction (1969: 218, 445, 478). Lévi-Strauss also speaks of open and closed structures, a single instance of matrilateral cross-cousin marriage being an open structure since it can form part of a chain of giving and receiving women, whereas a patrilateral cross-cousin marriage forms a closed structure, in that a woman is given from one group to another in one generation, and another is received back in the next generation, after which the system 'relapses to a point of inertia' (1969: 444).

Lévi-Strauss argues that the 'structure of reciprocity' may define itself in two ways: in parallel perspective, when all the marriages are between members of the same generation; or in oblique perspective, when, so it seems, marriages are between members of adjacent generations, or when a marriage in one generation is balanced by another in the next. Patrilateral cross-cousin marriage has some of the qualities of reciprocity in oblique perspective. A man of A receives a bride from group B in return for the woman (his father's sister) given by A to B in the previous generation. In many societies where patrilateral cross-cousin marriage is found, marriage with the groom's sister's daughter also occurs, again with the implication that a woman is being returned in recompense for a woman received in the preceding generation. The parallel perspective leads to

154

more satisfactory results in the regularity of the structure and the affective states it helps to bring about. But the exchange mechanism works with reference to the society as a whole, and not to the individuals immediately concerned. The oblique perspective results from an individualist and greedy attitude; as far as possible the link between what is given and what is received is kept as concrete as possible (1969: 447–448).

8   Filiation and residence

In Lévi-Strauss's view women are exchanged not by individual men but by groups of men, and in the models the whole of male society is divided into a number of discrete, mutually exclusive, enduring groups. He distinguishes three types of filiation or recruitment of groups. He uses the term *filiation* which the translators of *Les Structures* render as 'descent', for in the book he does not make the distinction drawn by Fortes between 'descent' and 'filiation' which we shall examine in the next chapter. With a rule of 'undifferentiated descent' ('indiscriminate descent' in Josselin de Jong 1952: 10), the two lines of filiation are interchangeable and 'may be merged in a joint exercise of their functions' (Lévi-Strauss 1969: 106); by this I understand the rules of some, perhaps of any, cognatic kinship systems. *Filiation bilatérale* in the first edition of *Les Structures* becomes *filiation bilinéaire* in the second edition, rendered as 'bilineal descent' (1949a: 135; 1967: 123; 1969: 106), and refers to systems of double unilineal descent. Lévi-Strauss stresses that although some recognition of both patrifiliation and matrifiliation is universal, double unilineal descent is a highly specialized form (1969: 419).

Lévi-Strauss wrote *Les Structures* at a time when the distinction between the recognition of filiation and the formation of groups was not as widely appreciated as it now is. Despite the changes introduced into the second edition of his book, his writing on this topic still has a curiously old-fashioned ring. He is essentially concerned only with unilineal and double unilineal systems,

155

and has little to say about other societies. The bricks in his models are unilineal groups, or subdivisions of these, and he is concerned with them primarily as units in the game of exchanging women. Hence problems of segmentary fission and fusion, seen as political problems, are left untackled. He is however concerned to show that the choice of patrilineal rather than matrilineal descent is not of great significance. It is an 'illusion of traditional sociology' to attach a decisive value to the mode of filiation (1969: 409). On the other hand, though a four-class system can survive shifts from one mode of filiation to another, the mode of filiation is a 'convention' 'which is basic to the structure of the social group once it is established, and cannot thus be regarded as a "detail"' (1969: 323).

His assertion that 'the mode of descent never constitutes an essential feature of a kinship system' (1969: 408) is reflected in his interpretation of indigenous theories of procreation. He notes that in many parts of eastern Asia it is believed that a baby gets his bones from his father and his flesh from his mother. He argues that these beliefs are incompatible with restricted exchange and provide strongly presumptive evidence for the existence of generalized exchange. There is no difficulty in seeing that these beliefs are compatible with generalized exchange, but I do not think that they provide a strong presumption for the existence of this kind of system. Likewise the incompatibility of these beliefs with restricted exchange is not clear. Lévi-Strauss says merely that 'In a system of restricted exchange, each group is both "bone" and "flesh", since, to employ the language of the Schools, it gives fathers and mothers at the same time and in the same respect' (1969: 393). But in fact, given either rule of unilineal descent, the relations entailed by the marriage of a man in the group are not the same as those entailed by the marriage of a woman member. We could argue that in restricted exchange what happens is that A and B exchange 'bone' and 'flesh' to make each other's babies.

But if it is difficult to see how beliefs about procreation may be correlated with one kind of exchange, it is easier to accept Lévi-Strauss's other contention, that they cannot be linked with one rule of unilineal descent rather than the other. In an early comment, he argues that a unilateral theory of conception may be sufficient to generate a dual organization, but notes that the patrilineal Jews had in the Talmud a maternal theory of conception (1944: 42, f.n. 7). In much the same vein, he observes that because of 'phychological drives' men feel warmly towards their wives' children even when they reject the notion of physiological paternity (1956a: 271).

In the first version of 'Social structure' (1953a: 530) there is a reference to the 'very important' possible demonstration by Murdock that patrilineal systems cannot change into matrilineal, though the reverse shift is possible, thereby introducing for the first time a 'vectorial factor' into social structure. Even though the validity of this demonstration has been queried, it is curious that in the revised version of this paper, published in 1958, this reference is replaced by something else (1963a: 287).

A more significant attribute of a society than its rule of descent is its 'regime', which may be either harmonic or disharmonic (1969: 215; cf. Josselin de Jong 1952: 19). Under a harmonic regime, the rule of descent and the rule of residence are either both patrilineal or both matrilineal, while with a disharmonic regime, one is patrilineal and the other matrilineal. The introduction of rules of residence into the models seems at first sight rather odd, for it is easy to think of these groups of men which interchange women living, as it were, on some air-conditioned Olympus. They marry, and give in marriage, but that is all. They toil not neither do they spin and their need for shelter for the night is not apparent. Why then is it significant where they live? This question is not discussed in *Les Structures*, though later Lévi-Strauss has argued that 'every ordered society, whatever its organization or degree of complexity, has to be defined, in one way or another, in terms of residence, and it is therefore legitimate to have recourse . . . to a particular rule of residence as a structural principle' (1963b: 36). But residence is not an attribute of the same logical order as filiation, for though every man has only two parents there are in general an unlimited number of residential possibilities open to him; he can move

157

during his lifetime from one place to another and he can maintain more than one residence simultaneously; he may have no
place to call his own or he may work in one place, eat in another,
and sleep in a third. These difficulties are ignored in *Les Structures* because residence is treated merely from a formal point of
view. Lévi-Strauss uses the traditional categories patrilocal and
matrilocal, and introduces residence initially in explanation of
why the Kariera have a four-class system when their matrilineal
moieties by themselves would adequately provide for their rule
of double cross-cousin marriage. Likewise the northern Aranda
system, with its eight sub-sections, is seen as a model for relating
two matrimoieties and four local groups. There is no suggestion
that a group of men with women to exchange needs to be localized so that it can conduct its affairs expeditiously, or that a
descent group with dispersed membership must have an internal
structure of authority differing from that of a localized descent
group (cf. Schneider 1961: 8–12, 19–20). What alone is significant is that an additional form of cross-classification has been
introduced. It is tacitly assumed that local groups are exogamous. If descent and residence are harmonic, then all the natal
members of a local group belong to one descent group, whereas
if the rules are disharmonic some of the members of each local
group belong to one descent group and others to another, and
each descent group contains members of more than one local
group. In other words harmonic regimes have one less degree
of freedom than disharmonic ones.

Another way of putting this is to say that in harmonic regimes,
a child belongs to the intermarrying group of one or other
parent, whereas in a disharmonic regime he belongs to a group
different from both his parental groups. For in a disharmonic
regime each matrimonial class of the system, the group that
follows a defined marriage rule, is formed by the intersection of
two larger groups, one of which is patrilineal and the other
matrilineal. Since each of these groups is exogamous, a man's
parents belong to different classes, and he in turn belongs to a
class different from both of theirs. If there are two patriclans
X and Y, and two matriclans p and q, such that a man's mother
158

is in X and p and his father in Y and q, then the man himself will be in Y and p.

Lévi-Strauss cautions against regarding patriliny, matriliny, patrilocality, and matrilocality as abstract elements that combine themselves at random, and he discusses the difficulties of men who live in the village of their wives (1969: 118; cf. 1963a: 322). But these considerations are irrelevant to the form of the model of marriage rules. In a model, filiation is contrasted with the rule of residence but residence has no content. As far as the model is concerned, a man's residential affiliation is only one more label in a series of labels. In fact there is no content in filiation either. For example, in his characterization of the Kariera, Lévi-Strauss notes that, like the Aranda, they are divided into two matrimoieties and two patrilocal groups. This ascription of matrilineal moieties to the Kariera follows Radcliffe-Brown's second discussion of this society (1930–1931: 55), and clearly Kariera social organization is compatible with the existence of matrimoieties. But I find it significant that in his report on this society published shortly after he had visited the area (1913), Radcliffe-Brown does not mention matrilineal moieties at all. At the time of his visit the Kariera were living as peons on cattle ranches, but he inferred that formerly they had lived in patrilineal hordes, and listed nineteen of these. Lévi-Strauss is merely following Radcliffe-Brown in saying that there were two categories of hordes (cf. Romney and Epling 1958). Thus both 'residence' and 'matrilineal filiation' are attributes with very little cultural content among the Kariera. Likewise we know that many of their religious activities are, or were, based on totemic beliefs. But the model is not concerned with these activities; the Kariera could all be atheists without affecting the formula of restricted exchange. In fact all we need for a model of a disharmonic regime is two contrasting rules of filiation, patrilineal for purpose alpha and matrilineal for purpose beta, provided only that alpha and beta are different and that neither is concerned with marriage. That purpose is reserved for the matrimonial classes formed by the intersection of the two kinds of categories.

THREE STYLES IN THE STUDY OF KINSHIP

The reduction of residence and descent to merely two procedures for classifying groups explains why Lévi-Strauss maintains that generalized exchange is usually harmonic whereas restricted exchange is usually disharmonic. Restricted exchange entails the division of society into pairs of intermarrying groups. Members of different pairs are not linked by marriage, and in a harmonic regime they are not linked by descent or locality either. Hence the society breaks down into a number of discrete sub-societies, each consisting of a pair of intermarrying local groups, and there are no links of filiation, marriage, or residential proximity between any one sub-society and any other. On the other hand, if the regime is disharmonic the marriage classes are not descent groups, each intermarrying pair of classes is linked by relationships of parent/child to other classes in the system, and an enduring global structure is possible.

By contrast, generalized exchange fits in well with a harmonic regime, for its long cycle of reciprocity runs through the whole society, however many groups it contains. A system of generalized exchange can begin only in a harmonic regime, and once established, may engender some amount of social inequality, referred to as 'feudal tendencies', since some groups are more successful than others in the speculation or risk-taking implied by the matrilateral version of generalized exchange. These groups marry polygamously and participate in more than one cycle of exchange (1969: 265-266).

In many societies a man Ego is associated in certain contexts with members of his own generation and with members of the generations of his grandparents and his grandchildren. This group is contrasted with the group formed by members of the generations of Ego's parents, children, great-grandparents, and great-grandchildren, and so on. This dichotomy of society into sets of alternating generations is found in many parts of the world and receives formal recognition in several Australian societies, where these groups are named. Radcliffe-Brown saw these as yet another variation on the basic four-section or eight sub-section model, some parts of the model which are elsewhere left unnamed being picked out and identified (Radcliffe-Brown in Lévi-Strauss 1969: 499–500). Lévi-Strauss sees this arrangement of 'endogamous moieties', as Radcliffe-Brown somewhat infelicitously called them, as arising from a disharmonic regime, for only in this kind of regime does a man belong to a marriage class different from those of both his parents (1963b: 36; 110–111, 352). An alternation of generations is also implied in the patrilateral cross-cousin model, with its reversal of the flow of women in each successive generation (1969: 202–203, 313–314). Yet when Radcliffe-Brown notes that certain categories are named in some Australian societies and left unnamed in others, his procedure is not very different from that of Lévi-Strauss when he speaks of the four-class systems of the Murngin and Mara being 'transfigured' into the eight-class Aranda system, and of the Mara and Aluridja systems being identical, except that one is explained in vertical and the other in horizontal terms (1967: 229; 1969: 200–201, 203). Although Radcliffe-Brown writes that 'The problem, therefore, is why these four divisions are sometimes named and sometimes not', this was a problem he did not worry much about. For Lévi-Strauss, the transformations of one structure into another demonstrate that his second criterion for structural models is satisfied. He does sometimes ask why a certain society has chosen one transformation rather than another, as for example with the Kariera. But the historic choices made by societies remain for the most part outside his range of inquiry.

Harmonic regimes are unstable in the sense, as I understand it, that if there are n unilineal groups in a harmonic regime linked in a system of generalized exchange, it is easy, both in the model and in actual practice, for the system to change to one with $n + 1$ or $n - 1$ groups (cf. 1969: 217, 265–266, 441). Disharmonic regimes are stable, in that the number of marriage classes is always four or eight or, conceivably, some multiple of eight, and some new principle of classification has to be adopted to shift from a four-class to an eight-class system (1969: 216–217). These adjectives, stable and unstable, refer primarily to the model rather than to any particular society that may 'have' the model, though at one point Lévi-Strauss does refer to the 'general instability' (presumably political instability) of European medieval society as a probable reason for a tendency to shorten marriage cycles (1969: 472). In typical vein, he writes that 'generalized exchange, while relatively unproductive in the matter of system (since it can engender only one single pure system), is very fruitful as a regulating principle', whereas direct exchange 'is extremely productive as regards the number of systems which can be based upon it, but functionally is relatively sterile' (1969: 441). Here we are clearly discussing matters at the level of 'fundamental' reality, and the world of empirical reality is far away.

9   Limiting conditions

Throughout most of *Les Structures* kinship systems and marriage rules are treated in isolation from empirical concrete reality, and hence from factors that relate primarily to aspects of that concrete reality other than marriage and filiation. We have already noted that residence is treated as another kind of affiliation rather than as arising from the need to have a roof over one's head and a garden to work in. Lévi-Strauss recognizes the impact of non-kinship on kinship in two contexts. On the one hand, we have the notion of the 'order of orders'. Perhaps with Radcliffe-Brown's picture of 'the network of social relations' as his anti-model, Lévi-Strauss says that '. . . anthropology considers the whole social fabric as a network of different types of orders' (1963a: 312). In other words, as well as a kinship structure we have structures of political ideology, mythology, ritual, art, etiquette, and cooking, all of which are 'partial expressions' of some society (1963a: 85). By 'order of orders', he means 'the formal properties of the whole made up of sub-wholes, each of which corresponds to a given structural level' (1963a: 333). The structures at different levels are not necessarily in harmony but they are related by transformations, which 'amount to formulas showing the number, magnitude,

162

direction and order of the convolutions that must be unravelled, so to speak, in order to uncover (logically, not normatively) an ideal homologous relationship between the different structural levels' (1963a: 334).

This last statement dates from 1956, and it is instructive to contrast this emphasis on the formal properties of models and their logical relationships to one another with the more functional approach followed in *Les Structures*. In the earlier work, kinship structures are influenced by, and are not merely logical transformations of, political structures. The relationship is worked out with reference to 'feudal tendencies'. The models presented in *Les Structures* are constructed with social groups that are homologous and unspecialized; the system looks the same to every member and there are no privileged positions. Thus no recognition is given in the models to differential social status and differential capabilities of exchanging women. In empirical reality, in some societies there are significant differences, and these are reflected in the marriage system. Lévi-Strauss speaks of 'feudal tendencies' when referring to inequalities in the distribution of wealth and power which lead to an accumulation of women at one point on the chain of exchange, and to a scarcity at some other point; or to the growth of status difference between groups which prevents intermarriage. Restricted exchange is based on the notion of a continuous return flow of women in exchange for women given, and patrilateral cross-cousin marriage on the return of a woman one generation later. But in the matrilateral version of generalized exchange, Lévi-Strauss argues, there is an element of risk, in that the return that group A gets for the women it gives as wives to group B comes only when group A receives women from the last group in the chain. The society adopting the system has to be ready, as it were, to speculate; subsidiary cycles of exchange tend to occur, and polygamy and unequal distribution of women result, thus contradicting the premise of equality on which the system of generalized exchange is based. Likewise, excessive splitting of the intermarrying groups may lead to a breakdown in the system. These conditions constitute the 'external limits' of generalized exchange (1969: 265–266, Chapter 17). The groups participating in the long cycles of exchange acquire differences in status, leading to hypergamy, and after a while the cycle breaks up into a number of intermarrying pairs, so that a system of generalized exchange is replaced by restricted exchange. Evidence from China and elsewhere is advanced in support of this line of evolution, while European kinship is said to have evolved out of generalized exchange into a complex kinship structure (1969: 474). Thus Lévi-Strauss is here postulating irreversible evolutionary processes rather than discussing purely formal transformations.

His later discussion of this issue is complicated by the introduction of the concept of transitivity, a concept not used in *Les Structures*. In his paper on 'Social structure' he describes a hypergamous society with matrilateral generalized exchange as having a transitive and non-cyclical order, with a girl at one end of the chain unable to marry because there is no man of higher status to take her, and at the other end of the chain a man who cannot marry because there is no woman of lower status (1953a: 547). Here relative social status is transitive, in the sense that group A is above group B which is above C which is above D and so on down to group Z at the bottom; and the order is non-cyclical, in that the long cycle of reciprocity is not closed, for the beggar of group Z does not marry the princess of group A. Lévi-Strauss says that the system will transform into an intransitive and cyclical order, which is formally the opposite of what it was, but which hardly fits either the restricted exchange or the complex structure postulated earlier. When the paper on 'Social structure' was revised in 1958, a sentence was added saying that 'either the society under consideration will succumb to its contradictions or its transitive and non-cyclical order will be transformed into an intransitive and cyclical one, temporarily or locally' (1963a: 311). Thus inexplicably the evolution or transformation postulated in *Les Structures* has been reversed. Lévi-Strauss refers in the revised version of the paper to fresh evidence of kinship changes in Malabar (Gough 1955) and of a non-transitive political hierarchy in Fiji (Hocart 1952), but his exact meaning remains obscure. In another paper of the same date, he argues that prescribed differences in status between wife-giving and wife-taking groups may contribute to equilibrium, in that every family occupies both positions (1958d: 28). His thesis that feudal tendencies are incompatible with matrilateral exchange systems, which are fundamentally egalitarian, has been heavily attacked by Leach (1961b: 76–80, 101; 1969).

Matching these 'external limits', Lévi-Strauss speaks of an antagonism between the bride's mother's brother and the groom's father's sister among, for example the Gilyak of eastern Siberia. The antagonism is so strong that the marriage system nearly breaks down; these conditions constitute the 'internal limits' of the system (1969: Chapter 18; Josselin de Jong 1952: 22–23). In another context, he argues that in societies with matrilateral cross-cousin marriage, marriage with the FZD 'represents the omnipresent danger but irresistible attraction of a "social incest", more dangerous to the group, even, than biological incest, which latter will never compromise the security of the system because it cannot be conceived of as a solution' (1969: 454). This reification of marriage systems may well be unacceptable to many empirically minded readers but is quite compatible with a view of models as the only true reality.

10   Validation

It might be thought that this elaborate array of concepts would be used to state a battery of propositions which could be submitted to test. This is not what has happened, nor what Lévi-Strauss intends. In reply to criticism by J. F. Revel, he writes:

> I ask to be judged on the basis of this typology, and not on that of the psychological or sociological hypotheses which Revel seizes upon; these hypotheses are only a kind of mental scaffolding, momentarily useful to the anthropologist as a means of organizing his observations, building his classifications, and arranging his types in some sort of order (1963a: 340).

Thus, in dramatic contrast to almost all his colleagues, Lévi-Strauss declares himself a typologist rather than a propositionalist. The value of his work, therefore, has to be assessed not primarily by the specific propositions he advances about the way in which one kind of marriage system may modify itself and become another, or about how the Murngin system actually works, but rather by the explanatory value of his typology of reciprocity, exchange, fundamental elements, and so on. By comparing institutions in several societies, we may 'succeed better in grasping the feelings, intentions and attitude of the native' (1963a: 338). His view of anthropology places it among the human sciences whose function 'seem to lie half-way between explanation and anticipation; they never – or very seldom – explain completely and they do not predict with complete certainty' (1964: 539). And yet, according to another statement, it is neither a natural science nor one of the humanities, but unique (1966b: 126). As Caws (1968: 82) notes, 'structuralism is not a humanism, because it refuses to grant man any special status in the world'. If anthropology is a humanism at all, it is humanism of a generalized form (Levi-Strauss 1956d).

There are difficulties with this stance on a disciplinary tight-rope. The schema advanced by Lévi-Strauss certainly makes sense of phenomena which previously have been awkward to classify and anomalous. His method of analysis is strikingly flexible and adaptable; nothing – or almost nothing (cf. Barnes 1971) – is safe from the structuralist approach. Yet if structural analysis explains everything, though only partially, the danger is that it explains too much. Like psychoanalysis, it delights in paradox and contradiction and, though it is hard to prove, it is equally hard to disprove. In fact, in seeking to verify Lévi-Strauss's assertions, we meet the same difficulty as with many of the claims of Freud, who, in Schneider's words (1965: 40) 'haunts the pages of Lévi-Strauss'. Leach (1965: 17) remarks that 'a number of Lévi-Strauss' more difficult arguments seem to parallel comparable obsurities in the Freudian system'.

Lévi-Strauss's own position is spelt out clearly in relation to myth, when he discusses what sort of correspondence there

166

may be between 'the unconscious meaning of a myth – the problem it tries to solve – and the conscious content'. Either the myth may borrow its elements from social life itself or, equally, it may be 'an inverted image of the social pattern actually present in the consciousness of the natives' (1960c: 356). But is there any difference between this argument and the 'clever dialectic' he protests against, whereby some anthropologists assert that an evil mythological grandmother either reflects the fact that grandmothers are actually evil or, if grandmothers are not actually evil, provides an outlet for repressed feelings? Lévi-Strauss comments that then interpretation becomes too easy (1963a: 207–208); cannot the same criticism be levelled against his own procedure?

But it will not do to argue by analogy and to say that because Freud was initially iconoclastic and had great difficulty, or perhaps no interest, in presenting his views in scientifically testable form, then Lévi-Strauss's views will eventually gain the general acceptance now accorded to those of Freud. For Lévi-Strauss is not, and never has been, an iconoclastic outsider. His notion of 'fundamental elements' is persistently present in anthropology, from Bastian onwards, and of course has its roots in Hellenic philosophy; the shift in level and sophistication is certainly significant but the generic idea was established long ago. If we wish to draw analogies we should turn to linguistics rather than psycho-analysis, and to do so is more in line with Lévi-Strauss's own thinking. The concept of the phoneme is a working tool in linguistics, whereas the fundamental elements of anthropological models have not yet been standardized and 'domesticated'. It does not take long to train a field linguist to the point where he can investigate a previously unknown language and draw up a reasonably complete list of its phonemes. The relation between the analytically derived phonemes and the concrete reality of people talking to one another can be defined operationally. More important, it is possible to argue about what the phonemes of any given language are, and how they are combined, and to reach firm and testable conclusions. There is not only the possibility of error in making phonemic

167

inquiries; there are also procedures for deciding between one interpretation and another. Thus we can say that in English there are forty-six phonemes. We can list them and can argue, and even disagree, that there are no more and no less than forty-six (Gleason 1961: 50). Despite continuing debates, phonemic analysis has become a standardized technique in a way that is only partly true of psycho-analysis and scarcely true at all of the structural studies of kinship we have been considering in this chapter. We are still in the realm of art rather than science.

This is, alas, no new event in anthropology. The wide range of the phenomena embraced by the theory, contrasting so markedly with the paucity of testing procedures, is matched by the earlier schemes put forward by, for example, Malinowski and Elliot Smith. Malinowskian functionalism and the heliocentric diffusionism of Elliot Smith were both schemes of great flexibility which made large explanatory claims; almost any piece of evidence could be interpreted in terms of the theory. The reader may well protest at this grotesque juxtaposition of two schemes of interpretation, the first of which is still current while the second is thoroughly discredited. My argument is merely that both were theories that tended to become closed systems, explaining too much rather than too little. Neither Malinowski nor Elliot Smith seriously consider the question: 'What hypothetical evidence would be needed to disprove my theory?' In my view, Lévi-Strauss's assertions have the same weakness. The explanations and interpretations provided by all three of these grand theorists fall short of Popper's criterion of the scientific status of a theory – 'its falsifiability or refutability, or testability' (Popper 1963: 37). Lévi-Strauss's 'fundamental elements' are postulated, not emunerated, though three are mentioned. The models 'explain' but it is not clear just what is being explained. The mechanisms whereby the model impinges on reality are for the most part unconscious, so that we have to postulate models rather than inspect for them.

It is clear that his own writing displays brilliantly those properties of binary opposition, of paradox and contrast, that he has argued are universal. For instance, in describing his reaction to a first visit to south Asia he writes:

The picture was this: against America of the Amazon region, a poor and tropical but underpopulated area (the latter factor compensating for the former) was set south Asia, again a poor and tropical but this time over-populated area (the second factor aggravating the first); in the same way that, of the regions with temperate climates, North America, with vast resources and a relatively small population, was a counterpart of Europe, with comparatively small resources but a large population (1951a: 772).

When writing about a topic more closely linked to the issues we have been considering in this chapter, the relationship between castes and totemic clans, he says:

In other words, both the caste system and the so-called totemic systems postulate isomorphism between natural and cultural differences. The validation of this postulate involves in each case a symmetrical and inverted relationship. Castes are defined after a cultural model and must define their matrimonial exchange after a natural model. Totemic groups pattern matrimonial exchange after a cultural model, and they themselves must be defined after a natural model. Women, homogeneous as regards nature, are claimed to be heterogeneous as regards culture, and conversely, natural species, although heterogeneous as regards nature, are claimed to be homogeneous as regards culture, since from the stand-point of culture they share common properties in so far as man is believed to possess the power to control and multiply them.

In totemic systems, men exchange culturally the women who procreate naturally, and they claim to procreate culturally the animal and vegetable species which they exchange naturally: in the form of foodstuffs which are interchangeable since any biological individual is able to dispense with one and to subsist on the others (1963c: 9; cf. 1962a: 165–166).

We cannot hope to resolve the myriad problems of human cultural complexity overnight, and yet we remain irresistably interested in ourselves and in the fruits of human thought and action. Any explanation of human behaviour, however partial and approximate, is better than none, unless a false and apparently complete explanation inhibits the search for a better one. Lévi-Strauss provides us with plenty of explanations and though he writes most of the time as if his explanations were the only ones possible, there are significant passages where he states that his views are only tentative and provisional. His style of writing attracts many readers in support of his arguments, and indeed the passages we have just quoted and many similar pieces of what might be called 'binary rhetoric' contribute to this strong appeal. Yet in this respect we cannot escape the suspicion that he has become the best advertisement for his own theories about mankind. It is interesting to note that in the contrast made by Lewin (1933) between Aristotelian and Galileian modes of thought, to which Lévi-Strauss refers (1963a: 301, 307), the use of Aristotelian dichotomous classifications features as one of the procedures characteristic of a young science that we should try to supersede. Lévi-Strauss has certainly made that shift from the study of objects to the study of relations between objects which Lewin regards as another difference between these two modes of thought and which, following Troubetzkoy (1933: 241, 243), Lévi-Strauss (1963a: 33) nominates as one of the specific characteristics of the structural method. But the pre-scientific dichotomous schemes of thought, typical of classical antiquity and the Middle Ages, which Lewin wished to leave behind, cannot be got rid of so easily. In Lévi-Strauss's view they have to be included under the rubric of 'primitive' thought (1962c: 215). Since the models that 'explain' human thoughts and actions are made up of fundamental elements which are present, consciously or unconsciously, in human thought itself, and not of artificially constructed analytical tools, it then becomes hard to develop any higher-order set of analytical constructs for use in 'super-models' that would explain the lower-order models. Instead, we are left with the fundamental binary oppositions that both characterize and explain human thinking, however regrettably Aristotelian this may be. This perhaps is a dialectical trap not yet fully explored. Though he may not be hung by his own petard, Lévi-Strauss may yet be caught by the cams of his own jigsaws.

One of the chronic difficulties in tying down Lévi-Strauss to simple propositions that can be tested is that he tends to move imperceptibly from statements of principle to statements of policy and back again, so that we cannot tell which we are dealing with. Thus his sustained reluctance to become too much involved in the world of events seems to be justified sometimes as a matter of principle – social anthropology is the study of rules – and at other times merely as the correct strategy for a young science. This ambivalence emerges clearly from the comments he makes on the assertion by Kunstadter and others (1963: 518) 'that no description of a marriage system, even in ideal terms, is complete without a statement of the demographic conditions within which that system operates'. Lévi-Strauss disagrees; the model must ignore demographic conditions. But then he goes on to say that 'Only when the rules of these difficult games are known and understood, may we venture to play them with models behaving like real populations' (1966c: 16–17).

Leach (1964b: 1112) suggests that Lévi-Strauss has tried to state in terms of binary oppositions relations that are ordinal (more or less) rather than dichotomous (yes or no). There is no doubt of Lévi-Strauss's fondness for discriminating among relations by the simple presence or absence of attributes. Warner (1931: 180) was perhaps the first writer to represent contrasting relations between kin in a code of plus and minus signs and Lévi-Strauss has developed this convention. His analyses of the relations within the 'global system' of a woman, her brother, her husband, and their son (the true atom of kinship) (1963a: 44–45, 48), the contrast between parallel cousins and cross-cousins (1969: 131), the structural differences between three societies (1963a: 160), and the relationships between social anthropology and some other disciplines (1963a: 286;

171

1964: 542) are all in dichotomous terms. Each cell of his tables can have one of two values. Though he uses the symbols plus and minus, these are employed purely qualitatively, and he does not, for example, give any cell the value $++$ to indicate an intensification of whatever quality is shown by a single $+$. Where signs appear to be combined (1963a: 73), this is merely a shorthand matrix notation. In fact the plus and minus signs add nothing to his argument and mislead the reader who thinks that there is some algebra that he should try to understand. Lévi-Strauss, like Warner before him, fails to develop a calculus of relationships (cf. Sahlins 1966; 134; Barnes 1967c: 29–30). We seem to have an example of that external and superficial borrowing of mathematical forms which we have been warned against from at least the time of Hegel (1929 (i): 231, cited in Murphy 1963: 18). The postulated universality of binary thinking finds support from linguistics, and it is understandably a fashionable belief at the beginning of the digital computer age. The principal thesis of *La Pensée sauvage* (1962a) is that human taxonomies are built up by successive binary contrasts, and it is easy to argue that a mechanism found so widely in taxonomies is to be expected in models of marriage systems; they are all products of *l'esprit humain*. Yet Lévi-Strauss's predilection for the binary mode of exposition, combined with the fact that taxonomies are conscious rather than unconscious models of empirical reality, forces one to be on one's guard against seeing a binary opposition under (or in?) every bed. As Worsley (1966: 157) says 'Once upon a time (from Vico to Hegel and beyond) it was triads. Now numerological fashion has changed . . .'

Ever since Malinowski's day anthropologists have stressed in their professional training the almost traumatic significance of face-to-face contact with an exotic culture. As Malinowski himself showed, there is always the danger that an anthropologist may come to see the whole primitive world or even the whole of human society in the light of the one or two exotic groups he has confronted at first hand. Indeed, it would belie the importance of personal fieldwork if this danger did not exist. Lévi-Strauss has not only done fieldwork but has demon-

172

strated in *Tristes Tropiques* that this experience has a great significance for him (cf. 1955a; 1963a: 326, 332). To summarize a complicated picture, we may say that the peoples he has studied intensively in South America live in small communities, with little inter-community political structure, with headmen leading villagers rather than chiefs ruling tens of thousands. They have no memory of long genealogies and no wide-range segmentary structure. Some of them are the heirs of a more complex way of life that has been preserved only in part and remembered only in part (cf. mainly 1936, 1948a, and 1948b). Hence it is not surprising that Lévi-Strauss has tended to see kinship systems as systems of terminology, of symbolism, and of attitudes, rather than as systems for organizing lower levels of political life, or as the mainstay of a major form of economic activity such as cattle-grazing. Because of the small scale of these South American societies, the acquisition of wives may well be one of the most important activities organized by groups of kin. Unlike the situation found in some other parts of the world, kinship does not there operate alongside other principles of organization in elaborate games in which the stakes are power over men, or merit for arranging feasts and dances, or high ritual status. Perhaps it is his own field experience that leads Lévi-Strauss to insist that kin categories have no meaning except in relation to marriages that are allowed or prohibited (1953b: 284; cf. 1966c: 14). Likewise his assumption that 'except for very rare exceptions, all known (kinship) organizations are unilateral' (1969: 408) must be seen in the light of his work in South America, coupled with the comparative paucity of good studies of cognatic societies available when *Les Structures* was written (cf. 1969: xxviii).

In *Les Structures* and in the works that have followed, Lévi-Strauss draws on ethnographic evidence from a vastly wider range of societies than those he has seen at first hand. Yet in *Les Structures*, outside Australia, India, and the Burma/eastern Siberia axis, he uses ethnographic evidence for 'apt illustration', as Gluckman (1961: 7) would say, rather than for systematic comparison. Leach (1969: 280) even accuses him of smuggling

173

back into circulation 'all the most notorious fallacies of the Frazerian comparative method'. It is indeed surprising that Lévi-Strauss classifies himself with Radcliffe-Brown and others who have tried to consider limited areas where dense information was available (1963a: 300–301). The geographical area of concentration in *Les Structures* is the home of more than half of mankind, while the kinship systems of the rest of the world outside this huge 'limited' area are treated in a few pages. In an article, Lévi-Strauss has summarized the salient features of kinship systems throughout the world in two pages (1951b; 1963a: 63–64).

Though the peoples he has studied personally may have led him to emphasize kinship rather than politics or economics, his interest in models has made him extol the Australian Aborigines he has never seen, 'whose physical appearance reminds us of adipose bureaucrats or soldiers of Napoleon's Old Guard, making their nudity even more incongruous' (1962a: 118). He criticizes those of his colleagues who are so fascinated by 'Australian Aristotelianism' that they assert that marriage classes belong to a more primitive mode of thought than kin-relations (1969: 410–411), and yet he himself argues that the Aborigines 'have gone further than empirical observation to discover the mathematical laws governing the systems, so that it is no exaggeration to say that they are not merely the founders of general sociology as a whole but are the real innovators of measurement in the social sciences' (1956c: 143; cf. 1969: 102, 110; 1955b: 1205–1206). Surely this is nonsense. The Aboriginal inhabitants of Australia have many admirable qualities, but if they invented general sociology and social measurement, these inventions must have remained inaccessible in an unconscious model.

There is more to this than an exuberant cultural relativism. It is possible to mistake the Australian Aborigines for the founders of sociology only if there is little more to sociology than the revelation of unconscious models. If we take the view that there are no acceptable analytical categories in sociology and anthropology other than the 'real' fundamental elements located in

174

the unconscious mind, and if our understanding of human society is based on the binary oppositions in terms of which each particular society explains itself to itself, then the Australian Aborigines have indeed a strong claim to be the founding fathers of the profession.

I certainly do not wish to suggest that Lévi-Strauss's structural view is useless or that it is merely idiosyncratic. Nevertheless his style of writing, fascinating as it is, shows clearly that he has a much keener eye than most for the paradox, the contradiction, the dialectical trap. These qualities enliven his writings but also colour his arguments, and what we admire in one perspective we must suspect in another. Writing about the art of British Columbia, he speaks of 'This dithyrambic gift of synthesis, the almost monstrous faculty to perceive as similar what all other men have conceived as different' (1943a: 180). This monstrous faculty may open our eyes to connexions we had never guessed at, but that is only the first stage; we have to devise prosaic ways of testing the truth of the connexion. On a couple of occasions (1950a: xxiv; 1960a: 9), Lévi-Strauss has cited the classic words of Mauss: 'We should . . . observe what is given. What is given is Rome or Athens or the average Frenchman or the Melanesian of such-and-such an island, and not prayer or law as such' (1950: 276; cf. 1954: 78). In applauding Lévi-Strauss's dialectic we are constantly in danger of forgetting the Melanesian who supplies him with ammunition. He claims for himself a 'neolithic intelligence', probing into unexplored territory, harvesting once or twice and passing on to leave behind a land laid waste (1955a: 44–45). Our task must be to determine what remains after he has moved on to other pastures. Now that the virgin forest has been cleared, the prospects for permanent agriculture seem good.

3 Irreducible principles

Kinship, in short, among the Tallensi as among many other primitive peoples, is one of the irreducible principles on which their organized social life depends.

Fortes (1949a: 340)

3 Irreducible principles

1 Scope and limits

In a comment on a paper by Eisenstadt, Meyer Fortes (1961b: 211) says that his 'instinct is to shy away from methodological discussion'. We should then not be surprised if in this chapter where I attempt a discussion of Fortes's own methods much of the characteristic quality in his work escapes my analysis. Nevertheless I think the exercise may have value for two reasons. First, Fortes's dislike of discussions of analytical procedures and conceptual schemes is shared by many of his colleagues who, like him, have contributed substantially to the study of kinship. If we are to understand the full implications of their achievements and to advance promptly from the salients of understanding they have brilliantly secured, we have to dissect their work, measure their imponderables, and system-atize their imaginative insights, even though this methodo-logical scrutiny may contrast sharply with their own preferred style of analysis. We can spontaneously recognize their achievements by reading their books and articles while sharing their distaste for arid scholastic pendantry; but we can utilize these achievements to the fullest extent only by taking their work to pieces to see what it is made of. I concur with Fortes when he says that it is only by the application of scientific methods that great advances in the study of human society were made during the first half of this century (1949b: vi). What is true for the first half is likely to remain true for the second; if progress is to continue our methods have to be stated explicitly so that we can the more easily use them and modify

---

them. Only in this way can we satisfy his contention that 'The new frame of reference for anthropological science will have to be worked out on the model of the experimental natural sciences' (1951a: 354).

Yet inevitably, in discussing his work, I shall find myself giving to his ideas a precision or a rigidity, whichever way we may choose to look at it, which Fortes himself does not intend. I shall in fact be doing the same as Eisenstadt, against whom Fortes protests in the comment first cited. Fortes says: 'I do not think our "models" and "mechanisms" are as systematically conceptualized as Eisenstadt's exposition suggests. They provide *directives* for field research and theoretical analysis rather than *operational rules*' (1961b: 211, his italics). In these terms, what follows here is an attempt to penetrate beyond the directives to establish a set of operational rules that are implicit in, or at least that can be derived from, Fortes's writings. My interest is avowedly typological rather than biographical and, as in the two earlier chapters, I shall use a corpus of publications to build up a polar or Weberian ideal intellectual position that may or may not be fully occupied by the eponymous author. Indeed, it is clear that even if I have been lucky enough to give an account of intellectual positions that the authors concerned will not repudiate outright, I shall at best have delineated only a part, and perhaps not the most important part, of the thoughts and ideas of my colleagues. The personal labels I give to these positions may be understood as mnemonics and not necessarily badges of ownership or signatures.

Fortes has published a great deal on kinship, but in almost all that he has written in strict professional guise, as a social anthropologist writing for an audience of social anthropologists, he dwells at length on kinship in only two societies, the Tallensi and the Ashanti, both of Ghana. To establish what he has to say about kinship in general we have to look at the observations of wider reference that are richly embedded in his writings on Tallensi and Ashanti, at the comments on data drawn from other societies to illustrate arguments mainly inspired by Tallensi and Ashanti, at the unspoken assumptions presumably underlying the looser phraseology necessarily used in his popular articles, and at the explicit statements in his few papers that are avowedly comparative or methodological. I think that we can assume that Fortes would accept the legitimacy of this procedure, for he has defended his practice of concentrating his attention on one, or two, societies rather than examining more rapidly a wider sample, as we have seen Murdock and Lévi-Strauss do. With the example of Mendel and his garden peas seen as supporting Malinowski's preoccupation with the Trobrianders, Fortes writes that 'the results have handsomely vindicated the procedure of testing, amending and adding to the generalizations which make up the body of social anthropological theory by intensive study of one society at a time'. Hypotheses, he argues, are commonly derived from studies of single societies, and only later is their range of validity tested by comparative methods (1953b: 191–192). Yet if this intensive uni-social procedure has advantages, it also has hazards, as Fortes recognizes. It has, he says, 'taken twenty years for the Trobrianders to be placed in a proper comparative perspective in British social anthropology' (1953a: 19). There is, I think, a similar danger that the Tallensi may also have to wait before they can be properly comprehended (cf. Banton 1964: 97), but perhaps one way of hastening this may be to separate, as far as it is feasible to do so, Fortes on kinship in general from Fortes on Tallensi kinship in particular.

As with the other writers we have considered, the study of kinship is for Fortes part of a wider study of many aspects of social life, and his aims and procedures in discussing kinship derive from his perception of the wider task. Fortes identifies himself unequivocally as a social anthropologist. In his formulation, social anthropology is 'the basic discipline concerned with custom and social organization', and studies mechanism and function rather than historical origins (1953c: 16, 22). It deals with 'the analysis of how primitive social systems work' (1951a: 339). This last definition appears in an essay where he states that in theory social anthropologists are concerned with all kinds of society but in practice they study mainly primitive societies because these are small and alien to the investigator (1951a: 333). The same restriction appears in his Cambridge inaugural lecture, where it is explained historically and where the analytically significant features of primitive societies are listed as homogeneity of culture, relative stability, and lack of institutional differentiation (1953c: 16, 38). Although he has contributed prefaces to two books (1953d, 1956b) describing family systems in societies that do not meet these criteria, the same emphasis on at least the heuristic superiority of primitive societies is seen in his comment that it is 'more instructive and less distracting' for the student 'to pay too little rather than too much attention to our own civilization' (1963a: 425). This is an issue that, we shall see, affects Fortes's approach to kinship as well as his view of the effective frontiers of his discipline. For in his view the advantage of the simpler societies for study is that with them it is possible for the ethnographer to carry out the operation, distinctive to social anthropology, of 'considering every institution in the setting of the total social system' (1956b: xiii). This requirement makes participation in the work of a team unsatisfactory for an anthropologist, for he is then 'not directly and responsibly concerned to know the whole society and its entire culture' (1963a: 435). To understand the field situation the ethnographer 'must, first of all, have the concept of a total social structure clearly in his mind' (1944: 362). He must have a conception 'of a people's culture as constituting a coherent whole' (1939: 129). All this sounds admirable, but it can have undesirable consequences. For these requirements do not merely limit the scope of the ethnographer's inquiries to those societies with structures simple enough to be grasped in the way Fortes requires; they also entail, or at least encourage, the use of notions of homogeneity, consistency, and, more treacherously, equilibrium and stability that come all too easily to be viewed as universal principles rather than as distinguishing characteristics of a strategically delimited set of social structures. Thus for instance when Fortes writes that 'Every custom and institution, whatever its history, has a functional value in relation to the whole system' (1951a: 340), it is not clear whether this proposition relates only to simple homogeneous nonliterate societies or whether the notion of function is to be understood in such a broad sense that the statement remains true, but no longer enlightening, with respect to all societies, however complex, heterogeneous, and 'maladjusted' they may be.

We shall return to this point later in our discussion of equilibrium and of the distinction between customary and actual behaviour. Here, we note merely that Fortes's definitions establish social anthropology as a generalizing discipline. Intensive studies of selected societies, he says, are aimed at eventually reaching scientific generalizations (1951a: 340). In his inaugural lecture he refers specifically to the relation between mother's brother and sister's son, and to Radcliffe-Brown's demonstration of this special relation as 'a regular feature of segmentary social structures with patrilineal descent and a means by which a moral tie of critical importance is maintained with the mother's kin'. This, says Fortes, is 'one of a series of verifiable generalizations about mechanism and function' (1953c: 27). Let us dissect this statement. The mechanism concerned is the special relation, the function is the maintenance of the moral tie. Verifiability presumably refers to the demonstrated presence of the relation fulfilling this function in all, or some, societies with patrilineal segmentary social structures, and generalization to the fact that the simultaneous occurrence of these features in these societies happens, as he says, '*irrespective* of period and place' (1953c: 30, 35; cf. 1955a: 24). We have here most of the tantalizing and perplexing elements in Fortes's generalizations: just exactly what is 'special' in the MB–ZS relation is left unstated, so that we do not know what has to be verified as a 'regular feature' (though this lack of specification may have been appropriate in the context of a brief inaugural lecture); 'regular' sounds weaker than 'invariable' and stronger than 'common' but its exact meaning is uncertain; the 'moral tie' is presumably part of the 'special' relation, so that to some extent the proposition is tautologous; and the generalization is potentially verifiable

183

rather than actually verified, for although Radcliffe-Brown marshalled a most impressive body of evidence to support his case, he never made any attempt to exhaust the ethnographic record (cf. Sweetser 1966). Indeed, although Radcliffe-Brown's views about the mechanism involved changed over the years, as Goody (1959: 61–63) points out, the constant feature of his hypothesis was the extension of sentiments from the mother to her brother. Fortes (1949a: 339) has repudiated this mechanism as set out by Malinowski, while retaining it in more sophisticated form as part of an interactive process between the individual and the society he grows up in (1938: 11; 1944: 363, f.n. 4; 1959a: 208; cf. Firth 1951: 158–159). His own explanation of the position of the mother's brother among the Tallensi makes use of 'the interaction of the principle of the equivalence of siblings and the principle of the cleavage between successive generations' (1949a: 305) in a way that is consistent with his interpretation of Radcliffe-Brown's later work.

Yet despite these difficulties in producing a testable and logically watertight proposition from his statements, it is apparent that Radcliffe-Brown's analysis has brought about some significant and meaningful change in our understanding of the position of the mother's brother in patrilineal societies. Fortes is, I think, quite justified to protest (1955a: 22) against the charge made by Evans-Pritchard (1951a: 57) that the generalizations produced by Radcliffe-Brown and his followers have so far 'rather easily tended to become mere tautologies and platitudes on the level of common sense deduction'. But if these generalizations are more than this, just what form do they take? The answer is not obvious. As we probe into Fortes's generalizations, it soon becomes apparent that we are not dealing with simple propositions that can be subjected to easy logical or statistical tests and promptly rejected or placed in cold storage. The transition from 'directives' to 'operational rules' is not a leap straight forward but rather has to be a cautious advance based on careful checking of the meanings of technical words and of the range of phenomena to which they are applied.

In his 1951 paper on 'Social anthropology' Fortes writes of the discipline as concerned with custom and social organization; the same pair of topics appear again in his 1953 inaugural lecture. What do these words mean? Custom is 'the behaviour that is standardized, expected and often enforced in a particular situation in the community' (1951a: 332; cf. 1962b: 54). In the 1953 lecture it is the observation of custom that distinguishes social anthropology from the other social sciences (1953c: 40), and by 1963 the phenomenon of custom becomes the 'paramount concern of social and cultural anthropology' (1963a: 429). This shift in emphasis doubtless reflects Fortes's increasing concern in recent years with problems of ritual and the moral order rather than with those of political and territorial organization that are discussed in his earlier publications. However, it also indicates a way out of the dilemma of actual versus ideal behaviour, and of statistical versus mechanical models, seemingly quite distinct from those essayed by Murdock and Lévi-Strauss. Unfortunately, the new escape route does not avoid all the old difficulties and, as we shall see, Fortes has had to develop his own methods for resolving the analytical puzzles he sets himself. Some of these puzzles he would have had to face even if he had stuck to a more conventional definition of his subject.

There is one other introductory issue to raise, Fortes's ideas about frames of reference. Fortes is not only a social anthropologist, he is also a structuralist, this term to be understood here as attaching to the tradition of analysis developed by Radcliffe-Brown and not to that exemplified by Lévi-Strauss's *Anthropologie structurale*. Furthermore, Fortes contrasts structural analysis with the type of inquiry carried on in social psychology. Hence, if we are to avoid becoming entangled unnecessarily over the status of, for instance, structuralist psychology, of which there are many variants (cf. Lacan 1966), we have to understand Fortes's structural frame of reference as limited to a particular kind of content. This content, so I assume, consists of principles of social organization. Fortes argues that structuralist theory 'provides the best conceptual apparatus and the most

185

satisfactory models for the initial "opening-up" of an analysis of any social system' (1963a: 433). His major work on Tallensi kinship, *The web of kinship*, is described as not 'a comprehensive account of family life and kinship'. In it, he says, 'I am concerned only with kinship in relation to the social structure' (1949a: viii). Yet we can never lose sight of the fact that before turning to anthropology, Fortes worked in statistical and experimental psychology (1963a: 423) and gained his doctorate with a thesis on mental testing (1932a: 281, f.n.). Hence it is understandable that he has shown to a greater extent than many of his colleagues a lively interest in the limitations of structural analysis, and has made significant forays beyond those limits into related but distinct analytical fields. One of his earlier publications is entitled 'Social and psychological aspects of education in Taleland', and there he says that the study of education as a function of society is 'primarily a problem of genetic psychology' (1938: 7), which in an alien society necessarily entails a preliminary inquiry by sociological analysis to discover the cultural idiom. In the same way, a psychological study of a ritual system can be carried out only after it has been studied sociologically (1955a: 29).

This early appreciation that sociological or structural analysis is distinct from psychological analysis becomes sharper in his later work. In his 1953 paper on unilineal descent groups he refers to the fact that a substantial minority of Tiv men dwell in proximity to kinsmen who are not their closest agnates and notes that the men give purely personal reasons of convenience and affection for living thus. Inquiry shows that all the kinsmen involved belong to a limited range of kin types (cf. Bohannan 1954: 12–14). Fortes comments that 'What purports to be a voluntary act freely motivated in fact presupposes a structural scheme of individuation' and describes this as an instance of moving between the frame of reference of the social psychologist and the structural frame without confusing data and aims (1953a: 34). A few years later, the main burden of his criticism of Malinowski's view of kinship is that Malinowski failed to do what Fortes was forced to do in confrontation with the reality

186

of Tale life, to 'distinguish between the jural and the personal: or psychological, components of kinship institutions' (1957a, 179). On the other hand he praises Radcliffe-Brown for his 'rigorously sociological' analysis, 'wholly purified of psychological implications in the sense of hidden assumptions about a conditioning process working on individuals'. He argues that Radcliffe-Brown, unlike Murdock, was resigned to the use of a plurality of frames of reference for the study of society (1955a: 20, 26, 27), and suggests that at least three frames are needed to deal with ethnographic observations. What is observed can be seen either as (1) facts of custom, or (2) of social organization or social structure. The same data can also be seen (3) in a socio-psychological or bio-psychological frame of reference (1953a: 21). A similar tripartite division of analytical labour he sees, in another context, as possibly giving rise to three interdependent disciplines, (1) the historical and comparative study of culture, (2) the analytical study of social organization, the third prong being in this case (3) 'the elucidation of culture and social organization in the light of psychology and psychoanalysis' (1951a: 351). There is an unstated assumption in both these schemes, so it seems to me, about the data that are being analysed. Whatever may be the data used in the third mode of inquiry according to either triad, the first two modes make use of 'ethnographic observations'. Fortes here seems to have in mind the kind of evidence that is abundantly reproduced in his own publications. There is the record of who did what with whom, what was said, and how others responded; statements about customs and beliefs elicited from or volunteered by informants; responses to questions about who is the father of whom, who owned what, and about what alternative course of action was chosen and what was rejected. Other classes of data, such as the results of Rorschach and similar projective tests, seem not to be included. Ethnographic data, it appears, are those that the field ethnographer who is not also trained in psychology can collect unaided when working in a simple homogeneous society. Although social and cultural anthropology is defined, in his 1963 scheme, as paramountly concerned with custom, the structural frame of reference would seem to be associated with the second rather than the first of the three disciplines, with the analytic study of social organization rather than the historical and comparative study of culture. The structuralist is not concerned with the study of culture or custom in their own right. For it is in the second approach, not the first, that 'We see custom as symbolizing or expressing social relations – that is, the ties and cleavages by which persons are bound to one another in the activities of social life. In this sense social structure is not an aspect of culture but the entire culture of a given people handled in a special frame of theory' (1953a: 21).

If this is the position in the study of homogeneous societies, other queries arise when we look at more heterogeneous systems. In a relative complex society like Ashanti, where 'the major groups of factors are now operating in relative independence', the anthropologist has to call in specialists like the economist and the geographer to collect data showing the effects of economic and ecological factors and to study 'specialized developments which are not susceptible of investigation, or perhaps even of being grasped by the anthropologist' (1948a: 150–151). This is a different division of labour, and its relation to the disciplinary trichotomy is not obvious, particularly as the 'major group of factors' assigned to the anthropologist in the second scheme is described as 'strictly social and psychological'. The economic and ecological groups of factors are said to be operating in the social system, so that we may guess that the structural frame of reference has to take them into account. Yet the fact that the working of these factors is seen by Fortes as lying outside the anthropologist's special range of professional competence even in the quite 'underdeveloped' conditions of Ashanti in 1945 suggests that these same factors are likely to be treated sketchily even in the simpler environment of Taleland. Fortes argues in *The dynamics of clanship* that in order to understand how the 'equilibrium' in Tale social structure is maintained, a further study of Tale economic organization would be necessary. He then goes on to
188

say that 'economic interests do not play the part of dynamic factors in the social structure' (1945a: x). The limitations of this view of the Tale scene have been examined at length by Worsley (1956) and there is no need to repeat his cogent re-analysis of the evidence. The point to note here is merely that, from the point of view of method, the divergence of opinion between Fortes and Worsley is about matters of fact and interpretation, rather than about modes of analysis. In discus-sing the 'strong economic elements in an individual's adhesion to the lineage', Fortes quotes the Tale saying, 'it is all a question of manure' (1949a: 263), and on a broader canvas he calls attention to the fact that 'In Africa one comes up against economics where in Australia and parts of North America one meets only housekeeping' (1953a: 18). The paucity of reference to economic factors in his analysis of the Tallensi, and his resort to specialist collaboration in the Ashanti inquiry, do not then spring in any way from an *a priori* view that economic considerations lie outside the structural frame of reference. They must spring instead either from a belief that these considerations happen to be unimportant among the Tallensi, yet are particularly complicated among the Ashanti; or alter-natively (and this I think is the more plausible explanation), from an intellectual preference for analysis which emphasizes non-economic factors or structural principles such as equili-brium, stability, consistency, reciprocity, and equivalence.

The third frame of reference, concerned with socio-psychological, bio-psychological, or psycho-analytical inter-pretations of ethnographic facts, appears to belong to an intellectual area where anthropologists, and perhaps even structuralists, rub shoulders with colleagues from other branches of learning. Fortes admits that the 'basic distinction between the *jural* aspects and functions of a kinship system and the *affective*, or if we prefer, psychological meanings of the customs and usages in which the system comes to expression, has been more difficult to establish than might be thought' (1955a: 21). On two occasions he presents this latter field of inquiry as if it were one of the legitimate branches of

189

anthropology (1951a: 351; 1953a: 21), though this opinion is only doubtfully maintained in his later recommendation that the graduate student in anthropology 'should at least have heard' of attempts to explore psychological and psychogenetic variables in custom and social organization (1963a: 429). After saying that religious rituals and beliefs are apparently derived from childish attitudes to, and fantasies about, parents, Fortes adds in a broadcast talk that anthropologists are keenly studying the circular process whereby beliefs generate moral rules which generate customs of education which reinforce beliefs (1956a: 79). Yet in another context, as we have seen, Malinowski's failure to discriminate between the jural and psychological components of kinship institutions is deplored, and, more significantly, Radcliffe-Brown is praised for producing a scheme of analysis 'wholly purified of psychological implications'. The need to discriminate two kinds of component can be readily accepted, but the explanatory utility of 'wholly purified' analyses cannot be assumed and has to be demonstrated. Indeed, it is Fortes's curiosity about questions that, in his view, lie beyond the structuralist boundary that illuminates the limitations of merely structural analyses.

The marginal status of these questions does not inhibit Fortes from suggesting answers, even if their marginality is indicated. Thus in a footnote in *The web of kinship* he gives as an explanation of rivalry between immediately adjacent Tale siblings the fact that the Tale infant is simultaneously weaned and affectively neglected by its mother when the next baby is born. This non-structural explanatory aside is allowed, as it were, because 'On the analogy of what is known to happen in our society, it can be surmised that . . .' (1949a: 255, f.n.). In his broadcast talk, he argues that in primitive societies customs 'provide a legitimate – one might also say a conscious – outlet for the contradictory emotions built up' during childhood (1956a: 794). Here he foreshadows his description of Malinowski's view that 'custom is in fact the equivalent of unconscious emotional forces' (1957a: 172). Several years later, writing for a professional audience, Fortes ends a discussion of ancestor worship, and in particular of the sacrifice that a Tale man makes to his deceased father, by saying that 'it may be a reassurance to himself to be able to make the kind of reparation to his displaced predecessor which the beliefs and practices relating to sacrifice make possible'. Fortes concludes: 'Here we trench on problems that call for psychological analysis, as indeed any comprehensive study of ancestor worship will be bound to do' (1965a: 141). This final sentence may perhaps be intended to evoke the echo of the final sentence of Evans-Pritchard's classic study of Nuer religion: 'At this point the theologian takes over from the anthropologist' (1956: 322). Even if we discount the possible polemical intention in Fortes's statement in the implied contrast of psychologist and theologian, we are still left with the view that any comprehensive study of ancestor worship, as of kinship, entails more than structural analysis.

Our problem is to determine how adequate is something that is less than comprehensive. Are there some customs, institutions, relations and processes, or interconnexions between these, that can be quite satisfactorily explained with a 'wholly purified' structural analysis, while other phenomena of the same class require explanation in a combination of structural and psychological terms? Or can all social phenomena be more fully understood by bringing in both kinds of analysis? I am not sure where Fortes stands on this issue. At least it is clear that, in his view, one kind of explanation cannot be reduced to the other, either way on. Writing of kinship institutions, he says they have only two major facets; they serve as a mechanism for organizing social activities and coordinating social relations, and they constitute the primary mould of the individual's psycho-social development. These are two different levels of organization and expression, and neither can be reduced to the other. *The web of kinship* is a study at only the first of these two levels. However, as noted earlier, Fortes holds that, in the study of educational processes and ritual systems, sociological analysis has to precede psychological analysis. His position emerges at its clearest when he adds: 'We have taken into account the genetic development in the individual of the modal patterns of thought, action, sentiment, and emotion which emerge in kinship relations, only in so far as this development is a dynamic factor in the social structure or can be directly correlated with the operation of kinship in standard and recurrent social relations' (1949a: 339). There is a world of difference between a theory wholly purified of hidden assumptions about a conditioning process working on individuals, shown in Radcliffe-Brown's work, and an analysis which explicitly invokes psychological mechanisms where appropriate. The problem then becomes: when is this appeal to psychology necessary – never, sometimes, or always? Fortes does not give an answer, perhaps because he holds that it can be answered satisfactorily not by *a priori* discussions of interdisciplinary metaphysics but only by empirical inquiry and a pragmatic search for explanations. This is suggested by his statement that we have to accept the inevitability of a plurality of frames of reference 'at least for a considerable time to come' (1955a: 28). What happens later is left open.

   Outside the structural frame, then, Fortes's personal affinity is with psychology, while within the frame he recognizes, but is not much enamoured by, economic considerations. On the other hand he recognizes and appeals to physiological or biological factors. Although Fortes is interested in both the 'productive and reproductive resources' (1958a: 5) of social groups, it is the reproductive resources that receive greater analytical attention. There are, he says, 'biological determinants' affecting social processes (1958a: 1), but among these the need for food and shelter, stressed by Malinowski, is little used in explanation. He writes 'Even if we think of sexual tendencies and habits as belonging to the biological factors that set limits to kinship forms rather than as directly constitutive of them, we can no longer overlook them' (1957a: 186). Elsewhere he lists the biological determinants as 'the life span of the individual' and 'the physical replacement of every generation by the next in the succession of death and birth' (1958a: 1). The elementary family 'may be regarded as a biological necessity'
192

because of the long infancy of man (1951a: 337). Descent, he continually stresses, is a jural and not a biological concept, but nevertheless he writes that among the Tallensi lineage membership 'is created by the bare physiological fact of patrilineal descent' (1945a: 134). 'All Tale genealogical connexions,' he says, 'go back to the fact of procreation' (1949a: 135). Among the Ashanti, 'The relations of father and child are rooted wholly and solely in the fact of paternity' (1950: 267). It is clear then that for Fortes structural analyses have to deal not only with social relations and moral imperatives, with customs and institutions, but also with 'bare physiological facts' which presumably exist independently of any cultural interpretation that may be put upon them. In the realm of kinship, and indeed throughout Fortes's writings, the most important of these bare facts are birth, copulation, and death. These are, as it were, inescapable facts in the sense that no human culture can ignore them; something must be done about them. As Fortes put it, 'Two "facts of life" necessarily provide the basis of every family: the fact of sexual intercourse is institutionalized in marriage, the fact of parturition is institutionalized in parenthood' (1959c: 149).

From these introductory remarks we can readily see that we have to deal with an author whose analytical apparatus does not lie exposed on the surface of his writings, and whose works abound with remarks that are superficially contradictory but which on careful scrutiny can be seen to be reconciled in some elliptically stated conceptual scheme. My method of exposition will be to discuss first what kinds of analysis Fortes aims at, and to describe his analytical toolkit. I then look at the way these tools are used in practice in analyses of structure and organization. A full examination of Fortes's intellectual position would require also an extended discussion of his views on how the individual is related to society and culture in which he grows up, as well as comments on Fortes's work on moral order and the ritual domain. Unfortunately an adequate treatment of these topics would take us beyond the bounds of this book.

2 Aims

In *The web of kinship* Fortes says: 'We shall not attempt a full-dress study of Tale family life; here we are concerned only with the structurally significant norms' (1949a: 78). He goes on to emphasize that no two people are absolutely alike, and to refer to 'the elasticity of actual social behaviour within the limits of the norms'. In another paper published in 1949, he gives four different meanings to the term 'norm' – the constant elements, the mean or mode, the lawyer's precedent, and the moralist's ideal pattern (1949c: 58) – and in the analysis of Ashanti households that follows he uses the term apparently in the first of these senses. Thus he writes that among the Ashanti 'there *appears* to be no fixed norm of domestic grouping' (his italics) and that 'the norm is that the structure of a woman's household is based primarily on her children, especially her daughters, and it is very little affected by their social maturation' (1949c: 61, 81). The norms thus appear to be invariant, or comparatively invariant, features of actual behaviour. The same emphasis on behaviour rather than on ideal pattern emerges in his inaugural lecture, where he argues that it is 'reasonable to suppose that human society exhibits regularities consistent with those found in the rest of nature' and that the mode of operation of each factor at work on any particular occasion in the life of a society can be foreseen within known limits of error (1953c: 34, 36). Yet Fortes is far from being a simple behaviourist, as can be guessed from his preference for the first, or constant, meaning for norm rather than the second, or statistical, usage. His position can be inferred from his discussion of Malinowski's work. He deals with the distinction frequently made by Malinowski between 'ideals' and 'reality', and shows how at least two distinct contrasts are involved. There is 'reality' in the sense of actions, feelings, and thoughts, directly observed by the ethnographer and admitted by the actors, contrasted with 'ideal', verbal statements by missionaries and native informants in response to generalized questions (1957a: 160). In this contrast Fortes, along with Malinowski, comes

194

down firmly in favour of reality. But for Malinowski there was also a contrast between the 'reality' of individual loves, hates and self-interest, sentiments and emotions, and the 'ideal' laws and morals, rights and duties. Here Fortes, unlike Malinowski, clearly prefers the 'ideal', and says that Malinowski's procedure 'is to turn the facts inside out, so to speak' (1957a: 164, 165). Thus in this context the regularities or norms that Fortes seeks to identify have to deal with laws and morals, rights and duties, but these phenomena emerge in observed social action rather than in response to abstract questioning. These are clearly social phenomena in that, for instance, the rights enjoyed by any individual exist only as part of a publically recognized system of rights, and persist, at least as a first approximation, independently of the use or abuse made of these rights by any particular individual. Other norms relate to the behaviour of one individual towards another, but again they are not necessarily identical with the actual behaviour of any given individual. Thus, after a discussion of the relation between a person and his real and classificatory parents, Fortes writes:

> We are defining the gradations that can be observed in the tone and emphasis of the child-parent relationship in the broadest terms. We are speaking of norms; and as we have previously remarked, the norms do not always emerge as simply as this in the actual relations of parents and children (1949a: 143).

Here 'gradations' refers to the relations with own parents, mother's co-wife, father's own brother, father's classificatory brother within the inner lineage segment, and so on. There are 'actual relations' between individual persons and their own and classificatory parents, and from a study of these there 'emerges' a range of norms. How this emergence occurs is not exactly clear, for the norm is neither the average nor the highest common factor of the aggregrate of observed relationships. For the actual relations, Fortes goes on to say, 'are subject to the distorting influence of many social and personal factors'.

What is clear is that norms are not merely matters of rights and duties; they have 'tone and emphasis' and embody emotional and ceremonial elements as well as jural and moral statements.

The same search for behavioural features that are frequent and approved and yet which are not necessarily identical with any behaviour actually observed appears in Fortes's discussions of the work of Radcliffe-Brown. Fortes mentions the distinction drawn by Radcliffe-Brown (1952: 190–199) between social structure and structural form and says that it is of doubtful validity; Fortes's 'structure' is equivalent to Radcliffe-Brown's 'structural form'. I think that here Fortes is wrong, and that Radcliffe Brown's distinction can be defended, but that is not what I want to stress. What is of interest is the argument Fortes uses here to criticize Radcliffe-Brown. Fortes argues that the distinction must be rejected because Radcliffe-Brown sees structure as an actually existing concrete reality, whereas in fact structure cannot be seen in this way. Structure is discovered by comparison, induction, and analysis, and is far removed from 'the tissue of actual social life'. When we describe structure 'We are, as it were, in the realm of grammar and syntax, not of the spoken word' (1949c: 54, 56, 59).

Thus we can see that Fortes is not dealing with simple observed behaviour, nor is he concerned only with explicitly stated customs or cultural themes. As he says of the structurally significant norm of filial piety, or pietas, among the Tallensi, 'It is not a formally elaborated doctrine, as among the Chinese, nor a dogma of faith, as among the ancient Hebrews, nor a legal principle, as in ancient Rome, but a diffused norm of conduct' (1949a: 171). Yet it would be quite wrong to infer that because structure is removed from concrete reality, Fortes holds that, in Lévi-Strauss's classic phrase, it has nothing whatever to do with concrete reality. On the contrary, it has a great deal to do with 'the tissue of actual social life'. The kind of relation envisaged between them can be glimpsed from Fortes's statements about Radcliffe-Brown and 'norms'. He argues that Radcliffe-Brown was concerned with, among other things, 'norms of conduct' required or permitted in different kin relations. Fortes says: 'The regularity – the standardization, if we like – of these norms is a necessary feature of the regularity of the relationships. They are matters of right and duty, as well as of standardized sentiment' (1955a: 24). Similarly he says that the form of Ashanti domestic organization derives from a paradigm or cultural 'norm' sanctioned by law, religion, and moral values (1949c: 60). We can see that in this formulation the term 'norm of conduct' comes to be synonymous with 'custom', or perhaps to include 'custom' as an explicitly institutionalized 'norm'. This usage may be adequate for an analysis of the simplest subsistence societies, but it requires refinement before it can be applied rigorously to more complex societies where what is sanctioned is sometimes different from that which occurs most frequently, and where the desiderata of law, religion, and moral values do not always coincide. This is the problem that Fortes tackles in his papers on Ashanti kinship, but while his work adds very considerably to our understanding of Ashanti, the concept of 'norm' still remains cloudy.

In highly diversified societies (Fortes puts Ashanti into this category) 'norms' cannot be discovered by inspection or haphazard comparison; rigorous methods of a statistical kind are needed (1949c: 59, 61). But, as Fortes himself realizes, a statistical analysis can tell us only how frequently various combinations of characteristics occur, and we have to turn to other sources for information about the sanctions of law and the like. The brilliance of Fortes's analysis lies in his choice of the right characteristics to measure, a choice clearly influenced by his prior knowledge of Ashanti culture. He records the age and sex of household heads, and contrasts their distribution with those of dependent household members. These are classified as lineage and non-lineage kin and by type of genea-logical relation. Women are classified by marital status, and so on. Tables of cross-classification provide a full statistical picture of Ashanti households. It is clear that many types of household exist, and that households with certain combinations of attributes are more common than others; some conceivable types do not occur at all. Fortes shows that in most households with female heads, the members belong to, or form, a matrilineal segment. Non-lineage members are found more frequently in households with male heads. As they grow up, sons tend to move out of households with male heads more than do sister's sons. No man lives under the same roof as his wife's brother. And so on. Fortes summarizes his analysis by describing the 'normal or model' household in the two localities included in his sample. He then describes the 'factors' which operate in varying force to produce the various norms, one factor being 'the tendency to seek a compromise between the opposed ties of marriage and parenthood on the one hand and those of matrilineal kinship on the other' (1949c: 83).

Fortes's analysis of Ashanti domestic arrangements is also noteworthy for his treatment of the notion of time and of the transition of particular households from one type to another with the passage of time. He uses analytical procedures developed in his books on the Tallensi, and carried further in more recent work; we shall have more to say about them later. Apart from these special features, his method of analysis may be summarized as follows. There is first a statistical examination of the relative frequency with which various combinations of social attributes occur in the population sampled. The characteristics selected for analysis are chosen because they are assumed to be meaningful in the culture of the people concerned, and the comparatively frequent or infrequent occurrence of various combinations of attributes is explained as due to the differential operation of various factors, these also being derived from the ambient culture. In other words, we construct a model of 'what actually happens' and explain its operation in terms of the values, sentiments, rights, and duties of the actors.

There is some circularity in this procedure, in as much as a characteristic in the statistical analysis may reappear unchanged as an explanatory factor, as with 'sex of household head' in this instance. There is also circularity or tautology to the extent that evidence for the strength of the various factors

198

is provided by the statistical results which are to be explained. Thus Fortes writes of married women that

> During the first two or three years of wifehood the great majority of young wives continue to reside with their own kin. Young and inexperienced, they cling to their mothers. As they advance in maturity the pull of conjugal ties increases and reaches its maximum at the peak of the childbearing years, in the thirties . . . The bias at Asokore is in favour of conjugal ties, but so strong are the ties of matrilineal kinship that nearly half of all married women, even at the peak of their child-bearing years, prefer to live with their own kin (1949c: 77–78).

In this passage, the first sentence repeats in words statistical information given more precisely though perhaps less accessibly in a table on the same page, but also makes use of information available elsewhere about the age of first marriage of Ashanti women. The second sentence draws on further ethnographic data to explain the first. In the third sentence we meet 'the pull of conjugal ties', but the only measure of this is the proportion of married women who are found to be living with their husbands rather than elsewhere. In the last sentence we have 'the ties of matrilineal kinship', and again the only available measure of the strength of these ties is the proportion of married women who live with their matrilineal kin. That these proportions are the only available measures seems to be clinched by the next sentence: 'At Agogo, . . . the pull of matrilineal kinship is three times as strong as that of marriage, at the peak of child-bearing.' 'Three times as strong' can only be another way of saying that of the 45 married women at Agogo, aged 31 to 40, 14 were living with their husbands while the other 31 were living away from their husbands, mainly with close maternal kin. Alternatively, the age range under scrutiny is 21 to 40, with 30 women living with their husbands and 103 living away from them. Whichever age range we take, we have merely a restatement of a statistical distribution in less precise but more vivid language, in more plausible and insightful

199

language perhaps, but not a correlation of household types with strengths of structural forces, as might appear at first sight.

But if we look past these quantified pulls and ties, we soon discover that Fortes delineates a most instructive model or picture of what in later publications he called the 'developmental cycle' of the Ashanti household. The notion of a developmental or growth cycle is set out in *The web of kinship*, where it is applied most fully to the joint family (1949a: 63–77). Fortes makes use of an idea found in the work of many of Malinowski's pupils, that temporal processes extending over many years may be studied during a delimited period of field-work by making observations in several localities or situations that conveniently happen to have reached different phases of the same process. Thus in the course of a few months of field-work the ethnographer can study infants, adolescents, young married couples, and aged widows and widowers, and from the data collected can infer the main characteristics of the seventy-odd year long process of growing up, marrying, and getting old. This technique of investigation received what was perhaps its most explicit statement in a paper by Richards (1932), and was often associated with the study of processes of social change due to persistent European influence in African tribal societies. In his early discussion of culture contact, Fortes (1936a: 53–54) attacks some aspects of this technique as it had come to be used, and stresses the advantages of studying processes of change by continuous observation over a period of years. His own application of what is essentially the same kind of analytical technique concerns processes of repetitive development, not non-repetitive social change, and the units undergoing the process are neither individuals nor whole societies but social units like joint families and nuclear lineages (1949a: 182–184). At any moment of time many different types of Tale joint family, or Ashanti household, are found to exist alongside one another. Earlier writers had sometimes interpreted evidence of this kind as indicating the presence of a diversity of genetically disjoint forms of social organization, or as evidence

200

for the persistence of traces of social organization from an earlier evolutionary phase. Fortes stresses that the various observed forms are not genetically disjoint but can be placed on a single or multiple sequence or cycle, such that any particular family or household changes with the passage of time and with the social maturation of its members from one type to another later in the cycle. As Fortes puts it, with reference to a study of families in British Guiana, 'where others have seen only a confusing medley of family "types" there is in reality a definite developmental sequence related to a few clear principles of conjugal and parental relationships' (1956b: xii). The process is analogous to the deduction of a sequence of stellar evolution from the contemporary evidence of stars of various brightness and sizes, as in a Hertzsprung-Russell diagram (cf. Sturve 1950: 31–46; Barnes 1967a: 89).

In his later work this technique is applied to domestic groups in general, with three main phases distinguished: expansion, from marriage to family completion; dispersion, from marriage of the first child to marriage of the last; and replacement, ending with the deaths of the founding parents (1956b: xii; 1958a: 4–5). In other words, we have a model in which cyclical time is an intrinsic dimension. The model is of 'what actually happens' or at least is based on 'what actually happens' rather than of ideas about what happens or ought to happen. Nevertheless the developmental process, having emerged from the empirical data, joins the conceptual universe of factors and forces and principles which, as we shall see, are the constituent elements of Fortes's models of society. Thus in the present context Fortes writes that 'Residence patterns are the crystallization at a given time, of the development process' (1958a: 3). Analytically posterior to the observed residence patterns, the development process becomes logically prior to them.

The notion of time, in one form or other, seems intuitively to be entailed in the concept of process, and Fortes is more aware than almost any of his colleagues of the need to recognize time as an indispensable analytical dimension (cf. 1944: 363). Custom and social organization, he says, are 'processes in

H

time' (1953c: 42) and recent research has displayed an 'endeavour to isolate the conceptualize the time factor' (1958a: 1).
He also sees the importance of distinguishing the various kinds
of time we have to handle in analysis and description. Lévi-
Strauss is perhaps the only other contemporary anthropologist
to write at such length on time (cf. Barnes 1971), and although
he and Fortes both derive their ideas to some extent from
Evans-Pritchard's work (1939; cf. Fortes 1945a: xi), they
diverge from one another and from him in terminology as well
as in emphasis. With Fortes this sensitivity towards the notion
of time seems to have sprung from his concern to recognize
certain kinds of time, but not all kinds, as necessary elements in
his analyses of social phenomena and yet not to waver in his
loyalty to the doctrine that as a social anthropologist in the
tradition of Malinowski and Radcliffe-Brown he is concerned
with synchronic analysis and not with historical reconstruction
(cf. 1953c: 25).

This dilemma shows itself in his remarks about the controversy which has continued sporadically for more than half a
century on whether or not anthropological studies belong to
history (cf. Evans-Pritchard 1961; Schapera 1962; Smith
1962). This, says Fortes, is a futile debate into which anthropologists are trapped (1953c: 28, 30). Yet by taking this stand,
he surely falls into the trap himself. His careful study of the
concept of time, and his discussion of synchronic versus
diachronic modes of analysis, convert the debate into something
far from futile. In his earliest exposition of the concept of time,
he says that it is 'a difficult methodological task to incorporate
the time dimension (which, be it noted, is not the same as
chronology) into a synchronic analysis' (1944: 363). His
commitment to synchronic analysis can be seen even in his
early paper on culture contract. This, he says, is a 'dynamic
process', a statement that can mean only that we are concerned
with a temporal sequence, and probably with the interaction of
'forces' as well. But in the same paper Fortes warns against the
danger of the anthropologist becoming a social historian, and
urges that investigators should study 'the dynamics of culture

contact as this is actually observable in the field' (1936a: 24, 53). In his later work, we have on the one hand his obvious concern with many aspects of time, as for example in the statement that 'The concept of social structure essentially implies ordered extension *in time* as well as ordered articulation *at a given time*' (1945a: 224, his italics; cf. 1944: 363; 1945a: 32). On the other hand we have the equally emphatic statements that synchronic study is 'the *sine qua non* of functional research' (1953a: 20), and that the essence of the social anthropologist's task is 'the investigation of *contemporaneous interconnections*' (1958b: 596, his italics). These statements appear less contradictory when we learn that 'the synchronic unit is not necessarily the year or two devoted to fieldwork' (1953c: 42). It covers at least three generations, corresponding to Marett's notion of 'the social present'. Thus the contrast he seems to have in mind is not between an instantaneous and a diachronic study but between an analysis using a model in cyclical time and one in which events are merely arranged in chronological sequence. His dislike of instantaneous analyses of social phenomena is suggested by his critical comment on what he calls 'billiard-ball sociology', dealing with 'individuals who are visualized as devoid of biography and therefore of social experience' (1957a: 160, f.n.1).

In his most explicit statement on kinds of time, Fortes distinguishes between time as duration, continuity, discontinuity, genetic or growth processes, and historical sequence (1949c: 54–55). Historical sequence seems to be merely an ordinal relationship between events, while duration relates to the fact that social events, such as ceremonies, do not happen instantaneously. Although they may take a day or a week or a month to complete, this duration 'is an extrinsic factor having no critical influence on the structure of social events or organizations'. By this, I understand Fortes to mean that the structure of these events would be unaltered if they took, say, two days or two weeks or two months to complete. His comparative lack of interest in economic factors, and hence in time or duration as a scarce good, is apparent here. Continuity, on the other hand, is 'an intrinsic and critical characteristic of some social events or organizations'. He exemplifies this by saying that 'all corporate groups, by definition, must have continuity'. Here I take him to mean that a significant feature of the description or analysis of a social phenomenon can be that it persists unchanged, as for instance when he says that 'the lineage tends to be thought of as a perpetual unit, expanding like a balloon but never growing new parts' (1953a: 31).

In an earlier context he distinguishes two kinds of continuity found within a lineage. Straightforward, cumulative continuity is seen in the notion of patrilineal descent, whereas dialectical continuity is manifest in the ousting and replacement of the paternal generation by the filial generation (1949a: 135). Dialectical continuity would seem to be what we have called cyclical change. The opposite of continuity, he says, is discontinuity, and here again I take him to mean that a significant feature of some phenomenon may be that at some point in time it changes abruptly. With growth processes, time, he says, 'is then correlated with change within a frame of continuity'. This might suggest that he is here referring to cyclical changes, and his use of the adjective 'genetic' as a synonym for growth supports this view, in the light of his references elsewhere to genetic psychology (1938: 7; 1949a: 339) and genetical analysis (1958a: 3; cf. 1957a: 169) focused on the maturing individual. But this seems not to be intended, for he says that growth processes are more marked in societies that are not in equilibrium, and that 'growth is the product of two kinds of forces symbolized by the passage of time, those of continuity (conservative forces) and those of non-reversible modification'. Thus Fortes seems to include both what I would call cyclical and irreversible processes under the rubric of genetic or growth processes. In his study of Ashanti households, he elucidates the cyclical processes that make up the developmental cycle of the household, and refers in particular to the results of the irreversible process whereby 'the social and cultural changes of the past thirty to forty years' have affected Asokore, one of the two townships studied, while the other, Agogo, has escaped disturbance from outside (1949c: 61, 63). Likewise he provides statistical evidence for a decline, during the same period of time, in the frequency of cross-cousin marriage, and attributes this to an increasing tendency to segregate the conflicting fields of conjugal and parental kinship and matrilineal kinship (1950: 282). But these irreversible processes of change are studied in their consequences rather than in themselves and in all his work cyclical processes retain the centre of Fortes's interest.

This emphasis on models in cyclical time can be seen in two features of Fortes's analysis of Tale society, the temporal continuity of the pattern of lineage segmentation and the extent of social differentiation. In most societies with an agnatic lineage framework we find typically that adults claim to be descended from a named ancestor n generations back from themselves. If this pedigree was a true record of events, then had the observer arrived twenty-five years earlier he would have found the same named ancestor placed $n - 1$ generations from contemporary adults, while if he arrived twenty-five years later the ancestor would be $n + 1$ generations back. It is usually assumed that the pedigree is not a true record, and that at whatever point in time the observer arrives he will find that the ancestor is placed n generations back from living adults. In almost all cases this assumption cannot be checked, for there are no contemporary records from the past and the observer observes only once (cf. Barnes 1967b: 120). For the Tallensi, Fortes says unequivocally that 'no historical validity can be attached to Tale genealogies beyond the time of the great-grandfathers. A genealogy maps out a particular set of lineage relations, it is not a true record' (1944: 370; 1945a: 36). The pedigree is kept constant in length by telescoping (1945a: 35). Structurally insignificant immediate ancestors are dropped from the list, just as genealogical links to collateral segments that die out are also forgotten (1944: 367, 1945a: 32; cf. 1953a: 32).

It seems to me significant that Fortes's interest is concentrated on the upper levels of the pedigree, which he postulates as unchanging, and on the lower levels, where cyclical processes can be directly observed. The middle levels, where telescoping and the irreversible process of fading away are presumed to occur, receive much less attention.

Fortes's analysis of the Tallensi is based almost entirely on his own field observations, for prior to his work very little had been published on the area and there seem to have been no significant contemporary colonial records. It is therefore on the basis of the oral testimony of his informants alone that he is able to make inferences about social conditions before he arrived in Taleland. In the introduction to *Dynamics* he says: 'I was impressed, in the field, with the apparent stability of Tale society over the historical time span consciously recognized by the natives, that is, five or six generations, and probably for a much longer period' (1945a: ix–x; cf. 1945a: 65). In the analysis that follows, this historical limitation tends to be overlooked. The analysis proceeds on the assumption that Tale society has in fact been stable for an indefinite period. The ground plan of the social structure is said to have been laid down 'in the distant past' (1945a: 33), and Fortes is not concerned with when this was or how it happened. This stance is of course in conformity with Radcliffe-Brown's rejection of the search for origins by the methods of conjectural history, but its effect is to give to parts of Fortes's model of Tale society eternal qualities that are just as conjectural, even if highly plausible. Tale lineage pedigrees go back beyond the six generations of ostensibly historical time-span (e.g. 1945a: 216, for nine generations at Tongo), and although some present clan settlements may be ten generations or two or three centuries old (1945a: 65; 1949a: 5) it seems clear that the upper levels of pedigrees stand for events or relations that are not necessarily conformal with those occurring now or in the recent past (cf. 1950: 276, f.n. 3). Fortes is obviously aware of this, as for instance when he writes that 'the ties claimed between corporate lineages are conceptualized as perpetual *kinship bonds* originating in matrilateral filiation' (1959a: 195, his italics). Here we are presented with the Tale model, which may or may not reflect the true

206

historical facts. Fortes makes no claim for historical accuracy when he reports that 'Tallensi think of the lineage as a continuous, even eternal, group. But then he goes on to say that 'A maximal lineage once established can never split into two or more independent (i.e. mutually exogamous) maximal lineages' (1945a: 201), and in the context it is not clear whether this is merely what the Tallensi think or Fortes's own view of what has actually happened. The question of how a new maximal lineage can be established except by splitting off an existing maximal lineage is left unasked and unanswered. In the same context Fortes writes that 'Segments of a clan or maximal lineage have the same structural position relatively to one another as they had in the beginning, only on a different scale; and in the beginning segmentarily related lineages sprang from brothers'. The examples he gives in his work of changes of scale (e.g. 1945a: 215–217; 1949a: 182–184) relate to the top or bottom rather than the middle of the segmentary hierarchy. Thus at the higher levels of segmentation, the Tale perception of segments as existing in perpetuity seems to cause Fortes to describe them as really existing unchanged for ever, while at the lower levels he tends to write in terms of developmental cycles rather than of non-cyclical changes due to population changes, exhaustion of the soil, and the like. This difference in treatment between higher and lower levels, a difference that to some extent is forced on the anthropologist by the kind of data that is available from acephalous societies without historical records and without any sense of cumulative history (1945a: xi), shows itself in Fortes's remarks on the 'architectural' way of looking at the structure of Tale society adopted in *Dynamics* (1945a: 232). He says, 'We have been analysing the product of social segmentation rather than the process itself.' In *The web of kinship* he is more concerned with the lower levels of segmentation and the study of process occupies a larger part of his analysis. The two parts of his analysis were published separately, four years apart, and hence it is easy, as with Evans-Pritchard's two books on the social system of the Nuer (1940 and 1951b), to overlook the possibility that between the two parts a crucial area of social and cultural relations remains unexamined (cf. Barnes 1967d).

Fortes infers that the Tale population has been increasing steadily in the recent past (1945a: 156). This inference is compatible with an increase in the population of each small segment as its apical ancestor becomes separated from the living members by an increasing number of generations. Fission within the joint family occurs in response to economic needs, among other things (1949a: 67), and these needs presumably are directly correlated with the number of mouths to be fed, so that a steady increase in total population entails continued fission at the lowest level of the segmentary hierarchy. But this in turn implies that although segments may preserve their structural position relative to one another, they do so not only on a different scale but also with increasing span (generational distance between the living and the apical ancestor) and rising degree of internal segmentation. Hence the number of orders of segmentation lying between the maximal and minimal levels must be also steadily increasing. These demographically determined phenomena, alas, require a quite different non-cyclical model of Tale society and cannot be accommodated in the eternal-cyclical model Fortes provides.

Throughout his books on the Tallensi, and when contrasting the Tallensi with the Ashanti, Fortes stresses the homogeneous quality of Tale society. He speaks of their 'almost complete absence of economic differentiation, by occupation or by ownership of resources, and in particular the absence of both material and institutional possibilities for capital accumulation or for technical advance' (1945a: x). In discussing fertility among the Tallensi, he says that 'except for a handful of chiefs and headmen, who are atypical of the general population in every respect owing to modern conditions, there is very little variation in the standard of living . . . or of hygiene' (1943: 99) and so he concentrates his attention on the typical population. His discussion of the pilgrim traffic to the Tong Hills in central Taleland which 'has brought violent competition into the sphere of the common ritual interests and values' of the Hill

208

Talis is relegated to a section on 'Modern factors of disequilibrium' at the end of *Dynamics of clanship* (1945a: 251–258) and does not form part of his main analysis. Likewise he mentions three Tale chiefs who have thirty, eighty, and perhaps a hundred wives (1949a: 72) and yet in another context writes that 'the social system of the Tallensi is so balanced that no single clan is likely to be able to draw more heavily on what might be called the total pool of marriageable women available in a given socio-geographical region than any other clan of that region' (1943: 112). These discrepancies do not necessarily invalidate his analysis, but it is apparent that Fortes's interest in any given situation is likely to lie in the analysis of those features that are characterized by homogeneity and persistence, rather than in a description of the possibly heterogeneous whole. His interest is firmly in 'what actually happens' but not in 'everything that actually happens'. In his first paper on the Tallensi he stresses that 'the political and legal behaviour of the Tallensi ... is as strongly conditioned by the ever-felt presence of the District Commissioner as by their own traditions', and the European influences among the Tallensi 'are so diffuse and pervasive that one has to take account of them in every routine observation of social practices, situations and institutions'. Yet despite this state of affairs, Fortes writes that 'the fundamental institutions, practices and beliefs of the community seem to be sufficiently vigorous to countervail the intrusion of contact influences' (1936a: 23, 46, 47, 49). What we have in Fortes's writings on the Tallensi is thus a penetrating analysis of these 'fundamental institutions, practices and beliefs' rather than a comprehensive account of Tale social life.

An interest in 'practices', however 'fundamental' these may be, explains Fortes's use of statistical data. We have seen how he employs statistics in his inquiry into Ashanti households, and in general he argues that 'elementary statistical analysis is indispensable for the elucidation of certain problems of social structure that arise in a society which is in the process of becoming socially diversified' (1949c: 83). He describes part of

209

his work in Ashanti as intended to show how far certain customary laws and conventional ideals are actually followed (1954a: 255). For instance, in his discussion of attempts in Ashanti to segregate the fields of matrilineal kinship and patrifiliation, Fortes refers to the common view that 'a child stays with its father till adolescence and then goes to his uncle, or, if a girl, to her husband'. The reader is at once reminded of the classic Trobriand model; but the temptation to import into the Ashanti picture Melanesian features that do not belong there is checked abruptly by Fortes's next sentence. 'Many individual cases conform to this generalization, but it is not universal; indeed not more than 10 per cent of adults fit the rule' (1950: 273).

In non-homogeneous societies, diversity in the pattern of social relationships makes measurement necessary (1948b: 166). Only numerical analysis can show what 'degree of freedom' if any exists in, for instance, the choice of where a couple should set up house after marriage (1958a: 4). Individual choice and initiative 'are not at variance with institutional prescription but are contained by it' (1963b: 62; cf. Leach 1962) at least in some instances, and the relative frequency of various possible choices not only indicates how an institution works in practice but can also bring to light some of its unstated features. Fortes maintains that surveys aimed at collecting data for numerical analysis cannot replace intensive studies. He adds that they can usefully precede intensive inquiries (1948c: 6), but his own work in Ashanti surely shows that it is only after detailed investigations have been made, not necessarily by the person conducting the survey, that a perceptive choice of characteristics for numerical analysis can be made. His Ashanti inquiry draws greatly on the inquiries made earlier by Rattray and others. For although many of the characteristics analysed are stock features such as age and sex, the object of statistical inquiry is, for Fortes, the elucidation of the working of institutions. Presumably these must be identified in broad outline before the survey can begin. Indeed Fortes states that his statistical results from Ashanti can be understood fully only

210

in the light of 'descriptive and qualitative data' (1948b: 169; cf. 1949c: 67–68).

Although most of Fortes's statistical work concerns the Ashanti, he also supplies some numerical information about the Tallensi, and presumably he would argue that in any society, however homogeneous, statistical inquiry can have confirmatory value even if it does not provide much fresh insight into the characteristics of the social structure concerned. In one passage, he argues that whereas 'culture' refers to the qualitative aspect of social facts (cf. 1945b: 221), the concept 'structure' is 'most appropriately applied to those features of social events and organizations which are actually or ideally susceptible of quantitative description and analysis' (1949c: 57). In this sentence, 'quantitative' could refer to frequencies and other measures summarizing the immediate results of numerical inquiry; alternatively, Fortes may be here referring to quantitative statements of a more abstract order, as for example the remark referred to earlier, that 'the pull of matrilineal kinship is three times as strong as that of marriage' (1949c: 78). Whichever construction is put on this contrast between structure and culture, it is difficult to make it tally either with a view of culture as 'the facts of custom and social organization' expressed in Fortes's inaugural lecture (1953c: 15), or with the more subtle notion, mentioned above, that social structure is 'the entire culture of a given people handled in terms of a frame of theory', the 'theory' being the interpretation of custom as symbolizing or expressing social relations (1953a: 21). A similar contrast drawn at one point between the 'form' of Ashanti domestic organization, derived from a paradigm or cultural 'norm', and its structure, which is 'governed by internal changes as well as by changing relations, from year to year, with society at large' (1949c: 60), is also out of line with the meaning Fortes usually gives to the concept of structure. I would argue that quantitative description and analysis are applicable to any social fact, whether or not the fact relates specifically to social relations. Any characteristic can be analysed numerically on a continuously variable scale, or digitally, or in terms of a simple binary present-or-absent choice. Whether or not the characteristic concerns social relations makes no difference. Likewise we have to look at the qualitative aspects of social relations in order to understand our numerical data, just as we have to with other features of culture and custom. Fortes's comment on the need to consult 'descriptive and qualitative data' to interpret numerical results seems to support this position.

The qualitative richness of Fortes's analysis of Tale social structure belies his equation of structure with that which may be analysed quantitatively. The ambivalence in his attitude towards statistical analysis seems to me to emerge strikingly in an exchange of views between Leach, Murdock, and Fortes which we have already examined from Murdock's point of view (above, pp. 38–39). After giving his hearty and enthusiastic agreement to Leach's assertion about social structures as the statistical outcome of multiple individual choices, Murdock continues with a criticism of Fortes's use of the notion of bilateral descent; this we shall look at later (below p. 241). In his reply, Fortes (1961c) refers to Murdock's support for Leach's conclusion as constituting 'common ground' between Murdock and himself. Even if we ignore my own contention that Murdock and Leach are actually saying quite different things, we still have to conclude that if Fortes agrees with Murdock and/or Leach on this point, then he must have changed his view significantly between 1949 and 1960. Leach says that for his assertion he is indebted to Fortes's 'highly germinal essay' of 1949, and Fortes draws attention to this. On my reading of the 1949 paper, however, it certainly does not entail Leach's conclusion, let alone Murdock's. On Leach's interpretation, Ashanti social structure would seem to be equated with the average or model pattern of social relations. Indeed, in his book on *Pul Eliya*, he writes that 'The social structure which I talk about in this book is, in principle, a statistical notion; it is a social fact in the same sense as a suicide rate is a social fact' (Leach 1961a: 300). But we have seen that Fortes's account of social structure among both Ashanti and Tallensi is far from this. When Fortes speaks of 'structurally significant norms' he is, as we have seen, using 'norm' in the first, invariant, sense and not in the second, statistical, sense as set out in his list of four usages. Leach's use of the concept of social structure seems to put it back into Radcliffe-Brown's realm of 'concrete reality' from whence Fortes has tried to rescue it.

It is perhaps Fortes's wish to operate at both levels simultaneously that accounts for the comparatively slight attention that he has given to the concept of social organization, particularly as developed by Firth (1964, Part I; cf. Stanner 1966). Indeed the effort 'to combine in a single account both structural and organizational analysis' causes, in Firth's view, most of the difficulties in *The web of kinship* (Firth 1951: 158). Fortes is, of course, aware of the analytical obstacles he has to overcome. He writes:

> The principles underlying the structure of a society are never embodied in a perfectly unambiguous way in its social institutions. Social life, even in the most stable and unprogressive of societies, demands continual reshufflings, readjustments, and revaluations of social relationships. (1945a: 183).

The detailed accounts of particular individuals acting on particular occasions which occupy such a large part of both the books on the Tallensi provide evidence for these reshufflings, readjustments, and revaluations, but the analysis, and the generalizations drawn from it, are concentrated on the principles underlying the structure and not on the readjustments themselves. In a later paper, Fortes gives us a brief analytical sketch of a generalized process of choosing a wife, using the language of the theory of games (1962a: 2–4), but this is exceptional. Almost all his other generalizations are concerned with structure rather than organization.

Occasionally these generalizations take the form of testable propositions. For instance he states that 'The more centralized the political system the greater the tendency seems to be for the corporate strength of descent groups to be reduced or for such corporate groups to be nonexistent' (1953a: 26). Other generalizations assert merely that one social fact 'fits in with' or 'is

213

THREE STYLES IN THE STUDY OF KINSHIP

related to' another, and although they may be enlightening they remain untestable. Thus he says that the identification of grandparent with grandchild 'fits in with the widespread concept of the completion of the cycle of the generations in three successive steps and with contrasting roles of grandparents and parents in the family system' (1955a: 19), and that 'The high value attached to fertility is related to many features of Ashanti culture and social organization' (1954a: 266). In connexion with the latter generalization, the importance of the matrilineage, the cult of lineage ancestors, and the need for sons for worship of the patrilineally specified *ntoro* are all mentioned.

So far are we still from a rigorous social science that statements of this kind are analytically valuable, even though they can scarcely be put into refutable form. Fortes seems to be aware of the primitive state of our science when he says, with reference to the two principles of the unity of the sibling group and the unity of the lineage enunciated by Radcliffe-Brown, that

> ... they are statements of laws of kinship organization which have a validity of the same order as the statements of general tendencies enshrined in such economic concepts as that of marginal utility, or such psychological concepts as that of the conditioned reflex ... These propositions have been verified by field observations (1955a: 20).

I cannot see how the principle of the unity of the sibling group can be treated as a verifiable proposition, any more than the concept of marginal utility can be verified. To me they are both analytical notions that have proved descriptively useful and which may be used as terms in testable propositions. We shall have more to say about principles in the next section along with other analytical notions used by Fortes.

3 Analytical armamentarium

Fortes describes his book *The dynamics of clanship* as 'a descriptive analysis' (1945a: viii), indicating that the book contains both descriptive data, mainly the transcription of observations of Tale social life made in the field, and an analysis of Tale social structure. The distinction that he has in mind is set out at length in his paper on 'Analysis and description'. Here he argues that 'The essence of description is that observations are grouped together in accordance with their actual relationships and contexts of time and place' (1953b: 1). In this sense, description would seem to be much the same as chronological narrative. However Fortes precedes the sentence quoted with a paragraph in which he says that a statement such as 'Among the Tallensi a first-born is prohibited from eating fowl' (cf. 1945a: 66–69) is analysis at a fairly elementary level and 'For practical purposes it can be regarded as description'. There is no actual relation set in time and place in the statement, so it seems that Fortes sees the two categories of analysis and description as overlapping. Analysis can proceed at more than one level. It makes use of 'ideal isolates', a term Fortes attributes to Whitehead. These isolates are theoretical constructions which collectively form, or should form, a theoretical system. 'The ideal isolates must have meaning in terms of the descriptive reality of social life', and must have a 'counterpart in social reality'. Fortes emphasizes that 'customs and institutions are not isolates' but like 'the family' and 'sacrifice' are descriptive units. On the other hand 'lineage' is an isolate, though of less generality than 'rights *in personam*' (1953b: 193). I find it difficult to understand why 'lineage' should be granted analytical status while this is denied to 'family' and 'sacrifice', particularly since Fortes describes sacrifice as 'The core of Tale ritual thought, doctrine, and performance' (1945a: 98) and devotes the final paragraph of his essay on ancestor worship to its analysis (1965a: 140–141). He also writes of 'such general comparative categories as matrilineal descent or segmentary political system' (1961b: 212), which may perhaps be thought of as jural isolates, while there are other comparative categories which are not jural. Thus he says that following Radcliffe-Brown we 'begin by establishing an analytical or paradigmatic isolate of social structure – e.g. a lineage system – or of ideology (thought, belief, value, etc.) – e.g. a totemic system'. He contrasts this procedure with that advocated by Malinowski in which the investigator has 'to begin from an empirical isolate of custom, e.g. the Kula, or the Chisungu' (1961b: 21). Here, 'empirical isolate', or 'activity' as he also puts it, would seem to be equivalent to his earlier 'descriptive unit'.

Analysis, we may say, is for Fortes a process of emancipation. We begin with empirical isolates, which I visualize as undiluted chunks of activity delimited only in space and time, and move towards statements about the relations between analytical isolates, each of which may be associated with a plurality of events that may be dispersed in space and time. The contrast is not so much between analysis and description as between analysis and 'concrete reality'. Description is needed to show how the analytical isolates correspond to the facts of concrete reality. For example, in Fortes's words:

> The method of analysis we have followed in this study has required, for purposes of description, the isolation of the lineage system from the domestic organization of the Tallensi. In the actual life of the natives, however, these two planes of social structure do not emerge in isolation from each other. Like blood and tissue in the animal organism, they constitute interpenetrating media of Tale social life. Membership of a family and membership of a lineage are equally and often concurrently decisive for the conduct of the individual and for the course of his life. Yet the analytical separation of these two planes of social structure is not entirely artificial (1949a: 12; cf. 1944: 372).

Here Fortes casts himself as a combination of surgeon and field geologist. How does the investigator decide where to cut into the tissue of time and space, along what planes of structural cleavage to strike? Fortes provides no general recipe, apart from the implicit advice to look for rights *in personam*. Also, by implication, he does not advise beginning with the analytical apparatus, or home-made model, such as it may be, used by the members of the society concerned. For instance, the concept of 'lineage', which dominates the analysis in both the Tallensi books, has no single analogue in Tale speech but corresponds to certain usages of three distinct terms, *vir* (house), *dug* (room) and *biis* (children) (1949a: 10–11).

In dividing up the job of analysis, Fortes uses in his later work the notion of 'domain'. This appears to be synonymous with 'plane' in the passage just cited, and with 'aspect' and 'level' at various other points in his work. Thus *The web of kinship* is said to deal with 'the domain of family life' (1949a: vii), and we have 'the internal system, or to be more specific, domain of the domestic group' contrasted with the external politico-jural domain (1958a: 6; cf. 1959a: 196, 210). There is 'the total genealogically defined domain of social relations', necessarily dichotomized into a kinship side and an affinal side (1962a: 2). Wider still are the domains of kinship (1949a: vii), non-kinship (1962a: 2), and ritual institutions (1958a: 13), as well as the internal domain of caste (1959a: 195) and the external domain of the political and the religious order (1962b: 65). 'In the study of kinship and descent,' says Fortes, 'we are dealing with institutions that operate in various fields, or as I now prefer to say, domains of social structure' (1959a: 195). In this taxonomy, internal and external seem to be purely relative terms, referring to the comparative scale of the social relations involved. The distinction he makes between internal and external structure, or aspects of structure, is similar (1959a: 194). By 'domain' I understand Fortes to mean a set of interconnected persons and groups such that any member's status is acknowledged consistently throughout the set. Thus he states that among the Lakher matri-determined rank is recognised in the internal lineage domain but not in the external politico-jural domain (1959a: 210). In general an individual is a member of several domains, a kinsman in the domain of kinship, a citizen in the politico-jural domain, a husband–father in the domestic domain, and so on. Domains are linked not only through overlapping or inclusive membership but also through a variety of institutions. Fortes specifically mentions classificatory kinship institutions, unilineal descent corporations, and age sets, along with the great variety of institutions and organizations through the medium of which

217

citizenship is exercised, as linking the internal domain of the domestic group and the external domain of the total social structure (1958a: 6). The admission of the adolescent child to membership of the politico-jural domain is commonly legitimated by *rites de passage* (1958a: 9).

Fortes sets out this analytical scheme in a paper published in 1958 and his subsequent papers conform to it. The terminology used in his earlier writings is somewhat different but the ideas are essentially the same. Thus the contrast he makes between the political and domestic 'aspects' of matrilineal descent among the Ashanti in his 1950 paper is essentially a contrast between the politico-jural and domestic domains (1950: 254, 261), though in another context 'anthropological aspect' (1948b) refers to the structural frame of reference, not to some anthropological domain. Elsewhere he refers to 'the plane of lineage relations' and 'the plane of domestic relations' (1949a: 45), and to the investigation of social structure at the 'levels' of local organization, kinship, corporate group structure and government, and ritual institutions (1953a: 29; cf. 1957a: 175). Here, planes and levels are domains; but when Fortes writes that 'It is easy and tempting to jump from one level of organization to another in the continuum of body, mind and society when analysis at one level seems to lead no farther' (1949a: 345), he is of course referring to different analytical frames of reference. The term 'field' is harder to pin down. When he writes that in analysis we must 'distinguish between the domestic field of social relations . . . and the politico-jural field' (1958a: 2; cf. 1953a: 26), 'field' is a synonym for 'domain'. However in other contexts Fortes writes of 'fields of clanship' (1945a: 61–65), a feature of the Tale politico-jural domain, and the 'field principle', which appears in the Tale domain of extra-clan kinship as well as in the politico-jural domain (1945a: 76–77, 102; 1949a: 286–293, 343; cf. 1962a: 4). These two notions are connected to each other and to a third notion, that of a 'field of social relations', to which Fortes gives a restricted meaning (1945a: xi, 233). Presumably the term 'domain' was introduced to provide an escape from these other connotations.

218

A domain is thus an analytically delimited part of the social structure. Fortes analyses or explains the pattern of social relations found within any domain by reference to 'principles' or 'axioms', the former relating to structure and the latter to culture. The field principle just mentioned is only one of a broad spectrum of principles which are invoked as required. Fortes often uses the word 'principle' in an everyday sense, as for instance when he writes of 'the basic principle of Tale exogamy, that consanguinity, however remote, is always a bar to marriage' (1945a: 97). The specialized and unspecialized usages may be found together, as when he writes that 'It is a cardinal principle of Tale social structure that every social grouping defined as a unit in one situation, or according to one principle, dissolves into an association of lesser and different-iated units in another situation or according to another principle' (1945a: 21). But in many contexts he identifies named principles that appear to enjoy some kind of conceptual discreteness and autonomy. In particular, in his comments on Radcliffe-Brown and on the structural frame of reference he mentions 'a limited number of principles of wide validity' (1953a: 39; cf. 1951a: 346; 1955a: 17) by which social systems can be apprehended as a unity. Fortes never attempts to provide an exhaustive list of these principles, and much of his discussion of Radcliffe-Brown's work turns on only two of this limited number, the principles of the unity of the sibling group and of the unity of the lineage (1955a: 18, 20; cf. 1949a: 234, 242–243; 1945a: 244). Radcliffe-Brown is also associated with the principle of functional consistency (1955a: 22, 24), and the principle of reciprocity (1949a: 198–203; cf. 1953 b: 193; 1957a: 174, 188) with Malinowski. Fortes himself appeals frequently to the principle of equilibrium (1940: 244, 271; 1945a: x; 1949a: 341) and of the equivalence of alternate generations (1949a: 275), and he contrasts the principles of descent, filiative kin right or filiation, and perpetual succession (1959a: 193, 212). Some principles are especially emphasized. For instance, patrilineal descent is 'the vertebral principle of Tale social organization' (1944: 336), kinship is 'the articulating principle' (1949a: 338;

cf. Firth 1957: 577), while among the Ashanti the rule of matrilineal descent is 'the dominant principle' (1950: 283). In the
analysis of religion Fortes appeals to Oedipal and Jobian
principles (1959b: 11). Sometimes principles are paired, as
when he writes of 'The principle of the unity of the sibling group
and its correlative the principle of the unity of the lineage'
(1955a: 20), and of 'The principle of segmentary differentiation
and the associated principle of dynamic coherence' (1949a: 2).
The two principles of patrilineal descent and maternal origin
'are always complementary in their action' and 'run like a cry
and its echo' through Tale social structure (1944: 379; 1949a:
30).

This partial list shows that we have to deal with a mixed
bag of principles, with some principles more general than others,
and with some associated with kinship and others not. The principle of, say, the equivalence of siblings is more specific than
the principle of kinship itself, and the principle of reciprocity
is said to be only a special case of the principle of equilibrium
(1949a: 215). We even have what might be regarded as a
meta-principle in 'that ever-recurring principle of Tale social
organization, the conjunction of polar forces, the synthesis of
tendencies that work in opposite directions' (1949a: 197).

Fortes uses these principles to describe and explain various
features of social life and social structure. For example, among
the Tallensi a widow may be inherited only by a man classified
as her dead husband's 'brother' or 'grandson' in his clan or in
a linked clan, or as his 'sister's son' in some other clan. Fortes
explains this by reference to the two principles of the equivalence of siblings and the equivalence of alternate generations. In
accordance with the first principle, a 'brother' of the dead husband is equated with the dead man himself, and hence may
inherit his widow. Any Tale woman, so the Tallensi say, might
have been a man but for the accident of birth; had she been a
man, she would have had the right to inherit the widow of her
dead clan 'brother'; because she is actually a woman she cannot
exercise this right herself, but it is exercised for her by her son,
who is 'sister's son' to the dead man. Thus this form of widow

inheritance is also explainable by appeal to the principle of the equivalence of siblings. Inheritance by a 'grandson' is explained by the principle of the equivalence of alternate generations (1945a: 52, 150–151; 1949a: 224–225, 274–275). Similarly the division of rights in a matrilineal society is explained by saying that 'A matrilineal father's rights over his children are based on the principle of filiation, the mother's brother's on the principle of descent' (1959c: 197). In more general terms, Fortes explains the dominance of the kinship principle in Tale social organization as due in part to the fact that their primitive technology 'puts a premium on principles of social organization that can be maintained in action by direct interpersonal relationships' (1949a: 344).

These then are at least some of the structural principles of wide validity. The crucial term here is 'wide', for it seems that the analytical procedure followed by Fortes is to appeal to the various principles as convenient, rather than to attempt to show that they are always operative. A good example of this is provided by his discussion of the ethnographic fact that among the Namoos, one of the major divisions of the Tale population, a man's first-born child, whether son or daughter, must not eat domestic fowl, and during his lifetime must neither wear any oɪ his garments or quiver nor look into his granary (1945a: 66). Among all Tallensi a first-born daughter may not uncover her mother's chief storage-pot while the mother is still alive (1949a: 223, 232). A first-born son who has reached marriageable age must not meet his father face to face in the gateway of their common homestead but a first-born daughter may do so (1949a: 225–226). These practices are explained by reference to the principle of the cleavage between successive generations, the principle of the equivalence of siblings, the fact that the granary symbolizes the sentiments and ideas associated with the struggle for food as well as the security of the domestic unit and is 'rigorously private' to the head of the household, the equation of the gateway with the 'ideological and jural dominance of the male line of descent', the identification of a man's granary, cap, tunic, bow, and quiver as emblems of his individuality, and so on (1949a: 55–61, 226–234). Fortes also gives the Tallensi explanation of tension between father and son in terms of the concept of *Yin*, which he translates as 'personal Destiny'.

This analysis is explanatory, in that it relates several superficially disparate customs to the operation of two principles which manifest themselves in Tale social life in many other ways, and to the symbolic associations of various material objects which likewise appear in many features of Tale culture. The analysis is also limited, in that it leaves many questions unanswered; for example, why is it that although a man is identified with his granary and his quiver throughout Tale society, it is only among the Namoos that his first-born son must taboo these objects? In other words, if the principle explains the custom, is there an antithetical principle to explain the absence of the custom? It is clear that Fortes does not intend his principles to be understood in this way. His explanations are not stated as testable propositions, and although they are 'verifiable' in as much as they make good sense and fit new data, they remain plausible and persuasive rather than proven. Fortes asserts that structural principles 'work together in mutual dependence' (1953a: 25) but, in my view at least, this working together amounts in Fortes's analysis to nothing more than a process of trial and error, and the explanatory principles are made to exert, as it were, an unpredictable and intermittent influence on the form of social structure. This is perhaps what Fortes has in mind when he argues that 'The combination of factors that make up a particular occasion in the life of any society are not predictable and never will be,' though holding that social laws can be stated as probabilities (1953c: 36). His view on this matter is stated again in connexion with the structural analysis of witchcraft accusations. He says that this method of analysis brings us nearer 'to understanding the machinery by which norms are made effective, not only in a particular primitive society but in a type of primitive society. It does not explain how the norms come to be what they in fact are in a particular society' (1953a: 38). At one point he states that 'Tale society is an organic society. That is to say, social organization is

222

governed by the same principles at all levels and in every sector of the social structure' (1949a: 341; cf. Gluckman 1963: 75–83). This suggests that he is contrasting Tale society with other societies that are not organic and where various principles operate only in delimited parts of the social structure.

Principles apply mainly to social organization and structure, while culture is described in terms of 'axioms' and 'absolutes'. Fortes uses 'axiom' in the sense of a statement or proposition, usually on evaluative statement, which the actors concerned accept without requiring further explanation or justification. Thus he writes that among the Tallensi, kinship 'furnishes the primary axioms of all categories of inter-personal and inter-group relations' and has an 'absolute, *a priori* character' (1944: 372, 376); Tale ritual observances go down 'to the axiomatic ideas and values that underpin the social structure' (1945a: 134); the starting-point of Tale lineage solidarity 'is the fundamental moral axiom of Tale social organization, the axiom that kinship is binding in its own right' (1945a: 249); kinship is 'the rock-bottom category' of Tale social relations. Unlike patrilineal kin, Tale 'Affines have no axiomatic ties' (1949a: 18, 119). More generally, every social system presupposes basic moral axioms, and 'Modern research in psychology and sociology makes it clear that these axioms are rooted in the direct experience of the inevitability of interdependence between men in society' (1949a: 346). In slightly different terminology, Fortes writes that in Tale thought the ancestors are the 'jealous guardians of the highest moral values, that is to say, the axiomatic values from which all ideal conduct is deemed to flow. The first is the rule that kinship is binding in an absolute sense. From this follows the second rule, that kinship implies amity in an absolute sense. The third rule is the fundamental one. It postulates that the essential relationship of parent and child, expressed in the parent's devoted care and the child's affectionate dependence, may never be violated and is, in that sense, sacred. It is indeed the source of the other rules' (1959b: 53). This passage brings out Fortes's mode of analysis well. We have three axiomatic values which, at first glance, might each be taken as a datum of

Tale culture that has to be accepted as input to the analysis, neither requiring an explanation nor capable of being explained within the structuralist framework. But it immediately transpires that the three so-called axioms are not of equal logical status, and that the first two are derived in some way from the third. Whether this derivation is made 'in Tale thought' or by Fortes in his analysis or both remains obscure, but the choice of the third axiom as the source of the other two suggests that Fortes is here again looking over his shoulder at that 'modern research in psychology and sociology' mentioned earlier, even if this lies outside his structuralist limits.

In this connexion, a critical notion used by Fortes is 'sentiment'. Radcliffe-Brown, who like Fortes received his early training in psychology, made great use of this notion in his analysis, as for instance in his statement that 'The cohesion of a social group . . . depends directly on the existence of a collective system of sentiments or affective dispositions that bind every member to every other' (Radcliffe-Brown 1948: 286; of Fortes 1955a: 26). Fortes uses the term in the same sense, and we have mentioned his use of 'norms' to include norms of 'standardized sentiment' (1955a: 24). The child's affectionate dependence is presumably an example of a standardized sentiment found in most or all human societies, while more specifically filial piety or pietas among the Tallensi is described as 'a complex of conduct and sentiment . . . felt to be an absolute norm of morality' and a 'binding moral principle' (1961a: 174–175; 1949a: 171). In his discussion of the work of Malinowski Fortes speaks of 'emotions and sentiments' as contrasted with 'laws and morals' or 'rights and duties' (1957a: 164, 169), but in his own work on the Tallensi it is usually sentiment alone that is contrasted with jural rights and duties. Thus he notes that the relation between a woman and her brother's child is 'devoid of a definite jural coefficient and is not subject to organized ritual sanctions' and does not have economic and domestic associations; hence 'A woman's bonds with her brother's children are fundamentally bonds of sentiment' (1949a: 334; cf. 1949a: 295). Radcliffe-Brown (1957: 45–52; 1958: 64; cf. Srinivas 1958: xiv) emphasizes the distinction between social anthropology and psychology, and does not relate his use of the term 'sentiment' to its technical meaning in psychology. However, it seems likely that he was aware of the work of McDougall (1908) and Shand (1914) and we know that Malinowski admired the work of these two psychologists (Fortes 1957a: 168). I assume that Fortes uses 'sentiment' roughly in the same sense as they do, though they disagree from one another in some respects. Sentiment is then a tendency or disposition to experience an organized system of emotions or feelings relating to some particular object. The objects that Fortes is principally concerned with are other individuals standing in specified kin relation to the actor, and symbols associated with these relations and with cultural axioms.

The three main ingredients on Fortes' analytical scheme begin to emerge. There is the social structure, whose characteristics can be explained by reference to various principles of different orders of generality, and to culturally determined symbols and values. Then there is the culture, consisting of axioms or premisses that are accepted, at least by the actors, as binding in their own right. Lastly there is the system of standardized sentiments or affective dispositions which presumably bears the same unresolved correlation to the emotions, thoughts, and feelings actually experienced by the actors as does the social structure to the actually existing relationships of concrete reality.

This tripartite division is, I believe, implicit in Fortes's analysis but, as expressed here, it is my construction rather than his design. I may have divided what Fortes sees as a continuum. For instance, it is obvious that the notion of kinship is not confined to one division, for it appears both as a principle and an axiom. Moreover, it is 'an irreducible principle' (1949a: 340) and also 'an irreducible factor in social structure that has an axiomatic validity as a sanction of amity and solidarity' (1959a: 209). It is difficult to give any precise analytical meaning to this use of the adjective 'irreducible'. Fortes mentions the 'irreducible facts of parenthood, siblingship and marriage' (1959a: 212); Ashanti think of the tie between mother and child as 'an ultimate and irreducible moral and psychological fact which needs no sanctions' (1949c: 72); the 'source (though not its *raison d'être)*' of peitas is 'the irreducible fact of parenthood' (1961a: 174); 'The *dug* (that is, a woman and her children by one man) constitutes the irreducible unit of Tale social structure, both jurally and morally' (1949a: 62); is there, he asks, 'something like an elementary "cell" of family organization susceptible of empirical identification and irreducibly necessary for the process of social reproduction' (1956b: xii)? There are many meanings here. With the Ashanti, Fortes presumably implies that they do not explain the mother–child tie in terms of anything else, and with the elementary cell, that it would have to be present in complete form in every society (cf. 1949a: 344–345). With the *dug*, I presume that he means that it is the smallest unit, whereas with parenthood we may be back among the 'bare physiological facts'. Perhaps siblingship and marriage fall into the same category, or perhaps it is merely that these are concepts found in all cultures. Whatever the right answer may be, it seems certain that Fortes does not mean that structural analysis can merely accept marriage, parenthood, and the rest as logically primitive input and output terms that it can rearrange but cannot dissect. On the contrary Fortes shows how these analytical terms can be related to folk concepts and physical events, and how they can be dissected and correlated. The fact that kinship emerges in his analysis as both a principle of social structure and an axiom of culture makes this plain.

4 *Structure and organization*

Both the societies studied by Fortes in the field have a system of lineages, patrilineal among the Tallensi and matrilineal among the Ashanti. When writing about these two societies Fortes has had to deal with a dual problem which many ethnographers face but which is not encountered by those social scientists who confine their studies to industrialized societies. He has had to separate analytically the small domestic family from the larger social groups which utilize the same descriptive

STRUCTURE AND ORGANIZATION

language and the same principles of recruitment and internal differentiation as the family and yet are quite unlike it in size, persistence, specialization, activities, and organizing sentiments; and at the same time he has had to elucidate the connexion between the real family and these pseudo-familial groups. In most industrialized societies a few traces of extra-familial familism continue: the king who is father of his people, the Mother Superior, God the Father and God the Son, Brother Brown of the Boilermakers Union, and my uncle who knows the right people. But these are merely traces; nepotism persists only in the interstices of social structure and descent is an organizing principle in neither the administration of justice nor the production of heavy machinery. Among the Tallensi quite other conditions prevail. Justice, warfare, religion, and agriculture all employ the same organizational language as the domestic family, for, as we have seen, Tale society is organic, and the same principles operate at all levels. The unit of organization for all large-scale Tale activities is the lineage, whose internal segmentation 'follows a model laid down in the parental family' (1953a: 32). Likewise relations between large lineages are in many instances 'couched in the idiom of kinship' (1945a: 97). Fortes distinguishes between 'kinship in the wide sense' and 'kinship in the narrow or strict sense' or 'consanguinity', these analytical terms corresponding, in many though not in all contexts, with the Tale categories *mabiirət* and *dɔyam* (1945a: 61, 117, 259). Relations of affinity are excluded from *dɔyam* (1949a: 16), whereas kinship in Fortes's narrow sense includes both 'consanguinity and affinity', in Morgan's phrase (cf. Radcliffe-Brown 1952: 51). With these distinctions in mind we can mark out somewhat arbitrarily four parts to Fortes's analyses of Tale and Ashanti social structure. First, there are those features that relate specifically to 'kinship in the wide sense', and which arise in that politico-jural domain where kinship, in this sense, either alone or in conjunction with others, operates as an organizing principle. Second, there are features which either are common to, or characterize in different ways, kinship in both senses; we are here concerned with the interconnexions

227

of the politico-jural, the internal lineage, and the genealogically defined domains. Third are those features that relate to what we might call 'the web of kinship in the strict sense', i.e. to the genealogically defined domain, and fourth we have the special features that appear in the family or domestic domain.

The political organization or, in his later terminology, the politico-jural domain, Fortes sees as the widest framework of social structure (1953a: 29) The notion of politics implied here is that of relations between or within large groups (1940a: cf. Fortes and Evans-Pritchard 1940: 5–7) or between corporations sole that are enmeshed in large-scale relations (1953a: 29–30), rather than the process of making alliances and competing for rewards which may pervade all parts of the social system (cf. Fallers 1963: 312; Barnes 1968: 107). 'Politicking' goes on throughout Tale society, as Fortes's books show vividly and in detail, but, as mentioned above, the study of political process, in this sense, lies outside his analytical objectives.

In the label 'politico-jural' the word 'jural' is used rather than 'judicial' to sharpen the contrast between the enforcement of law by constituted judicial machinery in a centralized state and the jural institutions of stateless societies based on the right of self-help (Fortes and Evans-Pritchard 1940: 14–15). Firth (1951: 157) criticizes Fortes for obscurity in the use of 'jural' in *The web*, and suggests that the word seems to refer to moral rights and perhaps to something more. Taking together all Fortes's writings up to 1949, the word seems to refer both to enforceable rights within the clan, or thereabouts, where some kind of 'rule of law' prevails – 'general observance of rights and obligations in property relations, in person-to-person relations, in intra- and inter-group relations subject to enforcement by explicit or implicit sanctions' (1945a: 235–236) – as well as rights outside the clan enforceable only by the sanction of self-help. In other words, it refers to the kinds of rights that courts might enforce, but for the fact that there are no courts. In his later writings, the contrast with 'judicial' is forgotten, and the politico-jural domain is used as an analytical concept both for those societies like the Ashanti where there are courts and

228

other constituted judicial machinery as well as for courtless
and stateless societies like the Tallensi.

The inhabitants of Taleland, numbering about 35,000, are
divided into some fifty or more named units designated maximal
lineages (1945a: 4, 109). These lineages are 'the smallest corporate units that emerge in political action'. In other words, the
political system is a system of maximal lineages and of unions
of maximal lineages. Our main interest is in kinship rather than
politics, and so little need be said here about the Tale political
system in this sense. The constituent maximal lineages unite in
two main forms. There are exogamous clans, 'the largest corporate units that act in political matters' (1945a: 103), and
fields of clanship. The largest clan, a Namoo clan called Mosuor
biis, is identical with the maximal lineage which has Mosuor
as its apical ancestor, and its male members live in several
spatially discrete settlements. Other clans are localized, and
most of them consist of two or more maximal lineages which do
not claim to be agnatically related to one another. The constituent lineages of a clan unite to perform funeral ceremonies
following the death of a clan member, and the clan has a common External Shrine. Every maximal lineage is also linked to
other maximal lineages in clans other than its own, and the
various lineages in a clan usually have distinctive sets of extra-
clan links. These extra-clan links Fortes refers to as 'ties of clanship' in order to indicate that they are similar to, though not
identical with, the links between the constituent lineages of a
clan. Ties of clanship entail exogamy and cooperation on specified occasions. More attenuated than ties of clanship are relationships between lineages which Fortes calls 'clanship-by-
courtesy' (1945a: 62, 64, 72, 82-91). We have therefore a system
of maximal lineages, joined in a network of three kinds of links,
though Fortes stresses that the three kinds are better thought of
as forming a continuum and that the link between two lineages
may change its quality with the passage of time (1945a: 85).
In addition to these links, lineages or whole clans are joined in
relations of cooperation in connexion with various cults and
politico-ritual offices (1945a: 109). Many links cross the major

cultural dichotomy in Tale society, that between the Talis and the Namoos. Fortes describes the pattern by saying that 'So complex is the overlapping of the fields of clanship of adjacent and neighbouring maximal lineages that the whole system might be compared to a piece of chain mail' (1945a: 87).

What part does kinship play in this? There are three ways in which the organic quality of Tale society emerges. Relations between lineages are often, but not invariably, stated in the language or idiom of kinship. Thus the Namoo maximal lineage Ŋkoog is said to be descended from a man who was a relative, possibly a son, of Mosuor, the founder of the largest Namoo clan. There is a tie of quasi-clanship between Ŋkoog and Tongo, one of the subclans of Mosuor (1945a: 74). The Talis maximal lineage Yakɔra of Zubiuŋ clan is said to have been founded by a man who was brother to the founders of the maximal lineages Gbizug of Gbeog clan and Ba'at-Sakpar of Ba'ari clan, and is linked to these two lineages by extra-clan ties of clanship. The same lineage is linked by clanship to Yiraaŋ lineage of Zoo clan, and this is said to be because the latter's founding ancestor was a 'sister's son' of the founder of Yakɔra (1945: 82). Gbeog proper and Gbizug, the two maximal lineages constituting the Talis Gbeog clan, are descended from men who are said to have been brothers, sons of a priest of the Earth (1945a: 87). In these examples, linkages between lineages are explained by a kinship connexion between their founders. However, other linkages are explained differently. For instance, Yakɔradɛm and Kpaɣara-yaɣardɛm are two of the three maximal lineages in Zubiuŋ clan, but the former is said to be descended from the founder of Gbizug in Gbeog clan and the latter from immigrants. Likewise, Zoo clan contains two maximal lineages, Yikpɛmdaan and Yiraaŋdɛm. The former is a Namoo lineage, whose founder is said to have been a kinsman of Mosuor, while the latter is a Talis lineage. There seems to be no myth joining the founders of the two lineages (1945a: 79, 71). Here then we have consti-tuent lineages of a clan without any kinship link postulated between their founders. On the other hand, Fortes gives an instance where a kinship link is postulated without the existence

230

of a tie of clanship. Nɔŋsuur yidɛm lineage, part of the large Namoo clan of Mosuor biis, live on land belonging to Zubiuŋ clan; it is said that the first member of the lineage to settle there was a 'sister's son' of the then Priest of the Earth of Zubiuŋ. Present members of the lineage are classified as 'sister's sons' of their host clan but their lineage has no ties of clanship with any of the constituent lineages of Zubiuŋ clan (1945a: 59, 78). However, it is significant that the fact of residential proximity exists in this instance to perpetuate the postulated kinship link, and that Nɔŋsuur yidɛm, although a lineage, is not a maximal lineage. There is little or no evidence for assertions of kinship links between the founders of lineages without the existence of some continuing linkage to sustain the memory of the connexion.

The second way in which the mechanisms of kinship emerge at the level of clans and maximal lineages is in the evaluation of the linkages in this network. The constituent lineages of a clan, and lineages linked by extra-clan ties of clanship, are said to be *sunzɔp*, the ordinary word for 'brothers'. Even where no kinship connexion between founders is postulated, the members of some linked lineages are said to be *dɔyam*, kinsmen by consanguinity, as in Zubiuŋ clan (1945a: 79). In general, Tallensi say that members of linked lineages should behave towards one another as if they were brothers. In action terms, this means that they should cooperate as members of their respective lineages in sacrifices, funerals, food distributions, and other secular and ritual affairs. There are specific injunctions against intermarriage, and raiding for cattle; the widows of the men of one lineage may be inherited by men of the other; in former times members of one lineage were liable to be raided by outsiders in retaliation for debts incurred by members of the linked lineage (1945a: 90). The attributes are found with varying distribution and intensity in different linkages. The greater the distance, measured by the number of intervening clans, between two lineages, the smaller the likelihood that there will be a linkage between them, and if there is a linkage, the more attenuated it is likely to be. Thus the obligations and rights arising from inter-lineage links follow the same broad pattern of attenuation with increasing spatial and genealogical separation found between agnatic relatives within any lineage.

The third manifestation of kinship at the clan level is in the construction of the constituent units. These are patrilineal lineages, each with a founder whose descendants are the members of the lineage concerned. Everywhere in the world, the most distinctive morphological feature of lineages, particularly patrilineal lineages, is that their internal genealogical framework makes possible, and even invites, internal segmentation at a plurality of levels. The generation levels, as well as the potential lines of cleavage between full and half brothers, are built into the framework, and one intermediate generation level looks much the same as any other. There is no inherent discontinuity between one level and the next, so that any segment may be expected to have much the same form and function as a segment from one level higher or lower. Where there is some necessary discontinuity, as for example in the operation of a rule of exogamy, it is likely to vary in its point of application by a level or two from one lineage to another. Hence it is not surprising to find among the Tallensi that the major segments of Mosuor biis act in many contexts as if each was an independent maximal lineage (1945a: 62), or that the three major segments of what Fortes refers to as Gbeog proper maximal lineage, itself part of Gbeog clan, have separate extra-clan ties of clanship and cult with other maximal lineages (1945a: 86–88, 108–110). It seems that there is no single Talni word for 'clan' or 'clanship' (1945a: 45, 61) any more than there is for 'lineage', and that these are essentially analytical notions used to describe connexions between various maximal lineages and major segments which are described, and presumably perceived, by the Tallensi in the idiom of kinship.

One last point on the clanship level of Tale social structure leads on to a consideration of features common to all levels. Some segments that participate as units in the network are what Fortes calls accessory lineages, in contrast to authentic lineages. There are two types of accessory lineage: an attached lineage is said to be made up of patrilineal descendants of a woman of the authentic lineage to which it is attached; an assimilated lineage is sometimes said to contain the patrilineal descendants of a man described as a 'kinsman' (in the wide sense) of the founder of the authentic lineage but 'it is whispered' that they are really the descendants of slaves or refugees (1945a: 40, 51–53). Although members of accessory lineages suffer ritual disabilities, some such lineages participate in the clanship network independently of the authentic lineage to which they belong. Thus for instance Pulien biis is an attached lineage belonging to Yakɔradɛm lineage of Zubiuŋ clan. Pulien biis has an extra-clan tie of clanship with a maximal lineage in Sakpee clan; this tie is not shared by the rest of Yakɔradɛm lineage (1945a: 79, 82, 84).

Even at the clanship level, then, we have to take account of the fact that a lineage is made up of a plurality of segments, and that each segment is divided internally according to the same plan as the lineage of which it is a part. The internal structure of the lineage is generated by the same principle operating at all levels. This is the principle of descent, and we have already encountered Fortes's insistence that this is essentially a jural concept. Among the Tallensi the rights and obligations that are entailed by segment membership concern, above all else, the cult of the ancestors but they extend to almost every form of collective activity. In every public event each man participates as a member of, or representative of, some lineage segment. The whole of the politico-jural domain, and not merely the clanship level, is characterized in this way, though below that level, so it would seem, there are no enduring linkages between segments belonging to different maximal lineages.

Fortes employs a comprehensive array of terms to identify segments of different kinds. To understand this array, we have first to grasp two general notions, span and order. In his book *The Nuer*, Evans-Pritchard (1940: 201) refers to the length of the genealogical line from the living members of a lineage segment back to their apical ancestor as the time depth of the segment; the totality of groups of living members within the segment constitute its width. Depth is always proportional to width among the Nuer. Fortes writes, in his first account of Tale political organization, of lineages of 'narrow span, i.e. with common ancestry placed four or less generations back' (1940a: 251), which suggests that his 'span' is equivalent to Evans-Pritchard's 'time depth'. This impression is reinforced by a sentence published four years later, where he says that 'Lineages vary in *span* proportionately to the number of generations accepted as having intervened between the living members and the founding ancestor from whom they trace their descent' (1944: 365). Fortes goes on to say that 'Lineages of the same order of segmentation are not all of equal span. The span of a lineage is a measure of its internal differentiation, whereas its order of segmentation defines its relations, as a corporate unit, with other units of a like sort' (1944: 370). The same two formulations are repeated in *The dynamics of clanship* (1945a: 30, 36). Fortes does not say so explicitly but I assume that the span of a lineage segment is found by counting its segmentary levels upwards from the bottom of the hierarchy, whereas the order of segmentation is found by counting downwards from the top. Since the number of segmentary steps from top to bottom is not always constant between one maximal lineage and another, or even between one part and another of the same lineage, it follows that there is no invariant relation between order and span. Much of the complexity of Tale social structure in the lineage domain seems to arise from the simple fact that the internal organization and activities of any segment are determined mainly by its span while its external relations are determined by its order of segmentation. Ancestors who are not the apexes of segments tend to disappear from Tale genealogies, as happens in most poly-segmentary systems, but some persist at least temporarily so that the number of generations between top and bottom of the hierarchy may be greater than the number of segmentary levels. Fortes claims that the putative time depth and the contemporary span of a lineage are perfectly correlated (1944: 364) but it appears from his own evidence that the time depth of a Tale segment may sometimes be greater than the minimum required for its span, due to the retention of segmentarily redundant ancestors in its pedigree.

Apart from the two parameters, span and order, there is a series of terms for segments at specific places in the hierarchy. A maximal lineage is the segment of widest span to which any of its members belong. A morphological minimal lineage consists of a living man and his children (1940: 243, f.n. 1; 1944: 365; 1945a: 30, 193, f.n. 1; 1949a: 4, 7, 9). These two end-points of the scale are easily fixed; difficulties arise only over the identification of intermediate points. In his early article on 'Kinship, incest and exogamy' segments were identified by generation depth and named in a descending hierarchy as clan, lineage, and sub-lineage (1936b: 239). This scheme of analysis was subsequently superseded (1944: 363, f.n. 2) and in later publications Fortes makes little use of generation depth as a parameter (cf. Schmitz 1964: 43). In his paper on 'The significance of descent', a segment one level below maximal is called a primary or major segment, and below this are secondary and tertiary segments (1944: 368). This series indicates order of segmentation rather than span. In *The dynamics of clanship* this series is repeated, with 'major' also used as a general indication of relative level (1945a: 31, 35). A third series is added, indicating span rather than order. The effective minimal lineage is defined as the segment of smallest span that emerges as a corporate unit in economic, jural, and ritual activities; this is the agnatic core of a joint family, and only very rarely contains members from four generations (1945a: 192, 198; 1949a: 9). Above that is the nuclear lineage, consisting of the male agnates of a single household or expanded family; its apical ancestor may be four to six generations back (1945a: 177–178, 205; 1949a: 9, 182–184). Two or more nuclear lineages constitute an inner lineage, this being the largest segment within which generational differences are consistently recognized. It is identified in Talni by the term *dug* used in a narrow sense, and its apical ancestor may be five to seven generations back. Two or more inner lineages form a medial lineage, though in some maximal lineages an intermediate level of segmentation is found (1945a: 205, f.n. 1).

Within a medial lineage, there is no common interest in land, and the seduction of a co-member's wife is not invariably considered to be a sin, as is the case within the inner lineage. A medial lineage is also known as *dug*, 'the wide *dug*' as Fortes puts it, and its apical ancestor may be six to nine generations back. A man cannot marry a woman who belongs to his mother's medial lineage. In some instances, above the medial lineage are major segments and above these maximal lineages; in other instances the major segment level is missing.

Fortes stresses that the assignment of a particular segment to one or other level in this third hierarchy may often be uncertain. He says that 'a lineage that functions as an inner lineage in one situation may be treated as a medial lineage in another' and that 'distinctions that hold at one period will not do so a generation later' (1949a: 10). Firth (1951: 158) argues that Fortes confounds two separate series, a morphological series of maximal, major, and minimal segments and a functional or organizational series of medial, inner, and nuclear segments. These terms I regard as constituting only one of Fortes's three series, and only the end terms appear to be morphologically, i.e. genealogically, specified. We have already noted that at the upper end of the scale, participation in the linkages of the field of clanship is not confined strictly to units that are maximal lineages, morphologically defined. Some major segments have their own sets of links, while in other cases whole composite clans participate as single units in the network. Moreover in some instances kinship links, even links of 'brotherhood' (*sunzɔp*) (1945a: 32) are postulated between maximal lineages without compromising their maximal status in Tale eyes. At the lower end, Fortes notes, in a paper published fourteen years after *Dynamics*, that his definition of the morphological minimal lineage as the children of one father has not been generally accepted (1959a: 207). Perhaps the reason for this is that units that are defined purely morphologically are, at least in Tale society, of no analytical utility. Relations between segments, and between members of segments as such, display constant properties only when the segments selected for comparison are defined functionally with respect to activities such as co-residence, farming, marriage, adultery, seduction, raiding, worship, affirmations of kinship, and the like in which these relations manifest themselves. The ethnographic evidence provided by Fortes indicates that a set of criteria involving these activities can be constructed to form a Guttman scale. What Fortes has done is to name the various portions of this scale. The Tallensi use the same scale, but have fewer names and label only part of the scale.

Taxonomic categories for lineage segments
Hierarchical dimension

Generation depth	Order	Span
clan	maximal	maximal
lineage	primary (*or* major)	major
	secondary	medial wide *dug*
	tertiary	[unnamed]
		inner narrow *dug*
		nuclear
		effective minimal
	morphological minimal	

5 Descent

As we have seen, the dominant principle operating in the Tale politico-jural domain is that of descent. We have also seen that it is not the only principle in this domain, even among the Tallensi; locality, slavery, political affiliation, and cultural affinity can also be seen operating at the level of clanship, and the relations between groups that this class of facts generate are, it seems, only partly translated by the Tallensi into the idiom of kinship. Furthermore, relations of 'sister's son' are found at this level as well as those of patrilineal descent; appeal is made to notions of kinship, in both the strict and wide senses, as well as to brotherhood. Nevertheless the concept of common descent is present, and below the segmentary level at which accessory lineages are attached, it is clearly the dominant organizing principle. The named positions on the segmentary hierarchy are defined by reference to a variety of criteria, but the existence of the hierarchy itself is due directly to the principle of descent.

In his paper on 'The significance of descent' and in *Dynamics*, Fortes has very little to say about descent as such; the word does not appear in the index of either Tallensi book. We hear a great deal of what it does but little of what it is analytically. In *The web of kinship* and in his Ashanti studies where he is more concerned with 'kinship is the strict sense', the concept of descent emerges more clearly, in contrast to filiation or maternal connexion. In his paper on unilinear descent groups in Africa he cites Radcliffe-Brown in support of the view that descent is fundamentally a jural concept, and that it provides the connecting link between the external and internal aspects, i.e. domains, of these groups (1953a: 23, 30; c.f. 1959a: 207). He returns to this theme in discussing Radcliffe-Brown's own ideas (1955a: 22), but it is not until 1959, in his paper on 'Descent, filiation and affinity', that Fortes discusses at length what he understands by the notion of descent. Here he argues that ambiguities have arisen because anthropologists have confused two distinct institutions, 'descent in the strict sense' and filiation (1959a: 206). This distinction only very roughly matches his earlier distinction between two aspects of kinship relations, that of lineage organization and that of interpersonal kinship ties (1949a: 340–341), and whereas the earlier distinction is easy to grasp, the later one is hard to pin down. His 1959 paper is fascinating but any certain definition of 'descent in the strict sense' can be teased out of it only with care (cf. Barnes 1962a: 408). Fortes says that descent (presumably in this strict sense) is descriptively defined as 'a genealogical connection recognized between a person and any of his ancestors or ancestresses' (1959a: 206), and he speaks of a descriptive as well as an analytical distinction between descent and filiation. This phrasing suggests that he considers that descent should be defined

238

analytically in terms different from its descriptive definition; but he does not provide a separate analytical definition. He qualifies his descriptive definition by limiting 'ancestor' to 'any genealogical predecessor of the grandparental or earlier genera- tion' (1959a: 207). Two persons whose pedigrees converge in common ancestor are said to be linked by descent; presumably this statement refers not to 'entire' pedigrees consisting of all ancestors in all lines but only those non-entire or partial pedi- grees used in any society 'for defining and identifying persons' (1959a: 206).

This descriptive definition makes no reference to descent groups, and it is this dissociation of descent from descent groups that has led to some confusion. Rivers (1924: 86) says bluntly: 'I will begin with *Descent*. Whenever I use this term it will apply to membership of a group, and to this only.' Most modern writers have followed Rivers in this regard, even when discarding other parts of his definition of descent, and Fortes has been misunderstood because he does not make explicit this break with recent tradition (cf. Leach 1962: 131; Scheffler 1966). It is only in isolation from the existence of groups that his statements about matrilineal descent among the Tallensi make sense. He says that 'matrilineal descent stands in con- trast to patriliny' and that 'the fact of matrilineal descent is given an institutional embodiment' in the concept of *soog* (pl. *saarɔt*), a word he translates as uterine kin. Likewise he stresses that the bond of uterine descent is maintained as a purely personal bond, and he refers to 'maternal descent' (1949a: 31, 32, 37, 161). These statements are made in *The web*, published ten years before he enunciated the distinction between descent in the strict and wide senses. Some of these references to descent may therefore be to what would later be described as 'descent in the wide sense' and to filiation rather than descent in the strict sense. Thus when he writes, in connexion with the physical layout of the Tale homestead, that it 'shows graphically the division of the family into two comple- mentary spheres . . .It is the line of cleavage between descent from the father (*ba dɔyam*) and descent from the mother (*ma*

239

dɔyam)' (1949a: 63), the reference is to filiation rather than
descent strictly understood. The other references cited from *The
web* cannot all, I think, be explained in this way and some must
refer to matrilineal descent *sensu stricto*, and not to matrifiliation.

There are no corporate matrilineal groups among the
Tallensi (1949a: 32) so that in this terminological scheme the
recognition in a given society of a specified mode of descent
does not in itself imply the existence of descent groups in the
same mode. However Fortes, in discussing the characteristics of
descent, argues that 'Since descent confers attributes of status
relating to a person's place in the external social structure it is
bound to operate by placing persons in categories or groups'
(1959a: 208). This is certainly true of patrilineal descent among
the Tallensi, but to what extent is it true of matrilineal descent
also? Though there are no Tale corporate matrilineal groups,
are there matrilineal categories? Or are there instances of that
twilight category, the non-corporate group? It is clear that
saarɔt is a matrilineal category. Every man knows who some of
his *saarɔt* are, but membership of the set is open, and Fortes
describes how men often encounter strangers only to discover
that they are really matrilineal kin (1949a: 40–41). For the
Ashanti, Fortes states that there are no jural or political rights
or duties derived from paternal descent (1950:267), but nevertheless a man is ritually and morally identified with all the
other descendants, by *successive steps of patrifiliation* of his own
father's father (1959a: 207). 'Successive steps of filiation' is
surely very close to 'descent'. In this case successive steps of
filiation serve to determine a closed category of agnates. Fortes
does not regard the Ashanti as having a system of double
descent (1963a: 58; cf. 1950: 253) and presumably the Tallensi
also, despite the recognition of both kinds of descent, are not to
be regarded as a double-descent society (cf. Goody 1961:
9–12).

On the other hand, the utilization of a given rule of descent
as the criterion of membership of a group does not necessarily
imply that the group is a descent group. Fortes is quite explicit

on this feature of his analysis, for he says that 'kinship or descent
may confer a title to membership of a political or cult or
economic "group". It does not make that "group" into a
kinship or descent "group" in any absolute sense' (1959a:
211). Unfortunately he does not give any clear examples of
this: indeed Scheffler (1966: 542) maintains that there are no
such groups. Fortes does state that citizenship in an Ashanti
chiefdom is acquired, at least by some of its members, by
descent (1959a: 207). An Ashanti chiefdom is made up of
several distinct matrilineal lineages and would not be classified
as a descent group, as commonly understood, but I am not
certain that Fortes would also exclude it. Likewise he says that
among the Tswana nobility, descent is the unequivocal source
of title to class (1959a: 208), and I can only assume that the
Tswana nobility do not constitute a descent group.

My uncertainty on this point springs from a consideration
of some of the hypothetical groups that Fortes does classify as
descent groups. He says that enclavement coupled with a rule
of compulsory endogamy, as with a caste or Jews in a ghetto,
or isolation as with Pitcairn Island, can produce a bilateral
descent group (1959a: 206), and that the Maori *hapu* would
have to be strictly endogamous for it to be a bilateral descent
group (1959a: 211). Murdock (1960a: 9–10; 1961) criticizes
Fortes for insisting on this endogamous requirement, though
this I think might be defended. The term 'bilateral' has never
been satisfactory; Fortes reads it in the strong sense of 'two-
sided, not one-sided' whereas most writers have used it in the
weak sense of 'one- or the other- or both-sided' (cf. Firth 1963:
22–23, 32, 35). Murdock's more telling criticism is that Fortes
in these instances seems to include in the category of 'descent
group' any group satisfying certain recruitment criteria, irrespective of how the group is organized internally. Fortes says
nothing about how an endogamous Jewish ghetto or a completely isolated island community would have to be internally
structured to qualify as a descent group and in his reply to
Murdock's first critical comment he (1961c) does not take up
this point.

Yet if some groups recruit their members by descent without thereby being descent groups, there must be additional criteria for deciding when a group is a descent group and when it is not. Recruitment by descent seems to be a necessary condition, though this is implied rather than stated; what are the sufficient conditions? To find an answer to this question there are five statements to consider. First, Fortes envisages the possibility of politico-jural marriage transactions, identical to those taking place between Kachin patrilineages, occurring 'between units not *internally* organized by a descent criterion' (1959a: 195, his italics). These hypothetical units might, I suppose, still be descent groups in Fortes's terminology, in as much as the hypothetical Pitcairn Island and Jewish communities are not internally organized by a descent criterion and yet constitute descent groups; but I think it more likely that Fortes intends here to make the point that political marriages can link non-descent groups, as for example the dynastic alliances of medieval Europe. Second, Fortes goes on to say that 'It is not enough to speak of descent or kinship or, in particular, of "groups", in general. It is essential to specify the structural domain to which the analysis refers' (1959a: 211). This suggests that a descent group must be a group in the domain of descent or, since descent is a jural concept, in the politico-jural domain; but this still leaves open the question of how to distinguish in this domain between descent and non-descent groups, since obviously in many societies there are non-descent groups in this domain, as for example in a European state. Third, Fortes says that he does 'not see how the concept of a "descent group" is applicable in the conditions of "ambilateral affiliation" described by Professor Firth for the *hapu*, for the "group" is never closed by a descent criterion' (1959a: 211; cf. Firth 1957; 1959: 110–114; 1963: 30–36). I interpret these three statements as meaning that for a group to be a descent group it must belong to the right domain and it must have members recruited by descent criteria, not by a mixture of descent and other criteria. The existence of marriage links between groups is not a sufficient condition for them to be descent groups. We have already seen that a necessary condition for a group to be a particular variety of descent group, namely a bilateral descent group, is that it shall be endogamous. Hence the existence of inter-group marriage links is neither sufficient nor necessary for the groups to be descent groups.

The last two statements about descent groups refer to pedigrees. Fortes says that 'Empirically, descent groups are constituted by the fact that all the members of a group in a given society have the same form of pedigree and all their pedigrees converge in a single ancestor or group of ancestors' (1959a: 208). This has to be reconciled with another statement that if there is obligatory endogamy as in a ghetto, enclavement 'can produce a common descent group none of the members of which need to know or establish their pedigrees in order to identify themselves or be accepted as members' (1959a: 206). The latter statement refers to a hypothetical group while the former begins with the word 'empirically', suggesting that the existence of common pedigrees merely happens to occur in those descent groups for which we have descriptions, rather than necessarily occurring because of the definition or nature of descent groups. This interpretation can scarcely be made to tally with the definition of descent as a genealogical connexion recognized between a person and any of his ancestors. Strictly interpretated, this entails identification of the ancestor and recognition of the connexion with him by means of a pedigree or some less specific device. If in the hypothetical ghetto there is nothing more than a shared belief that all members are in some way connected with unidentified ancestors by means of unspecified steps of filiation, it is stretching the definition to its limit to call it a descent group. It could then be argued, for example, that since according to Catholic dogma the whole of mankind is descended, in all lines but by steps unknown, from a known pair of ancestors, Adam and Eve, mankind as a whole, in the light of this dogma, constitutes an endogamous bilateral descent group. It seems better to me to stick to a narrower definition of descent.

The difficulty Fortes runs into on this point arises from his wish to separate the notions of descent group and descent, which is commendable, and from his apparent lack of interest, when constructing these definitions, in the internal structure of descent groups, which is surprising. His books on the Tallensi are as much concerned with the internal structure of lineages as they are with their external relations and with 'kinship in the strict sense', while even in the article we are discussing, he stresses that 'Surely the "ongoing structure" of any and every *unilineal* descent group, *looked at from within*, is determined by rules of descent' (1959a: 210, his italics). Again we meet the implied contrast between observed unilineal and postulated other, i.e. bilateral, descent groups. Pedigrees are met with even where no descent groups are present, as with the partly matrilineal pedigrees which link a Tale man with the ancestors of his Good Destiny shrine (1949a: 229–230; 1959b: 41–46), so that the existence of a pedigree is not a sufficient condition for the existence of a descent group. There seems to me to be no advantage in not making the existence of some kind of pedigree a necessary condition for the existence of a descent group, particularly when the analytical category of non-descent group with descent membership criteria is also available. Fortes' position seems to be that pedigrees are a necessary attribute of unilineal descent groups, but not of descent groups in general.

We can check the accuracy of this interpretation by looking at the examples of descent groups provided by Fortes. In 'Descent, filiation and affinity' he mentions that among the Ashanti, matrifiliation automatically creates title to lineage membership by descent, though for unencumbered citizenship an additional requirement must be met (1959a: 207–208), as we shall see later. A Tale jokes with his father's father when the operative relation is that of parent's parent to child's child, but does not joke when the operative relation is common descent in the lineage segment of which the father's father is head (1959a: 207). Fortes notes that the Kachin and Lakher have a social structure based on an association of exogamous corporate patrilineal descent groups (1959a: 209), and in his comparative article on unilineal descent groups (1953a) he refers to many other societies with lineages of the same general form as those found among the Tallensi and Ashanti. In effect Fortes's statements about descent groups, as distinct from descent, refer to two main types only: actually existing lineages, either patrilineal as among the Tallensi and Kachin or matrilineal as among the Ashanti; and bilateral descent groups hypothetically in ghettoes and on Pitcairn island. The lineages are exogamous and linked by marriage, while the bilateral descent groups are endogamous. The lineages constitute at least part of the politico-jural domain in their societies, whereas the area of operation of the bilateral descent groups is unspecified. Pedigrees are traced in the lineages, but need not be traced in the bilateral descent groups. From this summary it is apparent that these hypothetical bilateral descent groups lack the salient characteristic features of other descent groups, as Fortes defines them. Were they to exist, they would require separate analytical categorization. Since they are only hypothetical, I shall follow Murdock and say no more about them.

6 Filiation

We are left with unilineal descent groups. It is here that Forte's distinction between descent and filiation makes sense (cf. 1953b: 193). Therefore we shall forget about non-descent groups with descent membership criteria, descent groups without pedigrees, and the possibility or impossibility of bilateral descent, and shall concentrate on these societies where descent is unilineal and does determine the internal structure of groups. It is descent in this setting that Fortes writes about in his studies of the Tallensi and Ashanti, and in his comparative paper on unilineal descent groups in Africa.

The idea of filiation is used in at least two senses (cf. Barnes 1962a: 408) and is not to be confounded with affiliation (Fortes 1959a: 210; cf. Firth 1957: 2). Fortes quotes the dictionary meaning of filiation as 'the fact of being a child of a specified

245

parent' (1959a: 206). The reference is not to a simple physical relationship, either in the actors' or in the observer's eyes, but to a relationship that is culturally possible and socially validated, so it seems. Fortes writes that 'The fact of birth is only a necessary, not a sufficient, condition for kinship and descent status' (1962b: 85), and that it is because most societies give jural recognition to the parenthood of both parents that filiation is normally bilateral (1959a: 206). Hence there is both matrifiliation and patrifiliation. In one sense, descent and filiation refer to the same set of relations as in Fortes's statement that 'a rule of patrilineal descent states that only pedigrees made up exclusively of successive steps of patrifiliation are recognized as conferring descent for the particular social purposes in question' and that among the Ashanti 'matrifiliation follows automatically from the fact of birth and automatically *creates title to lineage membership by descent*' (1959a: 207, his italics). In this sense, it follows that 'filiation originates in the domestic domain, descent in the politico-jural domain, but filiation may confer title to status (which means right and capacities) in the politico-jural domain' (1959a: 208).

The other sense of filiation arises from the fact that wherever in a given society there is one and only one set of unilineal descent groups, one mode of filiation, patrifiliation or matrifiliation, is associated with the unilineal groups and the opposite mode is not. Under these conditions, Fortes refers to the unassociated mode of filiation as complementary, or as 'filiation on the non-corporate side' (1963b: 61). When he speaks of a contrast between descent and filiation, it is often complementary filiation that is to be understood. The adjective 'complementary' seems to carry no specialized meaning; thus in other contexts Fortes writes that a lineage 'emerges more precisely in a complementary relationship with or in opposition to like units' (1953a: 27), and that among the Ashanti individual choice and initiative are institutionalized 'by a mechanism of complementary redress that is rooted in the complementary conjunction at the structural level of matrilateral and patrilateral principles in status definition, and at the jural level of

246

legal and moral sanctions' (1963b: 62). More direct evidence
on the meaning of 'complementary' is provided by a sentence
in Fortes's article in 'The significance of descent' where he says
that among the Tallensi 'the two principles of patrilineal
descent and maternal origin are always complementary in their
action' (1944: 379). The passage in which this statement
appears is embodied in *The Web*, but here the statement is
revised to read that these two principles 'always work together'
(1949a: 30). The severely limited explanatory value of these
mechanical metaphors is well indicated by the fact that in
Dynamics we have a sentence flatly contradicting the one just
referred to: 'Patrilateral origin and matrilateral origin work in
polar opposition to each other' (1945a: 200). Yet Fortes makes
a valid point when he questions the usual terminology of
dominant and submerged lines or modes of filiation, arguing
that from the viewpoint of a person in a social system, the
'submerged line' may sometimes be dominant and the dominant mode of filiation submerged (1963b: 60).

When Fortes describes the rule in Periclean Athens restricting
the franchise to persons who could prove Athenian parentage
on both sides as introducing 'citizenship on the basis of bilateral
filiation', or that the normal source of title to membership in
a *hapu* for a free person is filiation to either parent (1959a: 207,
210), he is using filiation in the first sense, without reference
to whether filiation is dominant or complementary or neither.
Similarly his statements that 'filiation – by contrast with descent – is universally bilateral' (1953a: 33), and that 'filiation
is normally bilateral, or as we might even say, equilateral'
(1959a: 206) do not depend on the recognition of descent or
the existence of descent groups. On the other hand, when he
says that 'A matrilineal father's rights over his children are
based on the principle of filiation, the mother's brother's on
the principle of descent' (1959a: 197), he is referring to complementary filiation rather than filiation in general. It is difficult
to state the contrast between descent and filiation simply, and
my interpretation of what Fortes means is quite unlike the view
attributed to 'Cambridge anthropologists' by Leach (1962:

247

134). At least Fortes does not claim that the dominant mode of filiation is associated with descent groups in the politico-jural domain while the complementary mode of filiation is confined to the domestic domain. Both modes can determine status in the politico-jural domain, it seems, even when only one series of descent groups exist. Indeed, Fortes tends to take the existence of groups for granted, though the status an individual acquires is in fact usually membership in a descent group. The ethnographic facts are clear, but the analysis is baffling, though the points that baffle me are different from those that baffle Leach (1961b: vi, 114, 123). Writing of the Ashanti, Fortes says that 'Matriliny confers status in the politico-jural domain, patrifiliation only in the domestic domain' (1963b: 60-61). He refers back to his earlier article, where he says much the same, but in addition writes that complementary filiation 'is of peculiar significance in defining capacity for unencumbered citizenship . . . if his paternity is unknown or unacknowledged he is nevertheless socially defective . . . and in consequence ritually defective and jurally incomplete. This is a distinct handicap, if not an insuperable obstacle, to eligibility for lineage and political office' (1959a: 207–208). This suggests to me that among the Ashanti complementary filiation does indeed confer title to rights and capacities in the politico-jural domain. With the Tallensi and other peoples in mind, Fortes says 'in a segmentary patrilineal descent system matrifiliation endows a child with attributes of jural status subsuming claims on and obligations to its mother's lineage, without which it cannot be a normal jural person' (1959a: 209). Yet with reference to the Ashanti he states that 'the complementary opposition between matrifiliation and patrifiliation signifies the complementary opposition between a cluster of legally sanctioned and perpetually vested rights, duties and claims, on the one hand and a cluster of moral and contingent rights, duties and claims on the other sanctioned by religious beliefs' (1963b: 60), and this echoes his statement, in an earlier terminology, for both Ashanti and the Tallensi: 'The dominant line of descent confers the overtly significant attributes of social per-

248

sonality – jural status, rights of inheritance and succession to property and office, political allegiance, ritual privileges and obligations; and the submerged line confers certain spiritual characteristics' (1944: 380–381; 1949a: 32).

This characterization of the contrast must refer to relative emphasis, for the rights and obligations arising from patrilineal descent among the Tallensi and matrilineal descent among the Ashanti are supported by religious beliefs and practices, just as Tale matrifiliation and Ashanti patrifiliation have some significance in the politico-jural domain. Nevertheless there is a contrast, and in many segmentary societies (cf. Fortes and Evans-Pritchard 1940: 5–6; Middleton and Tait 1958: 6–8; Schneider 1965: 58–60) this takes a form similar to that found among the Tallensi and Ashanti. In many other societies, particularly societies that are not composed of lineages segmented at many levels, the contrast takes other forms or does not apply at all. Much of Leach's (1961b: 10, 114) criticism of the concept of complementary filiation derives from the fact that the societies he is principally concerned to analyse are dissimilar in this respect to the Tallensi and Ashanti (cf. Fortes 1967: 5–6).

The principle of complementary filiation is primarily associated in Fortes's analysis with the domestic domain, but there is one mechanism through which it operates on all levels of the Tale segmentary hierarchy. Fortes describes how in the polygynous domestic family full brothers tend to associate together more fully than do paternal half-brothers by different mothers. This leads to the division of small lineage segments into segments of lower order, each headed by a set of full siblings and identified by their mother. This type of segmentation is found at all levels. Fortes reports that the focal ancestor shrine of a segment is in some situations said to be the shrine of the founding ancestor of the segment and his mother, while in other situations it is said to be the shrine of the founder alone (1945a: 202). Thus for example the sub-clan of Tongo is divided into two major segments, Sɛyahɔg biis and Bɔyada biis, the descendants of Sɛyahɔg and Bɔyada respectively, these two ancestors being sons of Mosuor by different mothers. Fortes refers to these major segments as matri-segments, even though each mother, having produced only one segment-defining son, is segmentarily redundant. Another kind of matri-segment is Guŋ, consisting of the descendants of Sɛyahəg by one of his wives. Here the wife is not redundant, for she has three sons whose descendants constitute the three major segments of Guŋ (1945a: 214–216). Fortes does not distinguish clearly between these two types of segmentation, though to me they seem to be significantly different (cf. Barnes 1967f: 211–235). In one type, the apical and eponymous mother is the symbol for the contrast between the group formed by her sons and their agnatic descendants and the groups formed by the descendants of her co-wives. She is also the symbol of the unity of the group in contrast to the internal differentiation of the group into segments founded by her various sons. In the other type, the mother serves as a symbol in the first sense as before, but since she has only one son, the choice of her rather than him as the symbol of group unity has to be explained differently. Gluckman (1963: 63) comments that, at this point in his analysis, Fortes gives a wrong emphasis when he speaks of patrilaterality and matrilaterality working as polar opposites. Gluckman prefers the formulation given by Evans-Pritchard (1945: 64) for the Nuer: 'the social principle of agnatic descent is, by a kind of paradox, traced through the mother'. This Gluckman explains by reference to the inability of the patrilineal clan to reproduce itself without marriage to women of other clans.

7 Segmentation, incest, and exogamy

The main principle governing segmentation among the Tallensi is patrilineal descent, not matrifiliation. Here we are on more familiar ground. The general plan of patrilineal segmentation was being worked out by Evans-Pritchard for the Nuer while Fortes was beginning his work among the Tallensi, and since then there have been innumerable studies demonstrating the great similarities in morphology and process found among most patrilineal segmentary systems. Fortes's work has provided much of the analytical basis for these later studies and many of his ideas have been absorbed into the corpus of generally agreed analytical procedures of the discipline. For this reason we need say little about them, novel though they may have been when first enunciated. For example, we have the technique of contraposition, whereby 'a member of one social group identifies another social group or individual by comparison or contrast with his own social identity, and in terms of the most inclusive grouping which suffices to identify the latter unambiguously' (1945a: 17–18; cf. Smith 1956: 40–41); the principle of unit representation, or representative status, whereby any member of a segment may be called upon to act in relation to other segments as the representative of his own segment (1945a: 44, 246); the principle that in the corporate activities of a segment of any order, only the division into lesser segments at the level immediately below is recognized, and that each of these lesser segments must be represented (1945a: 31–32); the classificatory principle whereby one individual may substitute for another in intra-segment relations (1949a: 147–149). These and similar facts typical of the way in which all polysegmentary systems tend to work, at least of those which are based on a doctrine of descent (cf. Barnes 1962b: Langness 1964), are now well known largely as a result of Forte's demonstration of their presence among the Tallensi. Here in particular his publications bear out his contention that it is 'demonstration by facts open to general observation that turns intuition into discovery and so into the data of science' (1953a: 28).

Fortes describes the Tale ancestor cult as 'the calculus of the lineage system' (1944: 367; 1945: 33). He says that genealogies 'are relevant primarily as the mnemonics of the lineage system' (1944: 365; 1945: 31), are 'the conceptualization of the existing lineage structure' (1953a: 27), and are not true historical records (1944: 370; 1945a: 36). 'With few exceptions,' says Fortes (1944: 372; 1949: 13), 'social relations among the Tallensi always have a genealogical coefficient' (1944: 372; 1949a:

251

13). These metaphors indicate that the whole Tale field is, as it were, calibrated genealogically, and that the calibrations are published as ancestor shrines. To say this is merely to substitute one metaphor for another, and may not be helpful. But the substance of Fortes's contentions, in whatever imagery we view them, bears on his statements about pedigrees mentioned earlier. He does not distinguish between genealogies and pedigrees (cf. Barnes 1967b). It is clear that the genealogical calibration serves to bind together the various domains into which the social structure of any society like the Tallensi can be divided, in particular the politico-jural domain of clanship, the lineage domain and the domestic domain, and also the domain of ritual institutions. The same procedures are employed in all domains to identify and describe relations between individuals and between groups, whether this is a relationship of 'mother's brother' to 'sister's son' between two maximal lineages, or a relationship of brotherhood between cousins living in the same homestead. The calibration is genealogical rather than terminological (we might even say African rather than Australian), in that, although only a limited number of kinship terms are employed, the relations are spelt out step by step and carry a continuous gradation of intensity of jural, moral, and ritual content and of co-activity. It is a distinctive feature of genealogical reckoning that it can be extended indefinitely without discontinuity. Any system of descent groups that lacks a global genealogical framework has to deal with discontinuities between the various domains that are avoided in societies like the Tallensi.

The genealogical method of reckoning social distance permits and, strictly applied, entails the classification of persons by generation. Fortes has paid particular attention to the significance of generation. In his work on the Tallensi he emphasizes several times that generation differences are not recognized in large segments, for no attempt is made to equate generations in the genealogy of one sub-segment with those in another sub-segment. The limit comes at the boundaries of the inner or medial lineage (1945a: 225; 1949a: 141, 267) and affects the way in which segment heads are chosen, who may inherit widows, what kinship terms are applied, and other matters (1940: 251; 1949: 150, 156, 200, 267). At the other end of the scale, Fortes regards the opposition between successive generations, focused in the incest taboos, as the most important of all the forces generated by the social structure (1958a: 5). Whereas the classification of distant relatives by generation is a consequence of the recognition of descent, the recognition and institutionalization of differences between successive generations within the domestic domain follows from filiation. Indeed, Fortes says that in this domain filiation 'denotes the specific moral and effective ties and cleavages between successive generations (due allowances being made for sex differences) that arise from the facts of begetting, rearing and, above all, exercising responsibility in rearing a child' (1959a: 206).

Among the Tallensi, the cleavage between members of successive generations is held in check by the sanctions of filial piety (1949a: 195), but in more general terms actions in the domestic domain are controlled by sanctions emanating from the politico-jural domain. Thus the various domains are linked not merely because some of the same principles of organization, such as filiation and generational classification, apply in several domains, but also because sanctions that constrain in one domain are legitimated in another. Fortes argues that most societies give jural recognition to the parenthood of both parents, and that sanctions derived from the politico-jural domain ensure that a person succeeds, by right of filiation, to those components of his parents' jural status that are valid in the domestic domain (1959a: 206). In other words, the domestic domain is in no sense autonomous; the rules of the game within that domain are specific to it but they are validated by jural sanctions and moral ideas 'emanating' from the total social structure. Just what Fortes means by 'emanating' may become clearer when we discuss genetic processes (below, pp. 259–260).

At the core of the domestic domain is the domestic family. Fortes draws a contrast between the political, jural, and ritual interests and ends subserved by the Tale lineage system and the primarily economic and reproductive interests and ends subserved by the family system (1944: 372; 1949a: 12). We have already drawn attention to his emphasis on reproductive rather than economic interests, and this shows clearly in his description of the domestic group as 'the workshop, so to speak, of social reproduction', constituting its 'nodal mechanism' (1958a: 2). He draws an analytical distinction between the domestic group, 'a householding and housekeeping unit organized to provide the material and cultural resources needed to maintain and bring up its members', and the family in the strict sense. In the domain of the domestic group, 'kinship, descent and other jural and affectional bonds (e.g., of adoption or slavery) enter into the constitution of the group, whereas the family nucleus is formed purely by the direct bonds of marriage, filiation and siblingship'. The production of food and shelter and the non-material means for ensuring continuity are activities pursued in the domestic group, while the nuclear (or elementary) family is concerned with strictly reproductive functions (1958a: 8–9). Thus education or socialization would appear to belong to the domestic group rather than the nuclear family. *The web* predates the enunciation of this distinction, but here Fortes writes in similar terms of the domestic family as 'the focal field of kinship', with the parent–child bond 'the nodal bond of kinship' and the marital relationship 'a nodal relationship in Tale social life' (1949a: 16, 78, 81, 341). Furthermore, this 'focal field of kinship is also the focal field of moral experience; and the psychological and social factors that generate it are symbolically projected in religious beliefs' (1949a: 346). Later he writes that in patrilineal societies 'the relationship of fathers and sons is the nuclear element of the whole social system' (1961a: 170; cf. 1936b: 254).

These metaphors seem to have been chosen to bring out two points. First, the domestic family is a nucleus in that the values learned in it and the relations experienced in it provide models for values upheld and relations entered into in the wider world. Second, the distinctive activity or process carried on in the family is not the provision of food and shelter, or sexual activity, but social reproduction, the replacement of one generation by another. It is in the light of the latter proposition that Fortes has developed his view of the significance of incest prohibitions.

From his earliest papers onwards, Fortes has drawn a sharp distinction between incest and exogamy, arguing that treating them as equivalent phenomena is like treating the art of cookery and the institution of the market as equivalent because both relate to hunger (1936b: 255). In a paper published in 1949 he expresses support for Malinowski's interpretation of the incest taboo as 'the moral insulator of the family against the anarchic potentialities of sex' (1949d: 173), but in later publications he has stressed the divergence of his views from those of most of his colleagues. He argues that incest prohibitions are 'laid down in such a way as to ban sexual relations which might conflict with the right and duty of parents and their coevals to exercise discipline over the generation of their children' (1951a: 347). In *The web* Fortes is principally concerned with analysing why Tale rules of incest take their specific form, and in particular why sexual relations between a man and a distant clan 'sister' are treated with complete tolerance (1949a: 101, 111–117). In a talk on Freud given in 1956 Fortes presents Freud's interpretation of incest as a 'better theory' than those based on the primitive appreciation of eugenic advantage or the generation of sexual repulsion through childhood intimacy. He summarizes Freud as saying that parents impose inhibitions on childish wishes which serve to implant feelings of guilt which are necessary, for otherwise 'family organization would collapse in the struggle between fathers and sons for the possession of the mothers and daughters, and the task of training children in the knowledge and conduct they need to carry on social life would be impossible' (1965a: 794). Fortes does not say explicitly that he accepts Freud's view. His own understanding of the phenomenon emerges when he contrasts his opinion with those of Murdock and Lévi-Strauss. Fortes states his approval of the allocation of a whole chapter in Murdock's *Social structure* to sexual institutions and values, but he cannot accept Murdock's statement that 'incest taboos and exogamous restrictions of whatsoever sort seem clearly to be extensions of the sex taboos between parent and child and between brother and sister' (Murdock 1949a: 284). This statement, says Fortes, is 'pure Malinowski' and conflicts with Fortes's own view (1957a: 186–187). Likewise Fortes maintains that there is no ethnographic support for Lévi-Strauss's interpretation of the prohibition of incest as 'less a rule prohibiting marriage with the mother, sister or daughter, than a rule obliging the mother, sister or daughter to be given to others. It is the supreme rule of the gift' (Lévi-Strauss 1969: 481). Yet it seems that Fortes's divergence from Malinowski and Murdock is mainly about the way in which exogamy is connected with incest, and to a lesser extent about the way in which extra-familial incest prohibitions come to be accepted, rather than about the significance of incest taboos within the elementary family itself (cf. Fortes 1957a: 172–174). We have already mentioned his reference to 'the opposition between successive generations focused in the incest taboos' as the most important of the forces generated by the social structure which, among other things, determine the sequence of events in the developmental cycle of the domestic group (1958a: 5). This suggests that he still holds to his 1949 position, in alliance with Malinowski in this aspect of his views, and that his support for Freud can be safely inferred. He rejects Lévi-Strauss's view of incest rules as rules of giving, and writes that 'Only by stretching the term almost to the point of meaninglessness could it [marriage] be regarded as a form of exchange' (1953b: 194, 200). Yet he apparently accepts, in conformity to Malinowski (1927: 243–262), Lévi-Strauss's thesis that the adoption of incest prohibitions marks the transition from 'nature' to 'culture' (1969: 12; Fortes 1957a: 186). He also recognizes Lévi-Strauss's demonstration in *Les Structures* that, because of the rule of incest, there must be a dichotomy in the genealogical domain between a kinship side and an affinal side, bridged by marriage (1962a: 2). From this I infer that Fortes recognizes that, although incest is essentially a notion relating

256

to sexual intercourse rather than to marriage, the prohibition of incest does nevertheless entail the existence of institutionalized marriage and consequently a change of state whenever a marriage takes place.

But that is only part of the incest tangle. In Fortes's scheme of analysis the elementary family formed by a married couple and their children is characterized by tensions and cleavages of interest which are constrained by incest taboos and by all the other moral axioms that are accepted within the family but emanate from outside. In a society like the Tallensi, not only moral axioms but also structural principles are translated from the domestic domain to the lineage and clanship domains without discontinuity. The society is organic and the same structural features are to be found at all levels. Even in those societies where this is not the case, filiation is recognized and is employed in varying degrees through the mechanism of serial steps of filiation as the jural concept of descent.

We began this section at the level of clanship or, more generally, in the politico-jural domain, and moved progressively towards the nucleus of the domestic domain, the elementary family. To conclude, let us turn round and from the springboard of the domestic domain examine the interconnexions of one part of social structure with another. Fortes's view of incest may then become clearer.

In *The web* Fortes argues that 'all kinship institutions have only two major facets or, if we like, functions. They serve as a mechanism of organizing social activities and co-ordinating social relations . . . and at the same time they constitute the primary mould of the individual's psycho-social development' (1949a: 339). He goes on to attack Malinowski for giving primacy to the latter function and to stress that *The web* is mainly a study of the former, while stressing that 'A complete understanding of the significance of its institutions for a particular society calls for an investigation on both levels.' His criticism of Malinowski, Murdock, and others turns on what kind of connexion exists between these two facets, not on whether there is any connexion at all. Malinowski is criticized for holding that larger social groups are organized by extension from the initial situation in the parental family (1957a: 171, 175), and Fortes disagrees with both Malinowski and Murdock, as we have noted, when they maintain that rules of incest and exogamy are extensions of intra-familial sexual prohibitions (1957a: 187). Fortes's objections seem to be focused on the notion of a one-way process of simple extension from a smaller to a larger domain of social relations. His own idea of a two-way process of interaction between the family and the wider society appears in his statement that 'The tensions inherent in the structure of the parental family' are 'the result of the direction given to individual lives by the total social structure but they also provide the models for the working of that structure' (1953a: 34–35). The dominant term in the interaction is here the total social structure rather than the parental family, but a two-way process is implied.

Yet in several other contexts Fortes appears to give pre-eminence to the family, and even to postulate a one-way process of cause and effect, particularly in the religious domain. He writes that in Africa 'ancestor worship is a representation or extension of the authority component in the jural relations of successive generations' (1965a: 133) and that 'In the ultimate sense, perhaps, the concept of Predestiny among the Tallensi may be taken to designate tendencies that originate in organic sources and in the earliest experiences of infantile dependence' (1959b: 80). Likewise he states that 'There is a "feeding in" process by which the differentiation of persons in the domestic domain by generation, filiation and descent is projected into the structure of the unilineal descent group' (1958a: 6) and, as noted earlier, that 'lineage segmentation follows a model laid down in the parental family' (1953a: 32). These statements, taken by themselves, might suggest that Fortes is as much an extensionist as Malinowski or Murdock, though applying the notion in a slightly different context. Indeed, in his review of *The web*, Firth (1951: 158) criticizes Fortes for maintaining, in conformity with Radcliffe-Brown, that a person extends to his mother's brother the filial attitude he has to his mother, an assertion which Firth holds is refuted by the ethnographic evidence on the relationship to the mother's brother provided in the book.

The apparent contradictions between one statement and another are due partly to the style in which Fortes writes. Typically, the main conclusion of any argument is first stated in oversimplified and uncompromising form, and only later does it become clear that this opening statement is to be understood only as a first and inaccurate approximation to a subtle and carefully delimited intellectual position. Some of the discrepancies in statements about incest and exogamy are resolved when we remember the stress that Fortes puts on the notion of domain. As I see it, his main objection to Malinowski's mechanism of extension is that it assumes that a social phenomenon, whether it be a rule prohibiting sexual relations or the use of a kinship term, can be 'extended' without change from one domain to another. There is also the objection that, at least in Malinowski's looser statements, the 'extension' takes place with reference to the life history of the individual, so that social institutions are continually being recreated in the same image as new individuals grow up. Thus Fortes cites disapprovingly Malinowski's statements that 'the "origins of the clan system" . . . happen . . . under our very eyes . . . I have, myself, witnessed (them) . . .' and that 'In all primitive society, without exception, the local community, the clan or the tribe, is organized by a gradual extension of family ties' (Malinowski 1930: 25 and 1927: 221; Fortes 1957a: 170, 175). Whether 'gradual' is taken to refer to the passage of generations or to the maturation of the individual (I cannot see what other meaning it can have), I agree with Fortes that the statements are absurd.

Yet when we compare them with some of Fortes's own assertions such as 'We can uncover the roots of these religious beliefs in the family system and observe how their branches spread through the entire social structure' (1959b: 78), it is easy to think that the attraction of a good metaphor has led Fortes back to the Malinowskian position. With this statement,

259

as with so many others, we have to look at the argument as a whole, and soon discover that these beliefs are 'religious extrapolations of the experiences generated in the relationships between parents and children . . . their effect is to endow the critical components of filio-parental relationships with an external reality and representation that belongs to the whole society and not to the realm of individual thought and fantasy' (1959b: 78). Even though we might argue more readily that religious beliefs are in fact recreated afresh in the mind of each new believer than that a clan is recreated by each new recruit, this is not Fortes's argument. He attacks the prominence Malinowski gives to the technique of analysing kinship systems through a study of the life history of individuals, commenting that Malinowski made the notion of a genetic sequence the first principle of his theory of kinship. But Fortes goes on to qualify this by noting that 'the concept of genetic development was less a psychological hypothesis than a methodological one for Malinowski' (1957a: 169–170). In fact, Fortes rescues the notion of genetic development and the developmental mental processes it entails and uses them to link the domains of religion and the domestic family. His position is the same as Freud's, whose 'model of human nature' shows how moral rules 'emanate from society but are implanted by the parents through the agency of the inhibitions they impose on childish wishes and appetites' (1956a: 794). In the more mundane field of social organization, his position is essentially the same, and expressed in the same way. Thus we read that while from one point of view, 'fission in the domestic group can be regarded as the model and starting point of segmentation in the lineage', from another viewpoint 'differentiation and fission in the domestic group are reciprocally determined by norms and rules derived from the external domain' (1958a: 6–7). Only in a purely mechanical and metaphorical sense does Fortes postulate one-way processes, as in stating that 'The domestic family is the matrix of all the genealogical ties of the individual, the contemporary mechanism for ever spinning new threads of kinship' (1944: 373; 1949a: 14).

8   Assessment

The course followed in this chapter has differed from those traced when we were examining the work of Murdock and Lévi-Strauss, for we have had to handle a quite different corpus of writing. I do not think that even their greatest admirers would claim that either Murdock or Lévi-Strauss was an outstanding fieldworker, whereas even those who reject Fortes's analytical schemes along with his mechanistic metaphors will readily acknowledge the high quality of his fieldwork and his ethnographic reports. Only with monographs of the highest quality as ethnographic reports would a re-analysis of the kind carried out by Worsley on Fortes's Tallensi material be at all possible. Yet we cannot judge Fortes to be a first-class fieldworker and nothing more. He is no Junod, content to adapt accepted analytic categories to his own field experience in order to produce an outstanding monograph which can be interpreted by the pundits entrenched in their universities. On the contrary, Fortes has from his earliest publications sought to fashion his own version of anthropological theory, with his own concepts and his own technical vocabulary. Consequently, although his books on the Tallensi tell us almost all we might have wanted to know about their society and culture, this information is organized in terms of categories that are significantly different from those he might have been expected to use, given the time and place when the fieldwork was carried out and the professional training Fortes had received before going into the field. In the process, as a bonus, we are provided with much more information about the Tallensi than we might have expected to receive, more than is given for the Trobriand Islanders by Malinowski, and certainly more than Radcliffe-Brown provides for the Andaman Islanders or the Australian Aborigines.

However, Fortes has then followed in the steps of these two mentors and applied his scheme of analysis without substantial modification to society and culture everywhere. The fundamental and irreducible concepts of Tale and Ashanti culture

261

THREE STYLES IN THE STUDY OF KINSHIP

are transferred from emic to etic status and become universal ideas, liable to appear at any time and in any place. When this procedure of extension is limited to societies that are not so very different from either the Tallensi or the Ashanti, it works very well, as is shown notably in Fortes's paper on 'The structure of unilineal descent groups' (1953a; cf. Gluckman 1963; Chapter 1). But concepts refined among the Tallensi and applied successfully to a set of broadly similar African unilineal societies mainly studied in the field by a set of British-trained social anthropologists with broadly similar analytic interests begin to show their limitations even when matched, for instance, against the ostensibly unilineal societies of the New Guinea highlands. Aboriginal Australia appears to display even more clearly than the highlands of New Guinea the presence of notions of filiation and descent, and of unilineal descent groups, all reminiscent of Africa. Many writers have found no difficulty in describing the societies of New Guinea and Australia in terms of concepts that fit well in Africa. Yet intensive research carried out in the New Guinea highlands during the last fifteen years or so, and more recently in Australia, suggests strongly to me that there is more in these societies than meets the Africanist eye. Etic concepts may, indeed must, be developed that will be relevant to the analysis of all these societies, but it is in my view quite clear that the emic constructs which validate social institutions and forms of organization in these three areas are essentially different from one another (cf. Barnes 1962b, 1967c; Shapiro 1967, 1969; Peterson 1969).

With the experience of Malinowski before us, this failure might have been predicted. Yet though the attempt to comprehend the regularities and diversities of human society as a whole through the inspiration of one society alone was bound to fail, I think that it was necessary to make it. The analysis in our first chapter of the cross-cultural method practised by Murdock has demonstrated, I hope, that analytical categories designed *ab initio* for application to all cultures, as reported upon by ethnographers of all possible persuasions, are necessarily selected to classify ethnographic data in terms of attributes which are

262

the highest common factors of broad sets of real situations differing widely in cultural content and social arrangements. Because the attributes have to be applied widely, and the choice between them made 'objectively', i.e. with minimum reliance on informed insight, the discriminating criteria tend to be chosen for convenience of classification rather than for theoretical significance. The attributes tend also to be traditional categories, applicable to ethnographic reports written many years ago, rather than categories reflecting newly emergent theoretical interests; for this reason, for instance, the attributes tend to be classifications of enduring social and cultural arrangements rather than of repetitive social processes. One way of building new schemes of classification is to start with selected societies which have been analysed in detail, and to investigate how far the ideas, institutions, and processes found to be crucial in the operation of these societies are also relevant in others. The whole world cannot be fitted into a Trobriand or a Tallensi model, but our models of the societies and cultures of the world have to be designed so that one set of the parameters does provide us with an analytically adequate representation of the Trobriands, and another set of the Tallensi. We have noted that Fortes typically begins a discussion with a very simplified approximation to his final position, which is revealed gradually as the discussion proceeds. His statements about descent, filiation, patriliny, and matriliny, closely linked to the ethnographic context of Tallensi and Ashanti but applied without qualification to the world as a whole, seem to me to require interpretation as preliminary assertions only, to be gradually refined and developed to accommodate a wider range of peoples.

Fortes's work well exemplifies that interaction between ethnography and comparative analysis to which we referred in the first chapter. The ethnographer arrives in the field with a theory and an analytic toolkit which prove to be inadequate for coping with the ethnographic facts that crowd in upon him. He modifies his theory and develops new tools in the traumatic situation of first fieldwork, or in the sometimes equally traumatic situation of wrestling with his data to produce an analysis

263

that will stand up to the scrutiny of his colleagues. He then begins to apply the new form of analysis to other societies, and to teach his students to do likewise. The critical step in this helical process is insightful fieldwork imaginatively analysed, and Fortes shows just what is needed to take this step successfully.

Postscript

A comparative analysis of this kind is necessarily destructive in impact. We seem to have started with three serviceable, if imperfect, conceptual schemes and to have ended with only a few scraps and odd bits. Yet although a thorough-going synthesis would require the construction of a new meta-language into which we could translate the arguments and propositions of our three writers, a task that regretfully lies beyond the scope of this book, something may be saved from the wreck to keep us afloat for the time being.

All three styles of study seem to be based on the assumption that the distinction between culture and behaviour, though it exists, is not very important. Our writers assume that we have under scrutiny the orderly actions of homogeneous societies where norm and mean are closely in accord. Even if with Lévi-Strauss we concentrate our attention on thought rather than action, we are still dealing with homogeneous thinking, without serious cleavages of thought based on wealth or power. This preference for homogeneity, and hence for stability and equilibrium as well, is explicable by reference to the anthropological history of concentration on so-called simpler peoples, and has persisted longer in the study of kinship than in economic or political anthropology. In kinship we are in a terrain where there are no 'privileged positions', as Lévi-Strauss would say, and where therefore we can assume that each individual experiences the whole of his culture, and hence his culture reflects the whole of social life. Even Murdock, with his assertion that equilibrium and perfect integration is a rare condition, is not really concerned with radical disequilibrium or even with the major irreversible changes we recognize as general evolution; nor is he interested in diversity as a cultural characteristic. Fortes provides in his books the ethnographic evidence for a study of conflict, inequality, and political process but he uses this evidence to build up a picture of Tale culture that is timeless and repetitive. Lévi-Strauss does make use of the notion of instability, but the changes that follow the loss of stability in a marriage system seem to take place in a morphological museum or laboratory rather than in the real historical world. He is interested in the morphological consequences of instability rather than in the process of becoming unstable.

This preference for stable repetitive homogeneous societies shows itself in the poor development of diachronic models. Even if the models used are not completely static, they are still seen in terms of homeostasis. The models tend to have parameters defined qualitatively rather than quantitatively, for with homeostatic models the dogma of equilibrium makes measurement and calibration unnecessary. Indeed, though all three writers see the importance of the notion of time, no one of them seems to have produced an adequately rigorous set of concepts of different kinds of time. Likewise, though all three, each in his own way, recognize the need to measure, no one carries this out effectively. Murdock counts the wrong things, I argue, and Fortes links measurement with social structure in a way that implies homogeneity of cultural norm while admitting variety of customary practice. Lévi-Strauss seems sometimes to be fascinated by large numbers but he never really gets down to work with them. Numbers and symbols tend to have a mesmerizing effect, and statistical routines soon acquire ritual qualities, but nevertheless it should be possible in the study of kinship, and in other aspects of social science, to develop quantitatively defined models without falling into the errors of quantophrenia and sham mathematics attacked so vigorously by Sorokin (1956) and others.

All three authors have a preference, though not a prescription, for mechanical rather than statistical or stochastic

266

models, and for synchronic rather than diachronic models. All three make good use, in limited contexts, of models that are stochastic and/or diachronic, but none exploits fully the potentialities of this form of analysis. What is interesting is that for all three writers the contrasts of homogeneity and diversity, stability and instability, quality and quantity, determinism and probability, synchrony and diachrony, norm and behaviour, all call for attention. The answers they give are strikingly divergent and to me none seems entirely satisfactory. But this convergence of attention does suggest that these are the key contrasts in anthropological and sociological theory, and that from this strategically important area the building of a new synthesis might begin. Indeed, if social anthropology is ever going to complete the process of intellectual de-colonialization and come to grips with the contemporary world a satisfactory scheme for handling these contrasts is essential.

Another matter of common concern, and with divergent answers, relates less to data and analysis and more to the identity of the discipline. None of the trio adopts the Simon-pure neo-Durkheimian (or neo-Thomist?) view of the complete autonomy of sociological explanation but their attitudes towards other kinds of explanation vary greatly. None is a simple reductionist. Murdock advocates an eclectic but integrated theory of culture and behaviour in which there is no hierarchy of levels of explanation; Fortes seems to think in terms of areas of explanation, with fringe zones where some aspects of culture and social life cannot be understood except in terms of the theories of more than one related, but distinct, discipline, while rejecting the notion of a unified science of man (Fortes 1967a:5). Lévi-Strauss sometimes draws a hard and fast line between the study of infrastructures and superstructures, but he wanders across his own line from time to time, while even in his chosen domain of superstructures he maintains that he is really a psychologist, not a culturologist. Obviously this is another sensitive area. A new candidate for paradigm status must have a clear policy on whether, and if so in what sense, there is a distinctive level or area in which sociological and/or

267

culturalogical explanations apply; it must state what conditions of compatibility, reducibility, or complementarity must prevail on the borders of this area where it meets other disciplines. If Murdock is right, as I think he is, in his insistence on the need to develop a unified theory of behaviour, then some procedure for linking the existing disciplines better than his own trial-and-error pragmatic eclecticism seems to be called for. Here it is unfortunate that we have not been able to include an analysis of the Manchester school, for the most ambitious attempt to provide a theory of interdisciplinary relations has come from Gluckman and his colleagues (Gluckman 1964). But that attempt, like some others in recent years, seems to me to be aimed more at delimiting an intellectual niche for social anthropology rather than at finding the most satisfactory solutions to problems presented by data from the real world (cf. Barnes 1966).

Even if disciplinary territoriality is an anachronism, we are still left with the problem of demonstrating that the study of kinship, and of other aspects of culture and society, can form part of social science rather than of history and the humanities. What I have done continually in this book is to take material that was probably intended to be understood as literary and humanistic and to treat it roughly, as it were scientific. Perhaps this is unfair, for the authors I have discussed may not have intended their words to be interpreted in such a literal and deliberately unimaginative manner. Yet if the so-called social sciences aspire to become science one day, this rough and crude treatment may be necessary. When I called my analysis of the Murngin controversy *Inquest on the Murngin* I used the word inquest to suggest not only the end of a 'tribe that never was' but also the end of a style of analysis that seemed to me to be regrettably slapdash, casual, and impressionistic. The longer analysis attempted in this book suggests to me even more forcibly that the time has come when writers on kinship should stop holding their analytical cards so close to their chest. If we stated more openly, in pedestrian language, what concepts were being used, what contrasts were being drawn, and what propositions, if any, were being proved, then perhaps we would not end up in so many metaphysical muddles. This is not a plea for more jargon, and it is definitely not a plea for more pseudo-algebraic symbols; we still write in order to communicate and the clearer the message the greater the chance that its meaning will get through. But I believe that only when methodological rigour ceases to be merely an innovating act of ostentation and becomes accepted as a mandatory cultural attribute of our discipline can we begin to discover how much of a social science is possible.

References

ABERLE, David Friend
  1961 Matrilineal descent in cross-cultural perspective. *In* SCHNEIDER, David Murray, and GOUGH, Kathleen, eds. *Matrilineal kinship.* Berkeley: University of California Press. Pp. 655–727.

ALTSCHULER, Milton
  1967 Comment (*on* Köbben, The logic of cross-cultural analysis). *Current anthropology* **8:** 19–20.

APPELL, George Nathan
  1967 Observational procedures for identifying kindreds: social isolates among the Rungus of Borneo. *Southwestern journal of anthropology* **23:** 192–207.

Arc, L'
  1965a Bibliographie. *Arc* **26:** 79–84.
  1965b Principaux comptes rendus et discussions des travaux de Cl. Lévi-Strauss. *Arc* **26:** 85–87.

ATKINS, John
  1966 Review: Flament, Applications of graph theory to group structure. *American anthropologist* **68:** 1583–1584.

BANTON, Michael Parker
  1964 Anthropological perspectives in sociology. *British journal of sociology* **15:** 95–112.

BARNES, John Arundel
  1951a *Marriage in a changing society.* Capetown: Oxford University Press. 136 pp. *Rhodes-Livingstone paper* 20.
  1951b The perception of history in a plural society. *Human relations* **4:** 295–303.
  1962a Rethinking and rejoining: Leach, Fortes and filiation. *Journal of the Polynesian society* **71:** 403–410.

BARNES, John Arundel (*contd*)

1962b African models in the New Guinea highlands. *Man* **62:** 5–9.
1966 Review: Banton, Social anthropology of complex societies. *Man* n.s. **1:** 407.
1967a Feedback and real time in social enquiry. *Australian and New Zealand journal of sociology* **3:** 78–92.
1967b Genealogies. *In* EPSTEIN, A. L., ed. *The craft of social anthropology.* London: Tavistock Publications. *Social science paperbacks* 22. Pp. 101–127.
1967c Inquest on the Murngin. London: Royal Anthropological Institute. 50 pp. *Occasional paper* 26.
1967d Agnation among the Enga: a review article. *Oceania* **38:** 33–43.
1967e The frequency of divorce. *In* EPSTEIN, A. L., ed. *The craft of social anthropology.* London: Tavistock Publications. Pp. 47–99.
1967f *Politics in a changing society; a political history of the Fort Jameson Ngoni.* 2nd ed. Manchester: Manchester University Press. x, 245 pp.
1968 Networks and political process. *In* SWARTZ, Marc Jerome, ed. *Local-level politics: social and cultural perspectives.* Chicago: Aldine. Pp. 107–133.
1971 Time flies like an arrow. *Man* n.s. **6.**

BARRY, Herbert, III
1968 Regional and worldwide variations in culture. *Ethnology* **7:** 207–217.

BEAUVOIR, Simone de
1949 Les structures élémentaires de la parenté, par Claude Lévi-Strauss. *Temps modernes* **5:** 943–949.

BEFU, Harumi
1963 Classification of unilineal-bilateral societies. *Southwestern journal of anthropology* **19:** 335–355.

BLACKSTONE, William
1800 *Commentaries on the laws of England.* Book the second. 13th ed. London: Cadell and Davies. vii, 519, xix pp.

BOAS, Franz
1911 *Handbook of American Indian languages.* Washington, D.C.: Government printing office. Smithsonian institution, Bureau of American Ethnology, Bulletin 40. Part 1. vii, 1069 pp.

1927 Anthropology and statistics. *In* OGBURN, William Fielding, and GOLDENWEISER, Alexander Alexandrovitch, eds. *The social sciences and their interrelations.* Boston: Houghton Mifflin. Pp. 114–120.

BOHANNAN, Paul James
1954 Tiv farm and settlement. London: HMSO. iv, 87 pp. *Colonial research studies* 15.

BRAITHWAITE, Richard Bevan
1953 *Scientific explanation: a study of the functions of theory, probability and law in science.* Cambridge: Cambridge University Press. xii, 376 pp.

CAWS, Peter
1968 What is structuralism? *Partisan review* **35**: 75–91.

CHAPPLE, Eliot Dinsmore
1964 Comment (*on* Naroll, On ethnic unit classification) *Current anthropology* **5**: 294.

COLLINS, Paul W.
1966 Comment (*on* Driver, Geographical-historical *versus* psycho-functional explanations of kin avoidance). *Current anthropology* **7**: 149.

CONKLIN, Harold Colyer
1964 Ethnological method. *In* GOODENOUGH, Ward Hunt, ed. *Explorations in cultural anthropology.* New York: McGraw-Hill. Pp. 25–55.

COX, David Roxbee
1961 The role of statistical methods in science and technology. London: Birbeck College. 12 pp.

Current anthropology
1966 The published works (1936–1964) of Claude Lévi-Strauss. *Current anthropology* **7**: 128–129.

D'ANDRADE, Roy Goodwin
1966 Comment (*on* Driver, Geographical-historical *versus* psycho-functional explanations of kin avoidance). *Current anthropology* **7**: 149–153.

DE LINT, Jan and COHEN, Ronald
1960 One factor magic; a discussion of Murdock's theory of social evolution. *Anthropologica* (Ottawa) n.s. **2**: 95–104.

273

DRIVER, Harold Edson

1961   Introduction to statistics for comparative research. *In* MOORE, Frank William, ed. *Readings in cross-cultural methodology.* New Haven: HRAF Press. Pp. 303–331.

1966   Geographical-historical *versus* psycho-functional explanations of kin avoidance. *Current anthropology* **7:** 131–182.

1967   Integration of functional, evolutionary, and historical theory by means of correlations. *In* FORD, Clellan Stearns, ed. *Cross-cultural approaches: readings in comparative research.* New Haven: HRAF Press. Pp. 259–289.

DRIVER, H. E. and SCHUESSLER, Karl Frederick

1967   Correlational analysis of Murdock's 1957 ethnographic sample. *American anthropologist* **69:** 332–352.

EGGAN, Frederick Russell

1954   Social anthropology and the method of controlled comparison. *American anthropologist* **56:** 743–763.

ELWIN, Harry Verrier Holman

1947   *The Muria and their ghotul.* Bombay: Oxford University Press. xxix, 730 pp.

ERASMUS, Charles John, and SMITH, Waldemar R.

1967   Cultural anthropology in the United States since 1900: a quantitative analysis. *Southwestern journal of anthropology* **23:** 111–140.

EVANS-PRITCHARD, Edward Evan

1929   The morphology and function of magic. *American Anthropologist* **31**.

1939   Nuer time-reckoning. *Africa* **12:** 189–216.

1940   *The Nuer: a description of the modes of livelihood and political institutions of a Nilotic people.* Oxford: Clarendon Press. xii, 271 pp.

1945   *Some aspects of marriage and the family among the Nuer,* Livingstone: Rhodes-Livingstone Institute. 70 pp. *Rhodes-Livingstone papers* 11.

1951a   *Social anthropology.* London: Cohen and West. vii, 134 pp.

1951b   *Kinship and marriage among the Nuer.* Oxford: Clarendon Press. xi, 183 pp.

1956   *Nuer religion.* Oxford: Clarendon Press. xii, 336 pp.

1961   *Anthropology and history.* Manchester: Manchester University Press. 22 pp.

1963 *The comparative method in social anthropology*. London: Athlone Press. 30 pp.

FAGE, John Donnelly

 1961 Anthropology, botany, and the history of Africa. *Journal of African history* **2:** 299–309.

FALLERS, Lloyd Ashton

 1963 Political sociology and the anthropological study of African politics. *Archives européenes de sociologie* **4:** 311–329.

FIRTH, Raymond William

 1951 Review: Fortes, Web of kinship. *Africa* **21:** 155–159.

 1957 *We, the Tikopia: a sociological study of kinship in primitive Polynesia*. 2nd ed. London: Allen and Unwin. xxvi, 605 pp.

 1959 *Social change in Tikopia; a re-study of a Polynesian community after a generation*. London: Allen and Unwin, 360 pp.

 1963 Bilateral descent groups: an operational viewpoint. *In* SCHAPERA, Isaac, ed. *Studies in kinship and marriage*. London: Royal Anthropological Institute. *Occasional paper* 16. Pp. 22–37.

 1964 *Essays on social organization and values*. London: Athlone Press. vi, 326 pp. *London School of Economics monographs on social anthropology* 28.

 1968 Rivers on Oceanic kinship. *In* RIVERS, William Halse Rivers. *Kinship and social organization*. London: Athlone Press. Pp. 17–36.

FLAMENT, Claude

 1963 *Applications of graph theory to group structure*. Englewood Cliffs, N. J.: Prentice-Hall, 142 pp.

FORD, Clellan Stearns

 1967 Editor. *Cross-cultural approaches; readings in comparative research*. New Haven: HRAF Press. 365 pp.

FORDE, Cyril Daryll

 1941 *Marriage and the family among the Yakö in south-eastern Nigeria*. London: Lund Humphries. 121 pp. *London School of Economics monographs on social anthropology* 28.

FORTES, Meyer

 1930 A new application of the theory of neogenesis to the problem of mental testing. (Perceptual tests of 'g'.) University of London, Ph.D. thesis. Typescript, 231 pp.

FORTES, Meyer (*contd*)

1932a Perceptual tests of 'general intelligence' for inter-racial use. *Transactions of the Royal Society of South Africa* **20**:281–299.

1932b Translator. PETERMANN, Bruno. *The gestalt theory and the problem of configuration.* London: Kegan Paul, Trench, Trubner. xi, 344 pp.

1933a Notes on juvenile delinquency. *Sociological review* **25**: 14–24, 153–158.

1933b The influence of position in sibship on juvenile delinquency. *Economica* **13**: 301–328.

1936a Culture contact as a dynamic process: an investigation in the Northern Territories of the Gold Coast. *Africa* **9**: 24–55.

1936b Kinship, incest and exogamy of the Northern Territories of the Gold Coast. *In* BUXTON, Leonard Halford Dudley, ed. *Custom is king: essays presented to R. R. Marett on his seventieth birthday June 13, 1936.* London: Hutchinson's scientific and technical publications. Pp. 237–256.

1936c Ritual festivals and social cohesion in the hinterland of the Gold Coast. *American anthropologist* **38**: 590–604.

1937a Communal fishing and fishing magic in the Northern Territories of the Gold Coast. *Journal of the royal anthropological institute* **67**: 131–142.

1937b Marriage law among the Tallensi. Accra: Government printing department. 23 pp.

1938 Social and psychological aspects of education in Taleland. *Africa* **11** (4) Supplement. 64 pp. *International institute of African languages and cultures, memorandum* 17.

1939 The scope of social anthropology. *Oversea education* **10**: 125–130.

1940 The political system of the Tallensi of the Northern Territories of the Gold Coast. *In* FORTES, M., and EVANS-PRITCHARD, E. E., eds. *African political systems.* London: Oxford University Press. Pp. 238–271.

1941a Charles Gabriel Seligman, 1873–1940. *Man* **41**: 1–6.

1941b John Ranulph de la Haule Marett, 1900–1940. *Man* **41**: 20–21.

1943 A note on fertility among the Tallensi of the Gold Coast. *Sociological review* **35**: 99–113.

1944 The significance of descent in Tale social structure. *Africa* **14**: 362–385.

1945a *The dynamics of clanship among the Tallensi: being the first part of an analysis of the social structure of a Trans-Volta tribe.* London: Oxford University Press. xx, 270 pp.

1945b An anthropologist's point of view. *In* BRAILSFORD, Henry Noel, and others. *Fabian colonial essays.* London: Allen and Unwin. Pp. 215–234.

1948a Introduction. *In* FORTES, M., and others. *Ashanti survey, 1945–46: an experiment in social research.* Pp. 149–151.

1948b The anthropological aspect. *In* FORTES, M., and others. *Ashanti survey 1945–46.* Pp. 160–171.

1948c The Ashanti social survey: a preliminary report. *Rhodes-Livingstone journal* **6**: 1–36.

1949a *The web of kinship among the Tallensi: the second part of an analysis of the social structure of a Trans-Volta tribe.* London: Oxford University Press. xiv, 358 pp.

1949b Preface. *In* FORTES, M., ed. *Social structure,* Pp. v–xiv.

1949c Time and social structure: an Ashanti case study. *In* FORTES, M., ed. *Social structure.* Pp. 54–84.

1949d Sex and the family in primitive society. *In* NEVILLE-ROLFE, Sybil, ed. *Sex in social life.* London: Allen and Unwin. Pp. 158–173.

1949e Editor. *Social structure: studies presented to A. R. Radcliffe-Brown.* Oxford: Clarendon Press, xiv, 233 pp.

1950 Kinship and marriage among the Ashanti. *In* RADCLIFFE-BROWN, Alfred Reginald, and FORDE, Cyril Daryll, eds. *African systems of kinship and marriage.* London: Oxford University Press. Pp. 252–284.

1951a Social anthropology. *In* HEATH, Archibald Edward, ed. *Social thought in the twentieth century.* London: Watts. Pp. 329–356.

1951b Parenthood in primitive society. *Man* **51**: 65.

1952 Social effects of agricultural development in Africa. *Colonial review* **7**: 164–165.

1953a The structure of unilineal descent groups. *American anthropologist* **55**: 17–41.

1953b Analysis and description in social anthropology. *Advancement of science* **10**: 190–201.

1953c Social anthropology at Cambridge since 1900: an inaugural lecture. Cambridge: Cambridge University Press. 47 pp.

FORTES, Meyer (*contd*)

1953d Preface. *In* HENRIQUES, Fernando. *Family and colour in Jamaica*. London: Eyre and Spottiswoode. Pp. 3–8.

1953e Parenté et mariage chez les Ashanti. *In* RADCLIFFE-BROWN, Alfred Reginald, and FORDE, Daryll, eds. *Systèmes familiaux et matrimoniaux en Afrique*. Paris: Presses Universitaires de France. Pp. 331–372.

1954a A demographic field study in Ashanti. *In* LORIMER, Frank. *Culture and human fertility*. Paris: Unesco. Pp. 253–339.

1954b Mind. *In* EVANS-PRITCHARD, Edward Evan, and others. *The institutions of primitive society*. Oxford: Blackwell. Pp. 81–94.

1955a Radcliffe-Brown's contributions to the study of social organisation. *British journal of sociology* **6**: 16–30.

1955b Names among the Tallensi of the Gold Coast. *In* LUKAS, Johannes, ed. *Afrikanistische Studien Diedrich Westermann zum 80. Geburtstag gewidmet*. Berlin: Akademie-Verlag. *Deutsche Akademie der Wissenschaften zu Berlin, Institut für Orientforschung, Veroffentlichung nr.* 26. Pp. 337–349.

1956a The study of society. *Listener* **55**: 793–794.

1956b Foreword. *In* SMITH, Raymond Thomas. *The Negro family in British Guiana: family structure and social status in the villages*. London: Routledge and Kegan Paul. Pp. xi–xiv.

1956c Alfred Reginald Radcliffe-Brown, F.B.A., 1881–1955: a memoir. *Man* **56**: 149–153.

1957a Malinowski and the study of kinship. *In* FIRTH, Raymond William, ed. *Man and culture: an evaluation of the work of Bronislaw Malinowski*. London: Routledge and Kegan Paul. Pp. 157–188.

1957b Siegfried Frederick Nadel 1903–1956: a memoir. *In* NADEL, Siegfried Frederick Stephen. *The theory of social structure*. London: Cohen and West. Pp. ix–xvi.

1957c A history of the millennium: an anthropological footnote. *Cambridge review* **79**: 132.

1958a Introduction. *In* GOODY, Jack Rankine, ed. *The developmental cycle in domestic groups*. Cambridge: Cambridge University press. *Cambridge papers in social anthropology* 1. Pp. 1–14.

1958b Thinking about society. *Cambridge review* **79**: 596–8.

1959a Descent, filiation and affinity: a rejoinder to Dr Leach. *Man* **59**: 193–197, 206–212.

1959b Oedipus and Job in west African religion. Cambridge: Cambridge University Press. 81 pp.

1959c Primitive kinship. Scientific American 200 (6): 146–157.

1959d Review: Lystad, Ashanti. Africa 29: 211–212.

1960 Oedipus and Job in west African religion. In LESLIE, Charles, ed. Anthropology of folk religion. New York; Random House, Vintage Book. Pp. 5–49.

1961a Pietas in ancestor worship: the Henry Myers lecture 1960. Journal of the royal anthropological institute, 91: 166–191.

1961b Comment (on Eisenstadt, Studies of complex societies). Current anthropology 2: 211–212.

1961c Discussion and criticism (letter to editor). Current anthropology 2: 398.

1961d Radcliffe-Brown, Alfred Reginald. Encyclopaedia Britannica, 18: 874B–874C.

1962a Introduction. In FORTES, M., ed. Marriage in tribal society, Pp. 1–13.

1962b Ritual and office in tribal society. In GLUCKMAN, Max, ed. Essays on the ritual of social relations. Manchester: Manchester University Press. Pp. 53–88.

1962c Editor. Marriage in tribal societies. Cambridge: Cambridge University Press. vii, 157 pp. Cambridge papers in social anthropology 3.

1962d Review: Rose, Kin, age structure and marriage. British journal of sociology 13: 81–82.

1963a Graduate study and research. In MANDELBAUM, David Goodman, and others, eds. The teaching of anthropology. American anthropological association memoir 94. Pp. 421–438.

1963b The 'submerged descent line' in Ashanti. In SCHAPERA, Isaac, ed. Studies in kinship and marriage. London: Royal Anthropological Institute. Occasional paper 16. Pp. 58–67.

1963c Foreword. In HILL, Polly. The migrant cocoa-farmers of southern Ghana: a study in rural capitalism. Cambridge: Cambridge University Press. Pp. v–ix.

1964a (Contributor to) History, sociology and social anthropology. Past and present 27: 102–108.

1964b Le système politique des Tallensi des territoires du nord de la Côte de l'Or. In FORTES, M., and EVANS-PRITCHARD, E. E., eds., Systèmes politiques africains. Paris: Presses Universitaires de France. Pp. 203–233.

279

FORTES, Meyer (*contd*)

1965a Some reflections on ancestor worship in Africa. *In* FORTES, M., and others. *African systems of thought.* Pp. 122–144.

1965b Ancestor worship. *In* FORTES, M., and others. *African systems of thought.* Pp. 16–20.

1965c (Contributor to discussion) *In* CIBA FOUNDATION. *Transcultural psychiatry: Ciba foundation symposium.* DE REUCK, Anthony Vivian Smith, and PORTER, Ruth, eds. London: Churchill. Passim.

1965d Brenda Zara Seligman, 1882-1965: a memoir. *Man* **65**:177–181.

1965e Edipo e Giobbe in una religione dell'Africa occidentale. *In* LESLIE, Charles, ed. *Uomo e mito nelle società primitive: seggi di anthropologia religiosa.* Firenze: Sansoni. Pp. 23–68.

1966a Ödipus und Hiob in westafrikanischen Religionen. FIGGE, Hans, trans. Frankfurt am Main: Suhrkamp. 94 pp.

1966b Religious premises and logical techniques in divinatory ritual. *Philosophical transactions of the Royal Society of London,* ser. *B* **251**: 409–422.

1967a Totem and taboo. *Proceedings of the royal anthropological institute* 1966: 5–22.

1967b Tallensi riddles. *In* To honor Roman Jakobson: essays on the occasion of his seventieth birthday 11 October 1966. The Hague: Mouton. Vol. 1. *Janua linguarum, series maior 31.* Pp. 678–687.

1967c Bewusstsein. *In* FIRTH, Raymond William, and others. *Institutionen in primitiven Gesellschaften.* BÄRMANN, Michael trans. Frankfurt am Main: Suhrkamp. Pp. 93–106.

1967d Foreword. *In* ABRAHAMS, Raphael Garvin. *The political organization of Unyamwezi.* Cambridge: Cambridge University Press. *Cambridge studies in social anthropology* 1. Pp. ix–xii.

1968a On installation ceremonies. *Proceedings of the royal anthropological institute* 1967: 5–20.

1968b Seligman, C. G. *In* SILLS, David Lawrence, ed. *International encyclopaedia of the social sciences.* New York: Macmillan and Free Press. Vol. 14, pp. 159–162.

1969 *Kinship and the social order: the legacy of Lewis Henry Morgan* Chicago: Aldine. xii, 347 pp.

1970 *Time and social structure and other essays.* London: Athlone Press xii, 287 pp. *London School of Economics monographs* on *social anthropology* 40.

FORTES, Meyer, and DIETERLEN, Germaine
1965 Preface; I. The seminar: general review of the discussions; I. Indigenous religious systems; V. Islam in Africa; VI. Christianity in Africa. *In* FORTES, M., DIETERLEN, G., and others. *African systems of thought.* Pp. vii–viii; 1–6; 7–8; 28–30; 31–33.

FORTES, Meyer, DIETERLEN, Germaine, and others
1965 *African systems of thought: studies presented and discussed at the third international African seminar in Salisbury, December 1960.* London: Oxford University Press, viii, 392 pp.

FORTES, Meyer, and EVANS-PRITCHARD, Edward Evan
1940a Introduction. *In* FORTES, M., and EVANS-PRITCHARD, E. E., eds. *African political systems.* Pp. 1–23.

1940b Editors. *African political systems.* London: Oxford University Press, xxiii, 302 pp.

1964a Introduction. *In* FORTES, M., and EVANS-PRITCHARD, E. E., eds. *Systèmes politiques africains.* Pp. 1–20.

1964b Editors. *Systèmes politiques africains.* Paris: Presses Universitaires de France. xxiv, 268 pp.

FORTES, Meyer, and FORTES, Sonia Leah
1936 Food in the domestic economy of the Tallensi. *Africa* **9:** 237–276.

FORTES, Meyer, GOODY, Jack Rankine, and LEACH, Edmund Ronald.
1958 Preface. *In* GOODY, Jack, ed. *The developmental cycle in domestic groups.* Cambridge: University Press. *Cambridge papers in social anthropology* 1. P. vii.

1960 Preface. *In* LEACH, E. R., ed. *Aspects of caste in south India, Ceylon and north-west Pakistan.* Cambridge: Cambridge University Press. *Cambridge papers in social anthropology* 2. P. viii.

1962 Preface. *In* FORTES, M., ed. *Marriage in tribal societies.* P. vii.

1966 Preface. *In* GOODY, Jack, ed. *Succession to high office.* Cambridge: Cambridge University Press. *Cambridge papers in social anthropology* 4. P. vii.

1968 Preface. *In* LEACH, E. R., ed. *Dialectic in practical religion.* Cambridge: Cambridge University Press. *Cambridge papers in social anthropology* 5. P. vii.

FORTES, Meyer, and KYEI, T. E.
1945 Unpublished field data of the Ashanti social survey.
FORTES, Meyer, and MAYER, Doris Yankauer
1966 Psychosis and social change among the Tallensi of northern Ghana. *Cahiers d'études africaines* **6**: 5–40.
1969 Psychosis and social change among the Tallensi of northern Ghana. *In* FOULKES, S. H., and PRINCE, G. S., eds. *Psychiatry in a changing society.* London: Tavistock. Pp. 33–73.
FORTES, Meyer, STEEL, R. W., and ADY, Peter
1948 Ashanti survey 1945–1946: an experiment in social research. *Geographical journal* **110**: 149–179.
FOX, Robin
1966 Review: Goodenough, Explorations in cultural anthropology. *Man* n.s. **1**: 114–115.
FREEMAN, John Derek
1961 On the concept of the kindred. *Journal of the royal anthropological institute* **91**: 192–220.
GLEASON, Henry Allan
1961 *An introduction to descriptive linguistics.* Revised edition. New York: Holt, Rinehart and Winston. viii, 503 pp.
GLUCKMAN, Max
1961 Ethnographic data in British social anthropology. *Sociological review* **9**: 5–17.
1963 *Order and rebellion in tribal Africa: collected essays with an autobiographical introduction.* London: Cohen and West. xii, 273 pp.
1964 Editor. *Closed systems and open minds: the limits of naïvety in social anthropology.* Edinburgh: Oliver & Boyd. xxx, 274 pp.
GOODENOUGH, Ward Hunt
1956 Residence rules. *Southwestern journal of anthropology* **12**: 22–37.
1964 Editor. *Explorations in cultural anthropology: essays in honor of George Peter Murdock.* New York: McGraw-Hill. xiii, 635 pp.
GOODY, Jack Rankine
1959 The mother's brother and the sister's son in west Africa. *Journal of the royal anthropological institute* **89**: 61–88.
1961 The classification of double descent systems. *Current anthropology* **2**: 3–25.
1967 On the reliability of the ethnographic atlas. *American anthropologist* **69**: 366–367.

GOUGH, Eleanor Kathleen

1955 The changing structure of a Tanjore village. *In* SRINIVAS, Mysore Narasimhachar, and others. *India's villages.* (Calcutta); West Bengal government press. Pp. 82–92.

GUIART, Jean

1965 Survivre à Lévi-Strauss. *Arc* **26:** 61–64.

HAMMEL, Eugene Alfred

1968 Anthropological explanations: style in discourse. *Southwestern journal of anthropology* **24:** 155–169.

HEGEL, George Wilhelm Friedrich

1929 *Science of logic.* JOHNSON, W. H., and STRUTHERS, L. G., trans. New York: Macmillan. 2 vols.

HOBHOUSE, Leonard Trelawney, WHEELER, Gerald, and GINSBERG, Morris

1914 The material culture and social institutions of the simpler peoples: an essay in correlation. *Sociological review* **7:** 203–231, 332–368.

HOCART, Arthur Maurice

1952 The northern states of Fiji. London: Royal anthropological institute. xvi, 304, pp. *Occasional publication* 11.

HODGEN, Margaret Trabue

1936 *The doctrine of survivals: a chapter in the history of scientific method in the study of man.* London: Allenson. 192 pp.

HOLMBERG, Allan Richard

1950 Nomads of the long bow: the Siriono of eastern Bolivia. Washington, D.C.: Smithsonian Institution. iv, 104 pp. *Publications of the Smithsonian Institution, Institute of social anthropology* 10.

HOMANS, George Caspar, and SCHNEIDER, David Murray

1955 *Marriage, authority, and final causes: a study of unilateral cross-cousin marriage.* Glencoe: Free press. 64 pp.

JAKOBSON, Roman, and HALLE, Morris

1956 *Fundamentals of language.* 's-Gravenhage: Mouton. ix, 87 pp. *Jânua linguarum (series minor)* 1.

JORGENSON, Joseph G.

1966 Geographical clusterings and functional explanations of in-law avoidances: an analysis of comparative method. *Current anthropology* **7:** 161–169.

JOSSELIN DE JONG, Jan Petrus Benjamin de

1952 Lévi-Strauss's theory on kinship and marriage. Leiden: Brill

JOSSELIN DE JONG (*contd*)
(Ministerie van onderwijs, kunsten en wetenschappen). 59 pp. *Mededeingen van het rijksmuseum voor volkenkunde, Leiden* 10.

KLOOS, Peter
1963   Matrilocal residence and local endogamy: environmental knowledge or leadership. *American anthropologist* **65:**854–862.

KLUCKHOHN, Clyde Kay Maben
1939   On certain recent applications of association coefficients to ethnological data. *American anthropologist* **41:** 345–377.

KÖBBEN, André Johannes Franciscus
1952   New ways of presenting an old idea: the statistical method in social anthropology. *Journal of the royal anthropological institute* 82: 129–146.
1963   Comment (*on* McEwan, Validation in social anthropology). *Current anthropology* **4:** 173–174.
1967   Why exceptions? The logic of cross-cultural comparison. *Current anthropology* **8:** 3–34.

KUHN, Thomas Samuel
1962   *The structure of scientific revolutions.* Chicago: University of Chicago Press. xv, 172 pp.

KUNSTADTER, Peter, BUHLER, Roald, STEPHAN, Frederick Franklin, and WESTOFF, Charles Francis
1963   Demographic variability and preferential marriage patterns. *American journal of physical anthropology* **21:** 511–519.

LACAN, Jacques
1966   The insistence of the letter in the unconscious. *Yale French studies* 36/37: 112–147.

LANGNESS, Lewis Leroy
1964   Some problems in the conceptualization of Highland social structures. *American anthropologist* **66** (4: 2): 162–182.

LEACH, Edmund Ronald
1950   Review: Murdock, Social structure. *Man* **50:** 107–108.
1957   On asymmetrical marriage systems. *American anthropologist* **59:** 343.
1960a The Sinhalese of the dry zone of northern Ceylon. In MURDOCK, G. P., ed. *Social structure in southeast Asia.* New York: Wenner-Gren Foundation for anthropological research. *Viking fund publication in anthropology* 29. Pp. 116–126.

1960b Review: Udy, Organization of work. *American sociological review* **25:** 136–138.

1961a *Pul Eliya, a village in Ceylon: a study of land tenure and kinship.* Cambridge: Cambridge University Press. xv, 344 pp.

1961b *Rethinking anthropology.* London: Athlone Press. vii, 143 pp. *London School of Economics monographs on social anthropology* 22.

1962 On certain unconsidered aspects of double descent systems. *Man* **62:** 130–134.

1963 Comment (*on* McEwen, Validation in social anthropology). *Current anthropology* **4:** 174.

1964a *Political systems of highland Burma: a study of Kachin social structure.* London: Bell. xv, 324 pp.

1964b Telstar et les aborigènes ou 'La pensée sauvage'. *Annales* **19:** 1100–1116.

1964c Comment (*on* Naroll, On ethnic unit classification). *Current anthropology* **5:** 299.

1965 Claude Lévi-Strauss – anthropologist and philosopher *New left review* **34:** 12–27.

1966 Review: Murdock, Culture and society. *American anthropologist* **68:** 1517–1518.

1969 'Kachin' and 'Haka Chin': a rejoinder to Lévi-Strauss. *Man n.s.* **4:** 277–285.

LÉVI-STRAUSS, Claude

1936 Contribution à l'étude l'organisation sociale des Indiens Bororo. *Journal de la société des Américanistes* **28**: 269–304.

1943a The art of the northwest coast at the American museum of natural history. *Gazette des beaux-arts* 6th ser. **24:** 175–182.

1943b Guerre et commerce chez les Indiens de l'Amérique du sud. *Renaissance* (New York) **1:** 122–139.

1944 On dual organization in South America. *America indigéna* **4:** 37–47.

1945a L'analyse structurale en linguistique et en anthropologie. *Word* **1:** 33–53.

1945b French sociology. *In* GURVITCH, Georges, and MOORE, Wilbert Ellis, eds. *Twentieth century sociology.* New York: Philosophical library. Pp. 503–537.

1948a La vie familiale et sociale des Indiens Nambikwara. *Journal de la société des Américanistes* **37:** 1–132.

1948b The Tupi-Cawahib. *In* STEWARD, Julian Haynes, ed. The tropical forest tribes. Washington, D.C.: Government

285

LÉVI-STRAUSS, Claude (*contd*)

    printing office. Smithsonian Institution, Bureau of American Ethnology, bulletin 143. *Handbook of South American Indians*. vol. 3. Pp. 299–305.

1949a *Les Structures élémentaires de la parenté*. Paris: Presses Universitaires de France. xiv, 639 pp.

1949b Histoire et ethnologie. *Revue de metaphysique et de morale* **54:** 363–391.

1950a Introduction á l'œuvre de Marcel Mauss. *In* MAUSS, Marcel. *Sociologie et anthropologie*. Paris: Presses Universitaires de France. *Bibliotheque de sociologie contemporaine*. Pp. ix–lii.

1950b The use of wild plants in tropical South America. *In* STEWARD, Julian Haynes, ed. *Physical anthropology, linguistics and cultural geography of South American Indians*. Washington, D.C.: Smithsonian Institution, Bureau of American ethnology, Government printing office. bulletin 143. *Handbook of South American Indians*. vol. 6. Pp. 465–486.

1950c Les prohibitions matrimoniales et leur fondement psychologique. *Journal de psychologie normale et pathologique* **43:** 409.

1951a Foreword. *International social science bulletin* **3:** 771–775.

1951b Language and the analysis of social laws. *American anthropologist* **53:** 155–163.

1952 La notion d'archaïsme en ethnologie. *Cahiers internationaux de sociologie* **12:** 3–25.

1953a Social structure. *In* KROEBER, Alfred Louis, ed. *Anthropology today*. Chicago: University of Chicago Press. Pp. 524–553.

1953b (Contributions to discussions) *In* TAX, Sol, and others, eds. *An appraisal of anthropology today*. Chicago: University of Chicago Press. Passim.

1953c (Results of the conference from the point of view of anthropology) *In* LÉVI-STRAUSS, C. and others. *Results of the conference of anthropologists and linguists*. Baltimore: Indiana University, Waverly Press. *International journal of American linguistics* 19 (2) *Supplement. Memoir* **8**. Pp. 1–10.

1954 The mathematics of man. *International social science bulletin* **6:** 581–590.

1955a *Tristes Tropiques*. Paris: Plon. 462 pp. *Collection terre humaine*.

1955b Diogène couché. *Temps modernes* **10:** 1187–1220.

1956a The family. *In* SHAPIRO, Harry Lionel, ed. *Man, culture and society.* New York: Oxford University Press. Pp. 261–285.

1956b Les organisations dualistes, existent-elles? *Bijdragen tot de taal-, land- en volkenkunde* **112:** 99–128.

1956c Race and history. *In* UNITED NATIONS EDUCATIONAL SCIENTIFIC AND CULTURAL ORGANIZATION. *The race question in modern science.* Paris: Unesco. Pp. 123–163.

1956d Les trois humanismes. *Demain* **35.**

1957 Review: Briffault and Malinowski, Marriage past and present. *American anthropologist* **59:** 902–903.

1958a *Anthropologie structurale.* Paris: Plon. ii, 454 pp.

1958b Preface. *In* BOUTEILLER, Marcelle. *Sorciers et jeteurs de sort.* Paris: Plon. Pp. i–vi.

1958c Review: Firth, Man and culture. *Africa* **28:** 370–371.

1958d La geste d'Asdiwal. *Annuaire de l'école pratique des hautes études, VIe section (sciences religieuses)* 1958–1959: 3–43.

1960a Leçon inaugurale faite le mardi 5 janvier 1960. Nogent-le-Rotrou, Impr. Daupeley-Gouveneur. 47 pp. No. 31.

1960b Anthropologie sociale (Resumé des cours et travaux de l'année scolaire 1959–1960). *In* COLLÈGE DE FRANCE. Annuaire. 60e année. Paris: Imprimerie nationale. Pp. 191–207.

1960c Four Winnebago myths: a structural sketch. *In* DIAMOND, Stanley, ed. *Culture and history: essays in honor of Paul Radin.* New York: Columbia University Press. Pp. 351–362.

1960d On manipulated sociological models. *Bijdragen tot de taal-, land- en volkenkunde* **116:** 45–54.

1960e L'analyse morphologique des contes russes. *International journal of slavic linguistics and poetics* **3:** 122–149.

1961a *A world on the wane.* London: Hutchinson. 404 pp.

1961b Today's crisis in anthropology. *Unesco courier* **14**(11): 12–17.

1961c Comment (*on* Goody, Classification of double descent systems). *Current anthropology* **2:** 17.

1962a *La Pensée sauvage.* Paris: Plon ii, 395 pp.

1962b Les limites de la notion de structure en ethnologie. *In* BASTIDE, Roger, ed. *Sens et usage du terme structure dans les sciences humaines et sociales.* 's-Gravenhage: Mouton *Jânua linguarum, series minor* 16. Pp. 40–45.

LÉVI-STRAUSS, Claude (*contd*)

1962c Sur le caractère distinctif des faits ethnologiques. *Revue des travaux de l'académie des sciences morales et politiques* 4e ser. 115 (1): 211–219.

1962d (Contributions to) Compte rendu du colloque sur le mot structure. *In* BASTIDE, R., ed. *Sens et usage du terme structure.* Pp. 143–145, 150, 157.

1963a *Structural anthropology.* New York: Basic books. xvi, 410 pp.

1963b *Totemism.* Boston: Beacon press. 116 pp.

1963c The bear and the barber. *Journal of the royal anthropological institute* **93:** 1–11.

1964 Criteria of science in the social and human disciplines. *International social science journal* **16:** 534–552.

1966a *Mythologiques: du miel aux cendres.* Paris: Plon. 452 pp.

1966b Anthropology: its achievement and future. *Current anthropology* **7:** 124–127.

1966c The future of kinship studies: the Huxley memorial lecture 1965. *Proceedings of the royal anthropological institute* 1965: 13–22.

1967 *Les structures élémentaires de la parenté.* Deuxième edition. Paris: Mouton. xxx, 591 pp. *Maison des sciences de l'homme: collection de réédition* 2.

1969 *The elementary structures of kinship.* London: Eyre and Spottiswoode. xlii, 541 pp.

LÉVI-STRAUSS, Claude, and others.

1963 Résponses à quelques questions. *Esprit* **31** (ii): 628–653.

LEVY, Marion Joseph

1963 Comment (*on* McEwen, Validation in social anthropology). *Current anthropology* **4:** 175.

LEVY, Marion Joseph, and FALLERS, Lloyd Ashton

1959 The family: some comparative considerations. *American anthropologist* **61:** 647–651.

LEWIN, Kurt

1933 *A dynamic theory of personality: selected papers.* New York: McGraw-Hill. ix, 286 pp.

LEWIS, Oscar

1956 Comparisons in cultural anthropology. *In* THOMAS, William Le Roy jr., ed. *Current anthropology: a supplement to Anthropology today.* Chicago: University of Chicago Press. Pp. 259–292.

LOWIE, Robert Harry

1929 Relationship terms. *Encyclopaedia britannica* 14th ed. Vol. 19. Pp. 84–89.

1937 *The history of ethnological theory.* New York: Farrar and Rinehart. xiii, 296 pp.

1946 Review: Malinowski, A scientific theory of culture. *American anthropologist* **48:** 118–119.

1949 *Primitive society.* London: Kegan Paul. x, 453 pp.

MCDOUGALL, William

1908 *An introduction to social psychology.* London: Methuen. xv, 355 pp.

MCEWEN, William John

1963 Forms and problems of validation in social anthropology. *Current anthropology* **4:** 155–183.

MALINOWSKI, Bronislaw Kaspar

1927 *Sex and repression in savage society.* London: Routledge and Kegan Paul. xiv, 285 pp.

1930 Kinship. *Man* **30:** 19–29.

MAUSS, Marcel

1950 *Sociologie et anthropologie.* Paris: Presses Universitaries de France. lii, 389 pp. *Bibliotheque de sociologie contemporaine.*

1954 *The gift: forms and functions of exchange in archaic societies.* London: Cohen and West. xiv, 130 pp.

MAYBURY-LEWIS, David Henry Peter

1960 The analysis of dual organizations, a methodological critique. *Bijdragen tot de taal-, land- en volkenkunde* **116:** 17–44.

1965 Prescriptive marriage systems. *Southwestern journal of anthropology* **21:** 207–230.

MEAD, Margaret

1928 *Coming of age in Samoa: a study of adolescence and sex in primitive societies.* New York: Morrow, xv, 297 pp.

MIDDLETON, John Francis, and TAIT, David

1959 Editors. *Tribes without rulers: a study in African segmentary systems.* London: Routledge and Kegan Paul. xi, 234 pp.

MITCHELL, James Clyde

1967 On quantification in social anthropology. *In* EPSTEIN, A. L., ed. *The craft of social anthropology.* London: Tavistock Publications. Pp. 17–45.

MITCHELL, William Edward
  1963   Theoretical problems in the concept of the kindred.
          American anthropologist **65:** 343–354.
MOORE, Frank William
  1961   Editor. *Readings in cross-cultural methodology.* New Haven:
          HRAF Press. ix, 335 pp.
  1962   *Unpublished codings on type of natural environment.* New Haven:
          HRAF.
MOORE, Omar Khayyam, and OLMSTED, David Lockwood
  1952   Language and Professor Lévi-Strauss. *American anthropo-
          logist* **54:** 116–119.
MUKHERJEE, Ramkrishna
  1964   Comment (*on* Naroll, On ethnic unit classification). *Current
          anthropology* **5:** 301.
MURDOCK, George Peter
  1931   Introduction. *In* LIPPERT, Julius. *The evolution of culture.*
          London: Allen and Unwin. Pp. v–xxxii.
  1932   The science of culture. *American anthropologist* **34:** 200–215.
  1934a Kinship and social behaviour among the Haida. *American
          anthropologist* **36:** 355–385.
  1934b *Our primitive contemporaries.* New York: Macmillan. xxii.
          614 pp.
  1936   Rank and potlatch among the Haida. New Haven: Yale
          university press. 20 pp. *Yale university publications in anthro-
          pology* 13.
  1937a Comparative data on the division of labour by sex. *Social
          forces* **15:** 551–553.
  1937b Editorial preface. In MURDOCK, G. P., ed. *Studies in the
          science of society.* New Haven: Yale University Press. Pp.
          vii–xx.
  1937c Correlations of matrilineal and patrilineal institutions. *In*
          MURDOCK, G. P., ed. *Studies in the science of society.* New
          Haven: Yale University Press. Pp. 445–470.
  1938   Notes on the Tenino, Molala and Paiute of Oregon.
          American anthropologist **40:** 395–402.
  1940a The cross-cultural survey. *American sociological review* **5:**
          361–370.
  1940b Double descent. *American anthropologist* **42:** 555–561.
  1941   Anthropology and human relations. *Sociometry* **4:** 140–149.
  1943   Bronislaw Malinowski. *American anthropologist* **45:** 441–451.

1945 The common denominator of cultures. *In* LINTON, Ralph, ed. *The science of man in the world crisis.* New York: Columbia University Press. Pp. 123–142.

1947 Bifurcate merging: a test of five theories. *American anthropologist* **49:** 56–68.

1948 Baseball: it's waged in Truk. *Newsweek* **32** (9): 69–70.

1949a *Social structure.* New York: Macmillan. xvii, 387 pp.

1949b The science of human learning, society, culture and personality. *Scientific monthly* **69:** 377–381.

1950a The conceptual basis of area research. *World politics* **2:** 571–578.

1950b Family stability in non-European cultures. *Annals of the American academy of political and social science* **272:** 195–201.

1950c Feasibility and implementation of comparative community research. *American sociological review* **15:** 713–720.

1951a British social anthropology. *American anthropologist* **53:** 465–473.

1951b Outline of South American cultures. New Haven: HRAF Press. 148 pp. *Behavior science outlines, vol.* 2.

1952 Anthropology and its contribution to public health. *American journal of public health* **42:** 7–11.

1953 The processing of anthropological materials. *In* KROEBER, Alfred Louis, ed. *Anthropology today.* Chicago: University of Chicago Press. Pp. 476–487.

1954a Outline of world cultures. New Haven; HRAF Press. xii, 180 pp. *Behavior science outlines.*

1954b Sociology and anthropology. *In* GILLIN, John Philip, ed. *For a science of social man.* New York: Macmillan. Pp. 14–34.

1955 Changing emphases in social structure. *Southwestern journal of anthropology* **11:** 361–370.

1956a How culture changes. *In* SHAPIRO, Harry Lionel, ed. *Man, culture and society.* New York: Oxford University Press. Pp. 247–260.

1956b Political moieties. *In* WHITE, Leonard Dupee, ed. *The state of the social sciences.* Chicago: University of Chicago Press. Pp. 133–147.

1957a World ethnographic sample. *American anthropologist* **59:** 664–687.

1957b Anthropology as a comparative science. *Behavioral science* **2:** 249–254.

291

MURDOCK, George Peter (*contd*)

1958a Outline of world cultures. 2nd revised ed. New Haven: HRAF Press. xi, 227 pp.

1958b Social organization of the Tenino. *In Miscellanea Paul Rivet octagenario dicata.* Mexico City: Universidad nacional autónoma. Vol. I, pp. 299–315.

1959a *Africa: its peoples and their culture history.* New York: McGraw-Hill. xiii, 456 pp.

1959b Evolution in social organization. *In* ANTHROPOLOGICAL SOCIETY OF WASHINGTON. Evolution and anthropology: a centennial appraisal. Washington, D.C.: Anthropological Society of Washington. Pp. 126–143.

1960a Cognatic forms of social organization. *In* MURDOCK, G. P., ed. *Social structure in southeast Asia.* New York: Wenner-Gren Foundation for anthropological research. *Viking fund publication in anthropology* 29. Pp. 1–14.

1960b Typology in the area of social organization. *In* WALLACE, Anthony F. C., ed. *Men and cultures: selected papers of the fifth international congress of anthropological and ethnological sciences.* Philadelphia: University of Pennsylvania Press. Pp. 183–188.

1961 World ethnographic sample. (revised) *In* MOORE, F. W., ed. *Readings in cross-cultural methodology.* New Haven: HRAF Press. Pp. 193–216.

1963 Ethnographic atlas. *Ethnology* 2: 541–548.

1964a Comment (*on* Naroll, On ethnic unit classification). *Current anthropology* **5**: 301–302.

1964b The kindred. *American anthropologist* **66**: 129–132.

1965a *Culture and society: twenty four essays.* Pittsburgh: University of Pittsburgh Press. xii, 376 pp.

1965b Tenino shamanism. *Ethnology* **4**: 165–171.

1966 Cross-cultural sampling. *Ethnology* **5**: 97–114.

1967 *Ethnographic atlas.* Pittsburgh: University of Pittsburgh Press. 128 pp.

1968a Patterns of sibling terminology. *Ethnology* **7**: 1–24.

1968b World sampling provinces. *Ethnology* **7**: 305–326.

MURDOCK, George Pater, and GOODENOUGH, Ward Hunt

1947 Social organization of Truk. *Southwestern journal of anthropology* **3**: 331–343.

MURDOCK, G. P., and others

1950 *Outline of cultural materials.* 3rd revised ed. New Haven: HRAF Press. xxiii, 162 pp.

1961   *Outline of cultural materials*. 4th revised ed. New Haven: HRAF Press. xxv, 164 pp.

1962a   Editorial. *Ethnology* **1:** 1–4.

1962b   Ethnographic atlas. *Ethnology* **1:** 11–134, 265–286, 387–403, 533–545.

1963   Ethnographic atlas. *Ethnology* **2:** 109–133, 249–268, 402–405.

1965   Ethnographic atlas. *Ethnology* **4:** 114–122, 241–250, 343–348, 448–455.

1966   Ethnographic atlas. *Ethnology* **5:** 115–134, 218–232, 317–346, 442–448.

MURPHY, Robert Francis

1963   On Zen Marxism: filiation and alliance. *Man* **63:** 17–19.

NADEL, Siegfried Frederick Stephen

1951   *The foundations of social anthropology*. London: Cohen and West. xi, 426 pp.

1953   (Contributions to discussions) *In* TAX, Sol, and others, eds. *An appraisal of anthropology today*. Chicago: University of Chicago Press. Passim.

1955   Review: Gillin, For a science of social man. *American anthropologist* **57:** 345–347.

NAROLL, Raoul S.

1961   Two solutions to Galton's problem. *Philosophy of science* **28:** 15–39.

1962   *Data quality control – a new research technique: prolegomena to a cross-cultural study of culture stress*. New York: Free Press of Glencoe. 198 pp.

1964a   A fifth solution to Galton's problem. *American anthropologist* **66:** 863–867.

1964b   On ethnic unit classification. *Current anthropology* **5:** 283–313.

1965   Galton's problem: the logic of cross-cultural research. *Social research* **32:** 428–451.

1966   Comment (*on* Driver, Geographical-historical *versus* psycho-functional explanations). *Current anthropology* **7:** 154–155.

1967   Review: Coult and Habenstein, Cross tabulations of Murdock's World ethnographic sample. *American anthropologist* **69:** 103–104.

1968   Some thoughts on comparative method in cultural anthropology. *In* BLALOCK, H. M., and BLALOCK, A. B., eds. *Methodology in social research*. New York: McGraw-Hill. Pp. 236–277.

NAROLL, Raoul S., and D'ANDRADE, Roy Goodwin
1963   Two further solutions to Galton's problem. *American anthropologist* **65:** 1053–1067.

NEEDHAM, Rodney
1962   *Structure and sentiment: a test case in social anthropology.* Chicago: University of Chicago Press. ix, 135 pp.
1964   Descent, category and alliance in Siriono society. *Southwestern journal of anthropology* **20:** 229–240.

NISBET, Robert Alexander
1966   *The sociological tradition.* New York: Basic Books. xii, 349 pp.

NUTINI, Hugo Gini
1965   Some considerations on the nature of social structure and model building: a critique of Claude Lévi-Strauss and Edmund Leach. *American anthropologist* **67:** 707–731.

OGBURN, William Fielding
1922   *Social change with respect to culture and original nature.* New York: Heubsch. viii, 365 pp.

OLIVER, Douglas Llewellyn
1959   Review: Radcliffe-Brown, Natural science of society; Nadel, Theory of social structure; Lévi-Strauss, Anthropologie structurale. *American anthropologist* **61:** 506–512.

PARSONS, Talcott
1937   *The structure of social action: a study in social theory with special reference to a group of recent European writers.* New York: McGraw-Hill. xii, 817 pp.

PATAI, Raphael
1965   The structure of endogamous unilineal descent groups. *Southwestern journal of anthropology* **21:** 325–350.

PETERSON, Nicholas
1969   Secular and ritual links: two basic and opposed principles of Australian social organization as illustrated by Walbiri ethnography. *Mankind* **7:** 27–35.

PILLING, Arnold Remington
1962   Statistics, sorcery and justice. *American anthropologist* **64:** 1057–1059.

POPPER, Karl Raimund
1961   *The poverty of historicism.* London: Routledge and Kegan Paul. x, 166 pp.
1963   *Conjectures and refutations: the growth of scientific knowledge.* London: Routledge and Kegan Paul. xiii, 412 pp.

RADCLIFFE-BROWN, Alfred Reginald

1913   Three tribes of Western Australia. *Journal of the royal anthropological institute* **43**: 143–194.

1930–1931   The social organization of Australian tribes. *Oceania* **1**: 34–63, 206–246, 322–341, 426–456.

1948   *The Andaman islanders*. Glencoe, Ill.: Free Press. xiv, 510 pp.

1951   The comparative method in social anthropology. *Journal of the royal anthropological institute* **81**: 15–22.

1952   *Structure and function in primitive society*. London: Cohen and West. vii, 219 pp.

1953   Letter to Lévi-Strauss. *In* TAX, Sol, and others, eds. *An appraisal of anthropology today*. Chicago: University of Chicago Press. P. 109.

1957   *A natural science of society*. Glencoe, Ill.: Free Press and Falcon's Wing Press. xii, 156 pp.

1958   *Method in social anthropology: selected essays by A. R. Radcliffe-Brown*. SRINIVAS, M. N., ed. Chicago: University of Chicago Press. xxi, 189 pp.

RICHARDS, Audrey Isabel

1932   Anthropological problems in North-eastern Rhodesia. *Africa* **5**: 121–144.

RIVERS, William Halse Rivers

1914   *Kinship and social organization*. London: Constable. vii, 96 pp. *Studies in economic and political science* 36.

1924   *Social organization*. London: Kegan Paul, Trench and Trubner. xi, 226 pp.

ROMNEY, Antone Kimball, and EPLING, Philip Judd

1958   A simplified model of Kariera kinship. *American anthropologist* **60**: 59–74.

ROUSSEAU, Jean Jaques

1952   A discourse on the origin of inequality. *In* Montesquieu and Rousseau. Chicago: Encyclopaedia Britannica. *Great Books of the western world* **38**. Pp. 323–366.

SAHLINS, Marshall David

1966   On the Delphic writings of Claude Lévi-Strauss. *Scientific American* **214** (6): 131–132, 134, 136.

SAWYER, Jack, and LEVINE, Robert Alan

1966   Cultural dimensions: a factor analysis of the world ethnographic sample. *American anthropologist* **68**: 708–731.

SCHAPERA, Isaac

1953   Some comments on the comparative method in social anthropology. *American anthropologist* **55**: 353–362.

1962   Should anthropologists be historians? *Journal of the royal anthropological institute* **92**: 143–156.

SCHEFFLER, Harold

1966   Ancestor worship in anthropology: or observations on descent and descent groups. *Current anthropology* **7**: 541–551.

SCHMITZ, Carl August

1964   Grundformen der Verwandschaft. Basel: Pharos – Verlag Hansrudolf Schwabe. 134 pp. *Basler Beiträge zur Geographie und Ethnologie, Ethnologische Reihe, Heft 1. Regio Basiliensis, Ergänzungsheft.*

SCHNEIDER, David Murray

1961   Introduction: The distinctive features of matrilineal descent groups. *In* SCHNEIDER, D. M., and GOUGH, K., eds. *Matrilineal kinship.* Berkeley: University of California Press. Pp. 1–29.

1965   Some muddles in the models: or how the system really works. *In* BANTON, Michael, ed. *The relevance of models for social anthropology.* London: Tavistock Publications. *A.S.A. monographs* 1: Pp. 25–85.

SCHOLTE, Bob

1966   Epistemic paradigms: some problems in cross-cultural research on social anthropological history and theory. *American anthropologist* **68**: 1192–1201.

SELIGMAN, Brenda Zara

1927   Bilateral descent and the formation of marriage classes. *Journal of the royal anthropological institute* **57**: 349–375.

1928   Asymmetry in descent, with special reference to Pentecost. *Journal of the royal anthropological institute* **58**: 533–558.

SERVICE, Elman Rogers

1960   Kinship terminology and evolution. *American anthropologist* **62**: 747–763.

SHAND, Alexander Faulkner

1914   *The foundation of character.* London: Macmillan. xxxvi, 532 pp.

SHAPIRO, Warren

1967   Relational affiliation in 'unilineal' descent systems. *Man* n.s. **2**: 461–463.

1969   Miwuyt marriage: social structure aspects of the bestowal of females in northeast Arnhem Land. Australian national university, Ph.D. thesis. vii, 213 pp.

SIMONIS, Yvan
1968   *Claude Lévi-Strauss ou la 'passion de l'inceste': introduction au structuralisme.* Paris: Aubier montaigne. 380 pp. *Collection recherches économiques et sociales* 8.

SINGER, Milton
1953   Summary of comments and discussion. *American anthropologist* **55:** 362-366.

SMITH, Michael Garfield
1956   On segmentary lineage systems. *Journal of the royal anthropological institute* **86**(2): 39-80.
1962   History and social anthropology. *Journal of the royal anthropological institute* **92:** 73-85.

SNEDECOR, George
1946   *Statistical methods applied to experiments in agriculture and biology.* Ames, Iowa: Iowa State College Press. xvi, 485 pp.

SOROKIN, Pitirim Aleksandrovich
1956   *Fads and foibles in modern sociology and related sciences.* Chicago: Henry Regnery. viii, 357 pp.

SRINIVAS, Mysore Narasimhachar
1958   Introduction. *In* RADCLIFFE-BROWN, Alfred Reginald *Method in social anthropology.* Chicago: University of Chicago Press. Pp. ix-xxi.

STANNER, William Edward Hanley
1966   Firth's conception of social organization. *Australian and New Zealand journal of sociology* **2:** 66-78.

STEINER, Franz
1951   Review: Murdock, Social structure. *British journal of sociology* **2:** 366-368.

STEINMETZ, Rudolf
1896   Endokannibalismus. *Mittheilungen der anthropologischen Gesellschaft in Wien* **26:** 1-60.

STEPHENS, William Newton
1961   *The Oedipus complex: cross-cultural evidence.* New York: Free Press of Glencoe. xi, 273 pp.

STEWARD, Julian Haynes
1950   Preface. *In* STEWARD, J. H., ed. *Physical anthropology, linguistics and cultural geography of South American Indians.*

STEWARD, Julian Haynes (*contd*)
  Washington, D.C. Government printing office, Smithsonian Institution, Bureau of American Ethnology, bulletin 143. *Handbook of South American Indians*, vol. 6. Pp. x–xii.

STRUVE, Otto
 1950 *Stellar evolution: an exploration from the observatory*. Princeton: Princeton University Press. xiv, 266 pp.

STURTEVANT, William Curtis
 1964 Studies in ethnoscience. *In* ROMNEY, Antone Kimball, and D'ANDRADE, Roy Godwin, eds. Transcultural studies in cognition. *American anthropologist* **66** (3): Part 2. Pp. 99–131.

SUMNER, William Graham
 1906 *Folkways: a study of the sociological importance of usages, manners, customs, mores and morals*. Boston: Ginn. vii, 692 pp.

SUTTER, Jean, and GOUX, Jean-Michel
 1962 Évolution de la consanguinite en France de 1926 à 1958 avec des données récentes détaillées. *Population* **17:** 683–702.

SUTTER, Jean, and TABAH, Léon
 1951 Les notions d'isolat et de population minimum. *Population* **6:** 481–498.

SWEETSER, Dorrian Apple
 1966 Avoidance, social affiliation, and the incest taboo. *Ethnology* **5:** 304–316.

TEXTOR, Robert Bayard
 1967 *A cross-cultural summary*. New Haven: HRAF Press. xix, 208 pp., and printout.

TROUBETZKOY, Nikolai Sergieevich
 1933 La phonologie actuelle. *Journal de psychologie* **30:** 227–246.

TYLOR, Edward Burnett
 1889 On a method of investigating the development of institutions: applied to laws of marriage and descent. *Journal of the anthropological institute* **18:** 245–272.

UDY, Stanley Hart
 1964 Cross-cultural analysis: a case study. *In* HAMMOND, Phillip Everett, ed. *Sociologists at work*. New York: Basic Books. Pp. 161–183.

VOGT, Evon Zartmann
 1960 On the concepts of structure and process in cultural anthropology. *American anthropologist* **62:** 18–33.

VON NEUMANN, John, and MORGENSTERN, Oskar

1953 Theory of games and economic behavior. 3rd ed. Princeton: Princeton University Press. x, 641 pp.

WARNER, William Lloyd

1931 Morphology and functions of the Australian Murngin type of kinship. *American anthropologist* **33**: 172–198.

WHITING, John Wesley Mayhew

1954 The cross-cultural method. *In* LINDZEY, Gardner, ed. *Handbook of social psychology.* Cambridge, Mass.: Addison-Wesley. Pp. 523–531.

WHITING, John Wesley Mayhew, and CHILD, Irving Long

1953 *Childtraining and personality: a cross-cultural study.* New Haven: Yale University Press. vi, 353 pp.

WILLER, David

1967 *Scientific sociology: theory and method.* Englewood Cliffs, N.J.: Prentice-Hall. xx, 131 pp.

WILSON, Thurlow R.

1952 Randomness of the distribution of social organization forms: a note on Murdock's *Social structure. American anthropologist* **54**: 134–138.

WORSLEY, Peter Maurice

1956 The kinship system of the Tallensi: a revaluation. *Journal of the royal anthropological institute* **86** (1): 37–75.

1966 Groote Eylandt totemism and *Le totémisme aujourd'hui. In* LEACH, E. R., ed. *The structural study of myth and totemism.* London: Tavistock Publications. *A.S.A. monographs* **5**. Pp. 141–159.

WOUDEN, Franciscus Antonius Evert van

1956 Locale groepen en dubbele afstamming in Kodi, West Soemba. *Bijdragen tot de taal-, land- en volkenkunde* **112**: 204–246.

WRIGLEY, Christopher

1960 Speculations on the economic prehistory of Africa. *Journal of African history* **1**: 189–203.

YULE, George Udny, and KENDALL, Maurice George

1937 *An introduction to the theory of statistics.* London: Griffin. 570 pp.

ZELDITCH, Morris, jr.

1959 Statistical marriage preferences of the Ramah Navaho. *American anthropologist* **61**: 470–491.

Index

L *

INDEX

architectural view of social structure 207
areas, culture 84
Aristotle 138, 170, 174
Arnhem Land xxiii
art xv, 168
articulation, ordered 203
artificial units 87
Ashanti Chap. 3 passim, 135
Asia, south 169
Asokore 204
aspects 217: jural 189; non-structural 33; political & domestic 218; qualitative 211
assimilated lineages 233
association, statistical 51, 54
assumptions 23
astronomers 8
Athens 247
Atkins, J. 117
Atlas, Ethnographic 3, 91, 97
atom of kinship 117, 171
attached lineages 232f
attitudes 46, 113
attributes 12f, 60: compatibility of 46; lumping 57; rare 53
Australia, aboriginal: & alternate generations 160; & Aristotelianism 174; & descent 262; housekeeping in 189; & marriage classes 142, 152; & model-making 130f; & sociology 174; over-representation of 70, 92; & virilocality 22
Australia & Britain 16f
authentic lineages 232
authenticity 104
authority 158
average pattern 212
avoidances 80f, 96
avuncular marriage 149
avunculocal marriage 46, 53
axioms 219, 223
Azande 16

Ba'ari clan 230
Ba'at-Sakpar 230
balanced social system 209

302

Bali 16
Banton, M. P. 181
bare physiological facts 192f, 226
Barry, H. 20
Bastian, P. W. A. 167
Beauvoir, S. de 104
Befu, H. 61
behaviour 31ff, 194, 265: actual 183ff; & descent 35; instrumental 9 *see also* psychology, behaviouristic
beliefs, religious 259f *see also* procreation
bibliographies xxii
bifurcation 23, 52, 58
biis 217
bilateral: cross-cousin 146; descent 212, 241, 244
bilatérale, filiation 155
bilaterality: & filiation 247; & Fortes & Murdock 241; & residence 41; secondary 152
bilinéaire, filiation 155
bilineal descent 155
billiard-ball sociology 203
binary contrasts 168f, 170, 172
biography 203
biological factors 192
bio-physical frame of reference 187, 189
Blackstone, W. 124
Boas, F. xix, 63, 73: & models 130
Bohannan, P. J. 186
bones 156
Bororo 137
borrowing 37
boundaries 84f, 89: of disciplines 268
Bɔyada 249
Braithwaite, R. B. 118
British Columbia 9, 175
British social anthropologists: & history 9; & how society works 110; & intensive studies 9, 63, 64; & structuralists 38
brotherhood, links of 236
Burma 112f
Bushmen 12

disciplines 125; double unilineal 148; in human thought 116; in Lévi-Strauss's prose 168f; & ordinal relations 171f
Dieri 111
differences: & similarities 111; of status 163f
differentials, social 58
differentiation 182, 205, 220
diffusion: & equilibrium 79; as explanation 17, 73ff; theories of 20
digital parameters 61
direct exchange 154
directives 180,184
disciplines 11ff, 125: borders of 268; & Lévi-Strauss 125; & Murdock 20f see also psychoanalysis, sociology
discontinuity 111, 203; discontinuous exchange 154
discoveries 131
discrepancies 133
disequilibrium 208f
disharmonic regimes 157, 160f
dispersion stage 201
Disraeli, B. 88
distanciation 104
distinction, inherent 23, 58
distributional statements 15
District Commissioner 209
diversity: intra-unit 29f, 91; in sample 70, 93
division of labour: & change 83; & marriage 138; scale of 46; by sex 22, 40, 46; & social structure 19
divorce 32f, 51
Dobu 16
domain 217f, 238, 249: of models 125; politico-jural 228
domestic: family 14, 254f; group 254
dominant line 247
double cross-cousin 146
double unilineal descent: Ashanti & Tallensi 240; & filiation 155; & residence 46; & Mrs Seligman 132
double unilineal dichotomy 148

dɔyam 227, 231, 239f
Driver, H. E.: on cultural changes 20, 42, 74; on kin avoidances 80f; on regional evidence 18; on statistical tests 57, 60
drives see psychological d.
dual organization: & dualism 132, 136, 141; & marriage 150; & models 136; & procreation theories 157
duality 116
dug 217, 226, 237; narrow 235; wide 236
duration 203
Durkheim, É. 118
dynamic: coherence 220; factors 189; processes 202
dynastic alliances 242

ecological factors 188
economic factors 189, 192: & social structure 19; & time 189
economic: needs 208; organization 188; structure 126
economics 112, 174; economists 188
education 186, 190f
efficacy 53, 58
Eggan, F. R. 68
Egypt, ancient 16
Einstein, A. xvi
Eisenstadt, S. N. 179, 180
elementary: family 117; formula of exchange 148; kinship structures 114; structures 112, 116f, 126, 140f
elements, fundamental 114, 116f, 125, 133: & Bastain 167; postulated 168
Elliot Smith, G. 168
Elwin, H. V. H. 127
emic concepts 14, 261f
emotions 190
empirical: concrete reality 138, 162; isolates 216; observations 108
empty time 121
encoding see coding
endogamy 241, 243; endogamous moieties 161

Flower, W. H. 66
food 19, 22, 192
forces: polar 220; social 202; structural 200
Ford, C. S. 3, 59
Forde, C. D. 123, 127
form 44: structural 196; & structure 211; universal 139, 144
Fortes, M. Chap. 3 passim: on analytical scheme 45; on Ashanti marriage 135f; on developmental cycle 112; on incest and exogamy 139; on natural science xx; on time 120
Fox, R. 8
Fox (tribe) 47
frame: of continuity 204; of reference 185, 187, 189, 192, 257 see also structural f.
framework, circular 121
France 107, 123, 127
Frazer, J. G. 173f
Freeman, J. D. 124
French revolution 112, 125
frequency 55f, 138: & marriage 36
Freud, S. 21, 166, 255
function 51, 181, 183
functional: consistency 219; relations 18, 73; value 182
functionalism 96, 168
fundamental: mental structures 116, 126, 144; reality 114, 138 see also elements
funerals 231

Galileo 138, 170
Galton, F. 66, 73f
game: of exchanging women 139; theory 118f, 213
Gbeog clan 230, 232
Gbizug 230
genealogies 134, 205, 251f; genealogical specification 144
general: instability 162; systems theory xvi
generalizations 183: cross-cultural 98; & facts 63; statistical xvi

generalized exchange 138ff, 152f, 156, 160
generation: alternating 160; cycle of 214; as inherent distinction 23, 58; & segments 252 see also depth
genes xvii
genetic 72, 204: connexion 73, 79; development 192; explanation 4, 16; processes 203, 253, 259f; psychology 186; sequence 260
geography 20, 110, 188
Gestalttheorie 119
ghetto 243
Gifford, E. W. 134
gift, synthetic character of 116
Gilyak 143, 165
Ginsberg, M. 26, 67
Gleason, H. A. 168
Glick, P. B. xiii
global structure 150
Gluckman, M. xxiii, 223, 262: on apt illustration 173; on inter-disciplinary relations 268; on lineality 250
Good Destiny 244
Goodenough, W. H. xxii, 8: on Nakani 135; rule 64f; on Truk 9
Goody, J. R. 63, 184
Gough, E. K. 164
Goux, J.-M. 123
grammar 131, 134, 196; grammatical rules 32, 115
grandparent, identification with 214
gratifying culture 37
groups: number of 141ff see also corporate, domestic, local, pseudo-familial, sibling, unilineal g.
growth 200, 203
Guiana, British 201
Guiart, J. 104
guilt 255
Guŋ 250
gustemes 116
Guttman scale 237

Halle, M. 115
Hammel, E. A. xxii

hapu 241, 242, 247
harmonic regimes 114, 160f
Hawaii 16, 43, 56
Hegel, G. W. F. 172
heiresses 36
Heisenberg, W. 113
Henga 43
Hertzsprung-Russell diagram 201
Hiatt, L. R. xiii
Hima 28f
historians 202
historical: accidents 18; accuracy
207; anthropology 9, 20; arguments 111; explanations 17;
origins 181; problems 110; reconstruction 50, 202; sequence 203;
time 112, 206; validity 205
history 111f, 125: & anthropologists
9, 202f; & cumulative continuity 207; & functions 51; &
infrastructures 109; natural 97
see also conjectural h.
Hobhouse, L. T. 26, 67
Hocart, A. M. 164
Hodgen, M. T. 44
Holmberg, A. R. 8, 26, 51
hologeistic method 4
Homans, G. C. 51, 153
home-made models 118, 120, 216:
& consciousness 130; & reality
110
homeostasis 266
homogeneity 93, 209, 265: cultural
182; societal 70, 188; Tale 208f
homogenization 138
Hopi 107, 121
horizon 90
horizontal terms 161
households 197f, 200, 204
housekeeping 189
houses, shape of 65
Hull, Clark L. 8, 23
Human relations area files 3ff, 7,
97f: & cultural units 69
human sciences 110, 166
humanities 166
Humpty Dumpty xxi
Huxley memorial lecture 103

308

hypergamy 164
hypotheses 165
hypothetical societies xxiii

Iban 38
ideal: isolates 215; patterns 129,
194; types 180
ideals 32
ideational culture 37
ideology 162
idiographic explanation 4
idiom of kinship 227
'If I were a horse' 21
illusion: optical 153; of traditional
sociology 156
illustration, apt 173
Incas 16
incest 250ff: & culture 138f; &
exogamy 139f; as rule 116; &
sanctions 35; social 165; & trial
& error 37f; universality of 16,
21, 148
incipient forms 44, 46
inculcated culture 37
independent: trials 72ff; units 66f
indirect exchange 154
indiscriminate descent 155
individual man 110
industrial societies 30, 123
inequality 143, 160, 163
inertia 154
infantile dependence 258
informants 194
infrastructure 109, 267
inherent distinctions 23, 58
inner lineage 237, 252
innovation 37
instability 162
instinct, maternal 139
Institute of Human Relations 5
institutions, political 13, 30f
instrumental behaviour 9
integration 34, 37, 43f, 87f, 90: &
equilibrium 17f, 97; political 82
integrative culture 88f
intelligence, neolithic 175
intensive study 9, 63, 64, 181
internal limits 143, 165

telescoping 205
temporal processes 200
tendencies 24, 40, 53, *see also* feudal
t.
tentation 37
terminology, kinship 46, 65, 113:
classificatory 144f; cousin 43; &
descent 41; & Lowie 113; &
postulational method 22; &
residence 23
territory, size of 92f
testing, mental 186
tests *see* statistical t.
Textor, R. B. 15, 60, 66: on
dichotomous characteristics 57;
on economic factors 19; on
politics & sex 82f; on tendencies
40
theologian 191
theorems 23, 58
theories xxi, 11, 211: of culture 60;
of diffusion 20; & ethnography
62, 97; of games 118f, 213
thermodynamics 122, 124
thought, primitive 170
thought-of orders 110, 136
three degree rule 73
ties of clanship 229
Tikopia 56, 91f
time 39ff, 266: & Ashanti households
198; & custom 201f; depth 233f;
& economic factors 189; kinds of
120; & models 119ff; & process
201; & weighting 76 *see also*
continuative, cyclical, empty, historical, linear, non-reversible, progressive, reversible, stable, straight,
undulating t.; micro-time, macro-
time
Tiv 186
Todas 70
Tong Hills 208
Tongo 206, 230, 249
total social system 182
totems 159, 169
traits 12f
transfiguration 161
transformations 118, 164

transitional: forms 44; types 46
transitivity 164
translation 104
trials 37f, 72ff
tribe 68
triskelion 137
Trobriands: & Ashanti 210; &
Azande 68; data on 261; as
paradigm case 181; as unit 87f
Troubetzkoy, N. S. 170
true models 120, 132f
Truk 9
Tswana 48, 241
two-by-two tables 57, 84
Tylor, E. B.: on comparative method
4, 12, 65f; & Flower 66f; &
Galton 73f; on residence rule 41;
on sampling unit 26
types: cultural 28, 92 *see also* ideal,
polar, primary, stable, transitional t.
typologies 110, 165f

Udy, S. H. 7, 98
unconscious models 120, 130f, 174
under-representation 70
undifferentiated descent 155
undulating time 121
unified theory xxi
unilateral: filiation 173; transfer 148
unilineal descent *see* double u. d.
unilineal groups 142
union, privileged 149
unique cultures 70
unit *see* artificial, culture, ethnic,
etic, independent, natural, perpetual, sampling u.
United States government 6
universal: characteristics 110; explanations 148; forms 139, 144
universality *see* incest
universe, sampling 85
unstable regimes 161

validity, historical 205
value, functional 182
variation 37
vectorial factor 157